Heartfelt praise from the user community…

"All issues that occur when analyzing survival data in clinical trials are explained thoroughly and demonstrated using appropriate examples. This book can serve both as a reference for a medical researcher and as a teaching tool."

Karol H. Katz, M.S.
Department of EPH
Yale University

"Delightful, well written…a powerhouse of hands-on survival techniques! A must have resource for applied statisticians and data analysts in the field."

Jimmy Thomas Efird
Division of Epidemiology
Department of Health Research and Policy
Stanford University School of Medicine

§sas. | SAS Publishing

SAS®
Survival Analysis Techniques
for Medical Research

Second Edition

Alan B. Cantor

The correct bibliographic citation for this manual is as follows: Cantor, Alan B. 2003. *SAS® Survival Analysis Techniques for Medical Research, Second Edition*. Cary, NC: SAS Institute Inc.

SAS® Survival Analysis Techniques for Medical Research, Second Edition

Table of Contents

Preface.. v

Chapter 1 What Survivor Analysis Is About

1.1   The Nature of Survival Data...1
1.2   Exercises...5
1.3   Calendar Time and Study Time...5
1.4   Exercise..6
1.5   Example..6
1.6   Functions That Describe Survival...9
1.7   Exercises...11
1.8   Some Commonly Used Survival Functions..11
1.9   Exercises...12
1.10 Functions That Allow for Cure...13
1.11 Fully Parametric and Nonparametric Methods......................................15
1.12 Some Common Assumptions..16
1.13 Exercises...16

Chapter 2 Non-Parametric Survival Function Estimation

2.1   The Kaplan-Meier Estimate of the Survival Function............................17
2.2   Exercise...20
2.3   The Actuarial Life Table...20
2.4   The Variance of the Kaplan-Meier Estimator..23
2.5   Hypothesis Tests...24
2.6   Confidence Intervals...25
2.7   Some Problems with the Kaplan-Meier Estimator of S(t)......................25
2.8   Using PROC LIFETEST..27
2.9   Two Macros as Alternatives to PROC LIFETEST.................................32
2.10 Planning a Study to Control the Standard Error.....................................37
2.11 Example...39
2.12 The KMPLAN Macro..39
2.13 Exercise...42
2.14 Interval-Censored Data..42
2.15 Macros...48

Chapter 3 Non-Parametric Comparison of Survival Distributions

3.1   Notation...53
3.2   The Log Rank Statistic..54
3.3   More Than Two Groups...56
3.4   Other Linear Rank Tests..57
3.5   Using PROC LIFETEST..59
3.6   Exercises...64
3.7   A Test for Trend..64
3.8   Stratified Analyses..65
3.9   The Macro LINRANK..66
3.10 Permutation Tests and Randomization Tests...73
3.11 The Mantel-Byar Method..79
3.12 Power Analysis...84
3.13 Early Stopping Based on Conditional Power...92
3.14 Listings of Macros..95

Chapter 4 Proportional Hazards Regression

4.1   Some Thoughts about Model-Based Estimation and Inference 111
4.2   The Cox (Proportional Hazards) Regression Method........................112
4.3   The Hazard Ratio and Survival...113
4.4   Multiple Covariates 114
4.5   Defining Covariates 114
4.6   Scaling the Covariates 115
4.7   Survival Probabilities 116
4.8   Maximum Likelihood Estimation of the Coefficients....................116
4.9   Using PROC PHREG 117
4.10 Model-Building Considerations..131
4.11 Time-Dependent Covariates 134
4.12 More Complex Models 136
4.13 Checking the Proportional Hazards Assumption 136
4.14 Exercise 138
4.15 Survival Probabilities 138
4.16 Residuals..143
4.17 Power and Sample Size 145
4.18 Imputing Missing Values 148
4.19 Listings of Macros 150

Chapter 5 Parametric Methods

5.1   Introduction 153
5.2   The Accelerated Failure Time Model...................................155
5.3   PROC LIFEREG 156
5.4   Example Using PROC LIFEREG 156
5.5   Comparison of Models 159
5.6   Estimates of Quantiles and Survival Probabilities 160
5.7   The PROC LIFEREG Parameters and the "Standard" Parameters 163
5.8   The Macro PARAMEST 163
5.9   Example Using the Macro PARAMEST 166
5.10 An Example with a Positive Cure Rate................................169
5.11 Comparison of Groups..173
5.12 One-Sample Tests of Parameters 176
5.13 The Effects of Covariates on Parameters.............................176
5.14 Complex Expressions for the Survival and Hazard Functions 179
5.15 Graphical Checks for Certain Survival Distributions.................179
5.16 A Macro for Fitting Parametric Models to Survival Data..............180
5.17 Other Estimates of Interest 183
5.18 Listings of Macros 183

Appendix A..**187**

Appendix B..**193**

Appendix C..**209**

References **219**

Index **223**

Preface

Cox's proportional hazards regression model is one of the most popular methods used in survival analysis, and you will learn about it in Chapter 4, "Proportional Hazards Regression." Although Cox first described it in 1972, a search of Pub Med using the phrase "Cox Regression" finds the first article in medical literature using this method written in 1980. By the end of 1985, there were still only 69 such articles. During the 1990s, there were 1625 such articles. Of course, this simple search doesn't completely document the use of Cox regression during each of these time periods, but it does make the point that Cox regression, although an extremely useful tool for analyzing survival data, was not used much in medical literature until several years after it was published.

Now, you might think that this is a reflection of the slowness of biostatisticians to become aware of Cox regression. I don't think that this is the case. As a young assistant professor at a medical school in the late 1970s and early 1980s, I was aware of Cox regression but did not use it in a paper during those years. (I recall suggesting it once to a physician, but he rejected the idea as being too technical for a medical journal.) What augured against its use, by other biostatisticians and by me, was the difficulty of its implementation. Cox regression requires numerous matrix inversions and multiplications that make it impractical, in most real applications, to do by hand—even with a calculator. Computers were available in academic and research environments, but one would still have the task of writing a program in one of the popular languages of the time such as FORTRAN or BASIC.

With the implementation of Cox regression in commercial statistical software packages such as SAS software, and with the development of inexpensive desktop computers that could run this software, everything changed. Now, methods such as Cox regression, which would previously have required tedious calculation or computer programming, could be performed with a few lines of code on a computer sitting on the desk of a researcher or statistician. I'm convinced that this is why Cox regression became so much more widely used in the second half of the 1980s. Of course, this phenomenon has been repeated for a large number of statistical methods. As an experiment, you might want to note whether confidence bands for survival curves become more common in medical literature during the next few years. SAS is introducing them in Version 9.

While we are greatly indebted to those brilliant individuals who develop new methods that add to our armamentarium, we often fail to recognize the critical role of commercial software in allowing us to use these methods easily. Such software encourages the use of these methods by those who know about and understand them but who, in the absence of such software, would be reluctant to do the work required. But there is another, more insidious, effect as well. Such software enables those who do not understand the assumptions of a statistical method, or do not know how to interpret the results, to perform it anyway. This undoubtedly leads to a great deal of sloppy, and even misleading, reports in medical literature.

One of my goals in writing this book is to link the methods of survival analysis to the implementation of these methods in SAS software in a way that is accessible to those who are not professional statisticians. Hopefully, this will make some small contribution toward the remediation of the problem alluded to above. In doing so, I have not attempted to write "Survival Analysis for Dummies." I wouldn't know how to do that. The basic concepts of survival analysis cannot be understood without certain mathematical prerequisites. This includes some understanding of elementary differential and integral calculus. It also requires some understanding of statistics and probability. This includes the idea of likelihood-based estimation and inference.

In order to enable those without such a background to benefit from this book, I have included three appendixes. Appendix A provides the mathematical prerequisites for the material in this book. Appendix B presents the statistical background that the reader will need. Finally, because many readers will not have had experience with SAS software, Appendix C provides a brief introduction to SAS software. It is enough information to get started. I suggest that the reader glance through this material, and study those sections that are not already familiar. An instructor, using this book as a textbook, might want to look at the material in the appendixes and review, in the first part of the course, the subjects that the class needs.

A few other comments about this book are in order. First of all, SAS software is a moving target, so all I can do is provide information on the most up-to-date version. In mid-2002, when this book was nearing completion, that was an early release of Version 9. I am grateful to SAS for providing me with an early release of Version 9, and I've incorporated those new features that are related to survival analysis. Those readers who are using earlier versions will, of course, not be able to use them. Beginning with Version 7, SAS allows variable names with more than eight characters. Prior to Version 7, the limit was eight characters. In order to allow variable names to be more easily interpreted, I have used longer variable names in the macros, programs, and data sets that I included. To allow you to use the book's code without excessive typing, the code is provided on the SAS website. The details of how to download code are on the inside front cover. Users of earlier versions of SAS will have to find such variable names and shorten them. Readers of this book are strongly encouraged to download the programs and data sets and try them for themselves. You are also encouraged to make modifications and improvements. In addition to Base SAS and SAS/STAT, this book also makes extensive use SAS/GRAPH and SAS/IML software, so you should have those products installed. Finally, I make extensive use of the SAS macro language as well as of the IML procedure, two facilities that many readers will not be familiar with. That will not prevent you from using my programs, but you might want to spend some time studying their documentation to try to see how they work. It would be an additional benefit of this book if it leads to your learning these important skills.

Acknowledgments

In a book's preface, it is customary to thank those who have helped the author. Probably no author ever had more help from more people. I have been very fortunate to have had excellent instructors when I was a student. In addition, throughout my career I have learned a great deal from my colleagues. In this regard, some special words need to be said about Al Gross, with whom I worked from 1978 to 1983. Al, together with Virginia Clark, wrote the first widely used textbook on survival analysis. By doing so, they transformed the subject from a set of isolated articles in journals to a subject to be taught to students in graduate schools. In addition to his brilliance as a statistician, Al was known as a generous mentor to students and junior colleagues. His recent death was a source of great sadness to all who knew him.

I have also benefited greatly from my associations with biomedical researchers. For the past eight years, this has been at the H. Lee Moffitt Cancer Center and Research Institute. My colleagues probably thought that our primary relationship was that I was helping them. In fact, by providing me with challenging problems and constantly requiring me to enhance my skills, they helped me as much as I helped them.

The Survival Analysis class in the Department of Epidemiology at the University of South Florida in the Spring of 2001 deserves my special thanks as well. They served, without providing informed consent, as guinea pigs for much of the material in this book.

This book was vastly improved as a result of the critiques and suggestions of several reviewers, both external to and from within SAS. Their efforts are appreciated. As with the first edition, my thanks also go out to the folks at SAS, especially those in the BBU program. Their assistance has been vital.

And finally, my heartfelt thanks goes out to my dear wife Bootsie, for her support, encouragement, and love. Without that, this book, and much more in my life that gives me joy and satisfaction, would not be possible.

Chapter 1   What Survival Analysis Is About

1.1 The Nature of Survival Data 1
1.2 Exercises 5
1.3 Calendar Time and Study Time 5
1.4 Exercise 6
1.5 Example 6
1.6 Functions That Describe Survival 9
1.7 Exercises 11
1.8 Some Commonly Used Survival Functions 11
1.9 Exercises 12
1.10 Functions That Allow for Cure 13
1.11 Fully Parametric and Nonparametric Methods 15
1.12 Some Common Assumptions 16
1.13 Exercises 16

1.1 The Nature of Survival Data

Survival data are special and, thus, they require special methods for their analyses. Before going into what makes these data special and how they are analyzed, let's establish some terminology and explain what is meant by survival data.

Although you might naturally think of survival data as dealing with the time until death, actually the methods that will be discussed in this book are used for data that deal with the time until the occurrence of *any* well-defined event. In addition to death, that event can be, for example:

- Relapse of a patient in whom disease had been in remission
- Death from a specific cause
- Development of a disease in someone at high risk
- Resumption of smoking by someone who had quit
- Commission of a crime by someone after serving a prison term
- Cancellation of service by a credit card (or phone service) customer
- Recovery of platelet count after bone marrow transplantation to some predefined level
- Relief from symptoms such as headache, rash, and nausea.

Note that for the first six examples, longer times until the event occurs are better; while for the last two, shorter times are better. Nevertheless, the methods to be described in this book can be applied to any of them. Note also that the methods we will be discussing can be used in a variety of settings, some nonmedical. For simplicity, words like "survival" and "death" are used in describing these methods, but you should be aware of the broader areas of applicability.

1.1.1 Cause- and Non-cause-specific Death

This might be a good place for a few words about cause-specific death. When analyzing survival of patients with some form of cancer, you might want to focus on death caused by cancer, particularly in an older population in which we expect deaths from other causes as well. You would then count only those deaths that are caused by cancer as "events." A death from any other cause would be treated the same as if the patient had suddenly moved out of state and could no longer be followed. Of course, this requires that you establish rules and a mechanism for distinguishing between cause-specific and non-cause-specific deaths.

As an alternative, there are methods of dealing with death from one cause, in the presence of competing risks. We will not be discussing such methods in this book. In the New York Health Insurance Plan study designed to assess the efficacy of mammography (Shapiro, et al., 1988), women were randomized to a group who received annual mammography or to a group that did not. Since the study's planners realized there would be considerable mortality not related to breast cancer, they took as their endpoint death caused by breast cancer. A committee was created to determine whether the death of a woman in the study was due to breast cancer. This committee, which was blinded with respect to the woman's group assignment, followed a detailed algorithm described in the study protocol. It's interesting to note that a recent *Lancet* article (Olsen and Gotzsche, 2001) called into question this study and others that are the basis for the widespread use of screening mammography. One of the authors' contentions was that the determination of cause of death was biased. We won't attempt to deal with this controversy here. In fact, the issue of what should be the endpoint for a study of a screening modality is a difficult one. In fact, because of the problems in assessing cause-specific mortality, some have advocated overall mortality as a more appropriate endpoint for such studies.

What makes analyses of these types of data distinctive is that often there will be many subjects for whom the event has not occurred during the time that the patient has been followed. This can happen for several reasons. Here are some examples:

- The event of interest is death, but at the time of analysis the patient is still alive.
- A patient was lost to follow-up without having experienced the event of interest.
- A competing event that precludes the event of interest has occurred. For example, in a study designed to compare two treatments for prostate cancer, the event of interest might be death caused by the cancer. A patient may die of an unrelated cause, such as an automobile accident.
- A patient is dropped from the study without having experienced the event of interest because of a major protocol violation or for reasons specified by the protocol.

In all of these situations, you don't know the time until the event occurs. Without knowledge of the methods to be described in this book, a researcher might simply exclude such cases. But clearly this throws out a great deal of useful information. In all of these cases we know that the time to the event exceeds some known number. For example, a subject who was known to be alive three years into a study and then moved to another state and could no longer be followed is known to have a survival time of at least three years. This subject's time is said to be right censored. A subject's observed time, t, is right censored if, at time t, he or she is known to still be alive. Thus you know that this subject's survival time is at least t. A survival time might also be left censored. This happens if all that is known about the time to death is that it is less than or equal to some value. A death is interval censored if it is known only that it occurred during some time interval. Although there is a great deal of current research on ways to deal with left- and interval-censored data, most survival analytic methods deal only with right-censored data, since this is the type of censoring most commonly seen. Of the three SAS procedures that deal explicitly with survival data, two deal only with right censoring. This is the type of censoring most commonly seen in medical research. The third, PROC

LIFEREG, discussed in Chapter 5, deals with left and interval censoring as well. Except for that chapter, and a brief discussion in Chapter 2, this book will not consider left- or interval-censored times and the term "censored" will always mean "right censored" unless another form of censoring is specified.

1.1.2 Random Variables

Survival data, therefore, are described by values of a pair of random variables, say (T, D). They can be interpreted as follows:

- T represents the time that the subject was observed on study.
- D is an indicator of the fact that the event in question either occurred or did not occur at the end of time T. The values of D might be 0 to indicate that the event did not occur and 1 to indicate that it did. Then $D = 0$ means that the corresponding T is a censored time. Of course, other values are possible.

The SAS survival analysis procedures, as well as the macros presented in this book, allow you to specify any set of values that indicate that a time is censored. This is convenient when you have data in which a variable indicating a subject's final status can have several values that indicate censoring. Subscripts will be used to distinguish the subjects. Thus, if there are n subjects on a study, their survival data might be represented by the n pairs $(t_1, d_1), (t_2, d_2), \ldots (t_n, d_n)$.

Sometimes, in textbooks or in journal articles, survival data are reported with only the time variable. Adding a plus sign to the time indicates censoring. For example, reporting survival data as 2.6, 3.7+, 4.5, 7.2, 9.8+ would mean that the second and the fifth observations are censored and the others are not. You can also store information on both the survival time and censoring value with only one variable. Making the time negative indicates censoring. Using this convention, these data would be 2.6, −3.7, 4.5, 7.2, −9.8. A SAS DATA step can easily be written to convert such a data set to the desired form. This is illustrated by the following example and output:

```
proc print data=original;
title 'Original Data Set';
data; set original;
d=1;
if time<0 then do;
        d=0;
        time=-time;
        end;
proc print;
title 'Modified Data Set';
run;
```

Output 1.1

```
                     Original Data Set

                     OBS      TIME

                      1       2.6
                      2      -3.7
                      3       4.5
                      4       7.2
                      5      -9.8
```

Output 1.2

```
                    Modified Data Set

              OBS      TIME      D

               1        2.6      1
               2        3.7      0
               3        4.5      1
               4        7.2      1
               5        9.8      0
```

There is another way of thinking about the random variables T and D described earlier. Each patient in the study is really subject to two random variables: the time until death (or the event of interest) and the time until censoring. Once one of these happens you can observe that time, but not the other. The value, t, of the random variable T, which you can observe, can be thought of as the minimum of the time until death and the time until censoring. The value, d, of the random variable D indicates whether that minimum is the time until death ($d = 1$) or the time until censoring ($d = 0$). An important assumption in all of what follows is that time until death and the time until censoring are independent. This would generally be true, for example, if censoring were due to the ending of the follow-up period.

On the other hand, suppose you are analyzing the data from a study in which patients with some sort of cardiac disease are randomized to drug treatment or surgery. In some cases it might later be decided that a patient who has been randomized to drug treatment now needs to have surgery. You might be tempted to take the patient off study with a censored survival time equal to the time until surgery. However, if the decision for surgery were based on the patient's deteriorating condition, to do so would create bias in favor of the drug treatment. That's because such a patient's death would not be counted as a death since he had previously been censored. A better approach might be to anticipate this possibility when planning the study. You might plan the study as a comparison of two treatment strategies: immediate surgery vs. initial drug treatment with surgery under certain conditions that are established in advance.

Another feature of survival data that distinguishes them from other types of data is the importance to estimation and inference of the distinction between nonparametric and parametric approaches. You will recall that methods such as t tests and ANOVAs, which are based on normally distributed random variables, tend to be valid even when data are not normally distributed if the sample sizes are reasonable large. When we are concerned about the appropriateness of the normality assumption we can replace the t tests and ANOVAs with nonparametric methods, such as the Wilcoxon Rank Sum Test and the Kruskal-Wallis Test, that don't require that assumption. With survival data, there are also parametric and nonparametric methods and often we need to choose between them. However, in this context, we generally don't even think about the data being normally distributed. Other distributions, some of which will be discussed later, are sometimes used, but the correctness of the distributional assumption that we make can be much more critical. To avoid making this choice, we often prefer nonparametric methods. Of course, the cost of using nonparametric methods is typically a less precise analysis. We will return to this issue later.

1.2 Exercises

1.2.1 Think of three other potential applications for survival analysis. At least one should be nonmedical.

1.2.2 Why do you think the planners of the NY HIP mammography study decided to use cause-specific mortality as the major endpoint instead of simply considering the cases diagnosed and their stage distribution? The latter approach would have made the study much shorter and cheaper. What do you think about the idea of using overall mortality, instead of breast-cancer-specific mortality as an endpoint?

1.3 Calendar Time and Study Time

Another concept we need to discuss is how time is defined in survival studies. In most survival studies patients do not all begin their participation at the same time. Instead, they are accrued over a period of time. Often they are followed for a period of time after accrual has ended. Consider a study that starts accrual on February 1, 2000, and accrues for 24 months until January 31, 2002, with an additional 12 months of follow-up ending January 31, 2003. In other words, no more patients are entered on study after January 31, 2002, and those accrued are followed until January 31, 2003. Now consider the following patients:

- Patient #1: Enters on February 15, 2000, and dies on November 8, 2000.
- Patient #2: Enters on July 2, 2000, and is censored (lost to follow-up) on April 23, 2001.
- Patient #3: Enters on June 5, 2001, and is still alive and censored at the end of the follow-up period.
- Patient #4: Enters on July 13, 2001, and dies on December 12, 2002.

Their experiences are shown graphically in Figure 1.1.

Figure 1.1

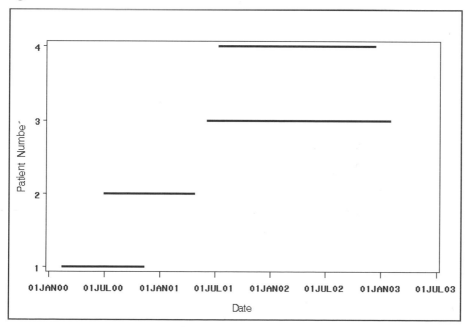

In survival analyses, all patients are thought of as starting at time 0. Thus their survival experience can be represented as in Figure 1.2. When reference is made to the number surviving or the number at risk at some time, the time referred to is the time from each patient's study entry—not the time since the study started. For example, of the four patients we just described, two of them (#3 and #4) are still at risk at 12 months. None are still at risk at 24 months. Both of these facts are seen in Figure 1.2. If, at some later date, you speak of those at risk at t = 6 months, that has nothing to do with the situation on July 31, 2001, six months from the start of the study. Rather you mean those who, as of the last date that the data were updated, had been on study for at least 6 months without dying or being censored.

Figure 1.2

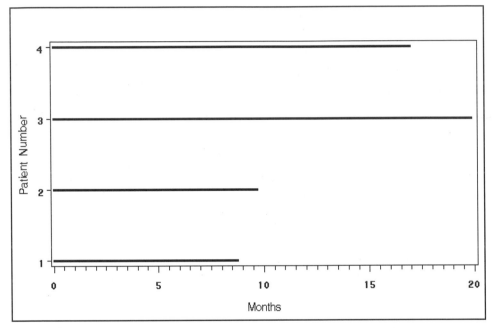

1.4 Exercise

For the data in the previous example, how many patients are at risk at 5 months? at 10 months? at 15 months? at 20 months?

1.5 Example

Sometimes, in studies involving follow-up of patients, there is interest in more than one time variable—for example, in an oncology study, time until death, which will be called survival time, and also time until death or relapse, which will be called disease-free survival time. The database will then have to contain information on both endpoints. Since SAS handles dates internally as numeric constants (the number of days before or after January 1, 1960) it is often convenient for the data sets to contain the dates of interest and to include in a SAS DATA step the statements to calculate the time values needed. As an example, consider a sample of patients treated for malignant melanoma. Presumably they are rendered disease-free surgically. Suppose that, in addition, they are treated with either treatment A or B, which are thought to inhibit relapse and improve survival. We might want to consider both survival and disease-free survival of these patients and how they are affected by treatment, tumor thickness, stage of disease, and tumor site. The first three records in the database might look like this:

Ptid	Date_of_ surg	Date_of_ relapse	Date_of_ death	Date_of_ last	Treatment	Site	Stage	Thickness
13725	10/5/95	11/6/96	1/5/97	1/5/97	A	1	III	1.23
25422	3/7/97	.	2/6/99	2/6/99	B	3	II	1.13
34721	9/6/94	.	.	3/18/2002	B	2	III	2.15

Note the inclusion of a unique patient identifying number, Ptid. While this number will play no role in the analyses of this data set, it is a good idea to associate such a number with each patient on a trial. This will facilitate merging with other data sets to add other variables of interest. Names are usually not good for this purpose because of the risk of spelling variations and errors. Also, we might want to exclude patient names in order to protect patient confidentiality. Note that Treatment, Site, and Stage are represented by codes or brief symbolic names. For obvious reasons we should avoid having long words or phrases for variables such as disease site or tumor histology. Treatment is a dichotomous variable. Although numbers are used for the possible sites, Site is categorical. The numbers used do not imply any ordering. Stage is ordinal with stages I, II, III, and IV representing successively more extensive disease. Finally Thickness is a continuous variable that is measured in millimeters. In later chapters, methods for dealing with all of these types of variables with SAS procedures will be discussed. In this case, missing values for date variables are used to indicate that the event did not occur. In order to analyze survival time and disease-free survival time, the following variables are needed:

Dfsevent   has the value 1 if the patient died or relapsed, 0 otherwise.

Dfstime   is the time, in months, from surgery to death or relapse if either occurred. Otherwise, it is the time that the patient was observed after surgery.

Survevent   has the value 1 if the patient died, 0 otherwise.

Survtime   is the time, in months, from surgery to death if the patient died. Otherwise, it is the time that the patient was observed after surgery.

The statements to add the variables needed to analyze survival and disease-free survival to the data set might look like this:

```
data melanoma; set melanoma;
   /*  Defining dfs time and event variables   */
dfsevent = 1 - (date_of_relapse EQ .)*(date_of_death EQ .);
   /*  Divide by 30.4 to convert from days to months */
if dfsevent = 0 then dfstime = (date_of_last -  date_of_surg)/30.4;
if date_of_relapse NE . then dfstime=(date_of_relapse -
date_of_surg)/30.4;
if date_of_relapse EQ . and date_of_death NE . then
dfstime=(date_of_death - date_of_surg)/30.4;

   /* Defining survival time and event variables */
survevent = (date_of_death ne .);
if survevent = 0 then survtime = (date_of_last - date_of_surg)/30.4;
else survtime = (date_of_death-date_of_surg)/30.4;
```

The divisions by 30.4 are simply to convert time from days to months, a more convenient time unit. Note that 30.4 is approximately 365/12. Also, when statements such as (date_of_relapse EQ .) or (date_of_death EQ .) are used in an arithmetic expression, they have the value 0 if false and 1 if true. The previous statements create the variables Dfstime and Dfsevent to be used in analyses of disease-free survival and the variables Survtime and Survevent to be used in analyses of survival. The first three observations of the resultant data set would look like this:

Output 1.3

PTID	DATE_OF_SURG	DATE_OF_RELAPSE	DATE_OF_DEATH	DATE_OF_LAST	TREATMENT	SITE	STAGE
13725	10/05/95	11/06/96	01/05/97	01/05/97	A	1	III
25422	03/07/97	.	02/06/99	02/06/99	B	3	II
34721	09/06/94	.	.	03/18/02	B	2	III

PTID	THICKNESS	DFSEVENT	DFSTIME	SURVEVENT	SURVTIME
13725	1.23	1	13.0592	1	15.0658
25422	1.13	1	23.0592	1	23.0592
34721	2.15	0	90.4605	0	90.4605

Now that these variables have been defined, there are several questions you might want to address. For example, you might want to estimate the survival and disease-free survival probabilities over time for the overall cohort and for subgroups defined by treatment, stage, site, and so on. Standard errors and confidence intervals for those estimates might also be desirable. This will be discussed in Chapter 2. You might also want to perform statistical tests to assess the evidence for the superiority of one treatment over the other. This can also be done. Methods will be discussed in Chapters 3 and 4. Now it might happen that the patients treated with treatment A were of worse prognosis (as seen by their stages, perhaps) then those treated with treatment B. If the treatment assignment was not randomized, this might happen if the treating physicians preferred treatment A for more advanced tumors. Even if the treatment assignment were randomized, it could happen by chance that one of the treatment groups had a higher proportion of patients with more advanced disease. You will learn how, using methods to be discussed in Chapters 3 and 4, to compare the two treatments after adjusting for stage. In addition, you will be able, if you make certain assumptions, to create a model that will produce estimated survival and disease-free survival probabilities for patients with specified values of three variables. Techniques for doing this are presented in Chapters 4 and 5. For example, you will learn how to estimate the probability that a patient with a stage II tumor of thickness 1.5 mm at site 1 treated by treatment A will survive for at least three years.

1.6 Functions That Describe Survival

1.6.1 The Distribution Function, Survival Function, and Density

The survival time of a subject being followed on a clinical study will be thought of as a random variable, *T*. As with random variables in other areas of statistics, this random variable can be characterized by its cumulative distribution function which, you will recall (see Appendix B) is defined by

$$F(t) = \Pr[T \leq t], t \geq 0 \tag{1.1}$$

That is, for any nonnegative value of *t*, F(t) is the probability that survival time will be less than or equal to *t*. Of course, you could just as well describe the random variable, *T*, in terms of the probability that survival time will be greater than *t*. This function is called the survival function and will be denoted S(t). We then have

$$S(t) = 1 - F(t) = \Pr[T > t], t \geq 0 \tag{1.2}$$

By convention, S(t) is usually used in survival analysis, although F(t) is more commonly used in other areas of statistics.

The density function, denoted f(t), is also used to describe a random variable that represents survival time. Recall that it is the derivative of the distribution function. Thus $f(t) = F'(t) = -S'(t)$.

1.6.2 The Hazard Function

Another very useful way of characterizing survival is by a function called the hazard function, which we will usually denote by h(t). It is the instantaneous rate of change of the death probability at time *t*, on the condition that the patient survived to time *t*. The formula for the hazard is

$$h(t) = \frac{f(t)}{S(t)} = \frac{-S'(t)}{S(t)}, t \geq 0 \tag{1.3}$$

Although the hazard at time *t* conveys information about the risk of death at that time for a patient who has survived for that long, you should not think of it as a probability. In fact, it may exceed 1.0. A way to associate the hazard, h(t), at time *t* with a probability is to note that from (1.3) and the definition of the density, f(t), as given in Appendix B, we have the approximation, when Δt is near 0 of

$$h(t)\Delta t \approx \frac{F(t + \Delta t) - F(t)}{S(t)} \tag{1.4}$$

The numerator in (1.4) is the probability that the patient dies by time $t + \Delta t$ minus the probability that he or she dies by time *t*; that is, the probability that the patient dies at time between t and $t + \Delta t$. As noted earlier, dividing by S(t) conditions on surviving to time *t*. Thus the hazard at time *t* multiplied by a small increment of time approximates the probability of dying within that increment of time after *t* for a patient who survived to time *t*. This is a handy approximation that will be used later.

By the Fundamental Theorem of Calculus, if we plot the graph of the function y = f(t), then for any value, t_0, of t, $F(t_0)$ is the area above the horizontal axis, under the curve, and to the left of a vertical line at t_0. $S(t_0)$ is the area to the right of t_0. Figure 1.3 illustrates this property for $t_0 = 2$ and an arbitrary density function f(t).

Figure 1.3

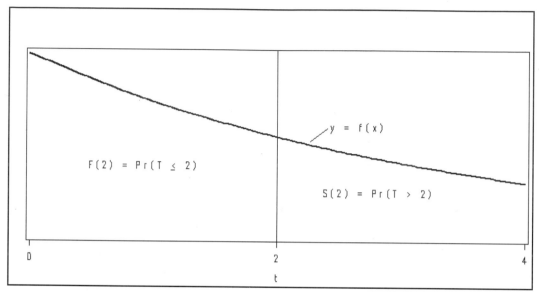

If we take the definition of h(t) in (1.3) and integrate both sides, we get

$$\int_0^t h(u)\,du = -\int_0^t \frac{S'(u)}{S(u)}\,du = -\log[S(t)].$$

So that   (1.5)

$$S(t) = e^{-\int_0^t h(u)\,du}.$$

The integral, $\int_0^t h(u)\,du$, in (1.5) is called the cumulative hazard at time t and it plays a critical role in long-term survival. If this integral increases without bound as $t \rightarrow \infty$, then S(t) approaches 0 as $t \rightarrow \infty$. In other words, there are no long-term survivors or "cures." If, however, the integral approaches a limit, $c < \infty$, as $t \rightarrow \infty$, then S(t) approaches exp(–c) as $t \rightarrow \infty$. In this case, we can think of exp(–c) as the "cure rate." Estimation of a cure rate is one of the most important and challenging problems of survival analysis. An approach to this problem will be presented in Chapter 5.

1.7 Exercises

1.7.1 Starting with a hazard function, $h(t) = \lambda t + \gamma$ for $\lambda > 0$ and $\gamma > 0$, find the associated survival function, S(t) and density, f(t).

1.7.2 Starting with a hazard function, $h(t) = \alpha\exp(-\beta t)$ for $\alpha > 0$ and $\beta \neq 0$, find the survival function, S(t), and density, f(t). What is the limit of S(t) as $t \to \infty$ if $\beta > 0$? What is the limit of S(t) as $t \to \infty$ if $\beta < 0$?

1.8 Some Commonly Used Survival Functions

1.8.1 The Exponential Function

The simplest function that we might use to describe survival is the exponential function given by

$$S(t) = \exp(-\lambda t), \quad \lambda > 0, \, t \geq 0. \tag{1.6}$$

This survival function has only one parameter, the constant hazard, λ. The median survival time, defined as the solution of S(t) = 0.5, is easily seen to be $t = -\log(0.5)/\lambda$. Also, if we assume a probability of p of surviving for time t, then λ is determined by $\lambda = -\log(p)/t$. Because of its simplicity, the assumption that survival data are exponentially distributed is very popular, although its validity is sometimes questionable. A graph of an exponential survival function is given as Figure 1.4.

Figure 1.4

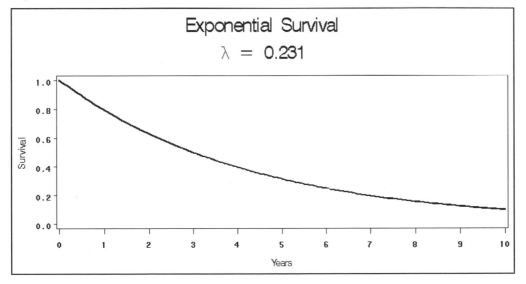

1.8.2 The Weibull Function

A more complex, but often more realistic, model for survival is given by the Weibull function

$$S(t) = \exp(-\lambda t^{\gamma}),\, t \geq 0,\, \lambda > 0,\, \gamma > 0 \tag{1.7}$$

Note that the exponential survival function is a special case of the Weibull with $\gamma = 1$. The hazard function is given by $h(t) = \lambda \gamma t^{\gamma-1}$. It increases as t increases if $\gamma > 1$ and decreases as t increases if $0 < \gamma < 1$. Graphs of survival functions of each type are shown in Figure 1.5.

Figure 1.5

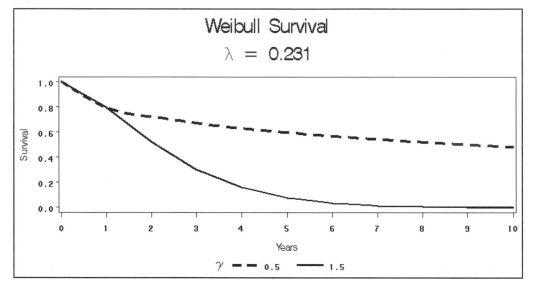

Other functions, such as the lognormal, gamma, and Rayleigh, are also sometimes used to describe survival, but will not be discussed in this chapter.

1.9 Exercises

1.9.1 Show that if $S(t) = e^{-\lambda t}$, the hazard function is the constant, λ, the density is given by $\lambda e^{-\lambda t}$, and the mean survival time is $1/\lambda$.

1.9.2 Find the value of λ and the median survival time for an exponential survival function if $S(3) = .4$.

1.9.3 Show that, for an exponential survival distribution, the probability of surviving past time $t_0 + t_1$ given that an individual has survived past t_0 equals the unconditional probability of surviving past t_1. In other words, the probability of surviving t_1 more units of time is the same at the beginning as it is after surviving t_0 units of time. This is often referred to as the "memoryless" property of the exponential distribution. Hint: In symbols, this means that $S(t_0 + t_1)/S(t_0) = S(t_0)$.

1.9.4 Show that the hazard function associated with a Weibull survival function is $\lambda \gamma t^{\gamma-1}$ and find the density function.

1.10 Functions That Allow for Cure

1.10.1 The Idea of "Cure Models"

The previously discussed survival functions are all based on proper distribution functions, that is $F(t) \to 1$ as $t \to \infty$. Of course this means that $S(t) \to 0$ as $t \to \infty$. Often, however, a model, to be realistic, must allow for a nonzero probability of indefinite survival—that is, a nonzero probability of cure. Suppose you were analyzing survival data for a cohort of children who had Hodgkin's Disease. You might find that a considerable number of patients were alive, apparently free of disease, and still being followed after ten years and that no deaths had occurred after four years. It would be reasonable to surmise that a nonzero proportion had been cured in this case. A survival function that goes to zero with increasing time would not be a good model for such data.

1.10.2 Mixture Models

One way to model such data is to assume that the population being studied is a mixture of two subpopulations. A proportion, π, is cured and the remaining proportion, $1 - \pi$, has a survival function as in Section 1.10.1. If, for example, the survival function of the non-cured patients is exponential, the survival of the entire population might be given by

$$S(t) = \pi + (1 - \pi)\exp(-\lambda t), t \geq 0 \tag{1.8}$$

The graph of such a survival function approaches a plateau at $S(t) = \pi$ as $t \to \infty$. Goldman (1984) and Sposto and Sather (1985) have studied this model. Of course, the exponential function in (1.8) can be replaced by any survival function. For example, Gamel et al. (1994) have considered such a model based on a lognormal survival function for the noncured patients.

1.10.3 The Stepwise Exponential Model

Another model that can allow for cure is the piecewise exponential model as described by Shuster (1992). This model assumes that the hazard is constant over intervals, but can be different for different intervals. For example, we might have $h(t) = \lambda$ for $0 \leq t < t_0$ and $h(t) = 0$ for $t \geq t_0$. For this model the survival function is given by

$$S(t) = \exp(-\lambda t) \ \text{ for } 0 \leq t < t_0$$
$$S(t) = \exp(-\lambda t_0) \ \text{ for } t \geq t_0 \tag{1.9}$$

1.10.4 The Gompertz Model

Still another model for survival that allows for cure is given by the Gompertz function defined by

$$S(t) = \exp\{-\frac{\gamma}{\theta}[\exp(\theta t) - 1]\} \ \gamma > 0, t \geq 0 \tag{1.10}$$

Although this function appears to be rather complicated, it follows by (1.7) from the assumption that $h(t)$ is increasing or decreasing exponentially with rate θ as t increases. In fact, this function was first used by Gompertz (1825) to describe mortality in an aging male population in which he observed an exponentially increasing hazard. With $\theta < 0$ it's not hard to see that $S(t) \to \exp(\gamma/\theta)$ as $t \to \infty$. This function was first used to describe survival of patients by Haybittle (1959). It has also been studied in this context by others (Gehan and Siddiqui, 1973; Cantor and Shuster, 1992; Garg, Rao, and

Redmond,1970). $S(t) \to \exp(-\gamma t)$ as $\theta \to 0$, so that the exponential function can be thought of as a special case of the Gompertz function with $\theta = 0$.

Figures 1.6 through 1.8 give graphs of each of these three types of survival functions allowing for cure. For purposes of comparison, the parameters in each case are chosen so that the cure rate is 30% and the non-cures have a median survival time of one year.

Figure 1.6

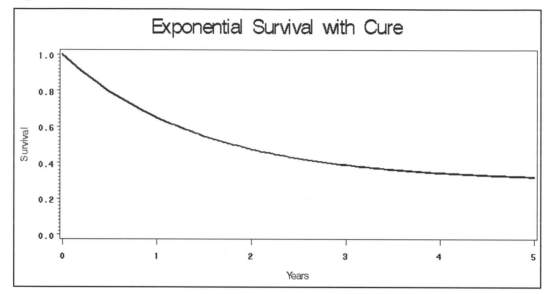

Figure 1.7

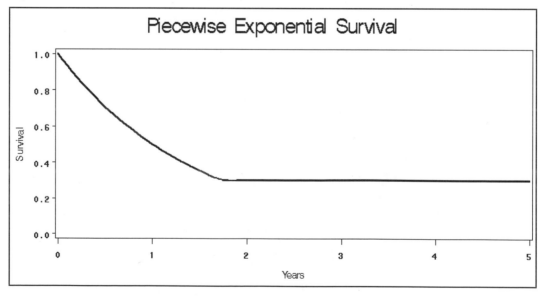

Figure 1.8

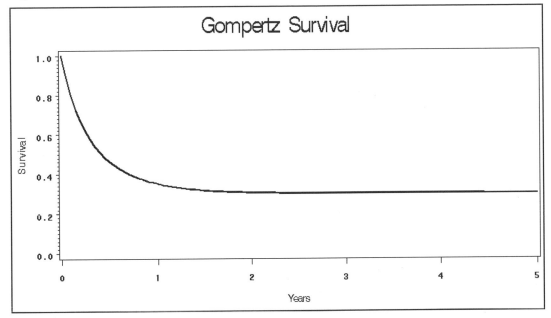

1.11 Fully Parametric and Nonparametric Methods

If you are willing to assume that survival can be described by a distribution of one of these types, or some other, then the way to use a set of sample data to make estimates or inferences about the underlying population is clear. You need to obtain estimates of the parameter(s) that determine the distribution. Then the desired estimates follow almost immediately. For example, let us assume that survival in a particular cohort can be described by the exponential model (1.6). Then if λ is estimated, by methods to be described later in this book, to be 0.043 where the unit of time is years, then $\exp(-3\times0.043) = \exp(-0.129) = 0.879$ is the estimated probability of survival for at least three years. Furthermore, if the standard error of the estimate of λ is known, then the delta method, as described in Appendix B, permits us to calculate the standard error of the estimate of $S(t)$ and confidence intervals for $S(3)$. Similarly, if exponentiality is assumed for survival of patients in each of two treatment arms, then the superiority of one of the treatments is equivalent to its having a smaller λ. These matters will be discussed in more detail in Chapter 5.

Often, however, statisticians are reluctant to base analyses on assumed types of distributions, for reasons explained earlier in this chapter. Thus we would rather make statements that hold whatever the underlying distribution. Because of this, we often prefer nonparametric methods. As you will see in Chapters 2 and 3, these methods are often quite simple and intuitive. Yet under certain conditions they have almost as much power as the competitive parametric method. Most SAS survival analysis procedures, and most of this book, will be based upon such methods. Between the fully parametric and nonparametric methods we find methods that, while not assuming that a density or survival function has a specific form, do make certain assumptions about the survival distribution. Such methods are frequently called semiparametric.

1.12 Some Common Assumptions

In the analysis of survival data, we are frequently concerned with the effect of a variable on survival. The treatment to which a patient is assigned might be such a variable. Other variables might be demographic—age, race, sex for example. Still others might be associated with the patient's disease—stage of disease, number of blocked arteries, Karnofsky performance status, and so on. There are many ways in which a variable can affect survival. Suppose a variable that is thought to affect survival is observed and let $h(t, x)$ be the hazard at time t for a patient with a value of x for that variable. The survival function has the proportional hazards property if for some positive number, r, we have for all values of t and x

$$\frac{h(t, x + 1)}{h(t, x)} = r \tag{1.11}$$

According to this assumption, the effect of the variable is multiplicative on the hazard function. Specifically, a change of one unit in x multiplies the hazard (at all times) by some constant, r (which is called the hazard ratio). Then, whether the hazard is increasing, decreasing, or not affected by increasing values of the variable depends upon whether that constant, r, is greater than, less than, or equal to one, respectively. It can be shown that (1.11) implies that $h(t, x) = h_0(t)e^{\beta x}$ where $h_0(t)$, which is $h(t, 0)$, is called the "baseline hazard function" and β is the logarithm of r. Alternatively, we can write $\log[h(t, x)] = \log[h_0(t)] + \beta x$. This creates a linear regression type of problem. The estimation of β is the key to describing the effect of the covariate x on survival. This will be discussed in Chapter 4.

Another possible assumption is that a variable might accelerate (or decelerate) mortality. Let $S_1(t)$ and $S_2(t)$ be the survival functions for two values of a variable. Often this variable will be the treatment a patient received, so that $S_1(t)$ and $S_2(t)$ are the survival functions for the two treatments. Then, for some positive number, b, we might have $S_1(t) = S_2(bt)$ for all nonnegative values of t. In other words, the probability of surviving to time t for one value of the variable is the same as the probability of surviving to time bt for the other. This is called the accelerated failure time assumption. Whether the value associated with $S_1(t)$ is better than, worse than, or equivalent to the value associated with $S_2(t)$ depends upon whether b is less than, greater than, or equal to one respectively. Now the estimation of b is the key to describing the relationship between the two survival distributions. This will be discussed in Chapter 5.

While, as we shall see, there are statistical methods that do not require such assumptions, often these assumptions are reasonable and can lead to more powerful and informative analyses. Assumptions such as these, which attribute certain properties to the underlying survival distribution without specifying its form, are said to be semiparametric. Methods based on such assumptions occupy a place between the nonparametric and parametric methods.

1.13 Exercises

1.13.1 Show that if the proportional hazards assumption holds with a change of one unit associated with a hazard ratio of r, then a change of two units would be associated with a hazard ratio of r^2.

1.13.2 Suppose the proportional hazard assumption holds for treatments 0 and 1 with hazards $h_0(t)$ and $h_1(t)$, respectively, so that $h_1(t)/ h_0(t) = r$ for all $t \geq 0$. If $S_0(t)$ and $S_1(t)$ are the survival functions, show that $S_1(t) = S_0(t)^r$. This is known as the Lehmann alternative.

1.13.3 Show that if two treatment groups (say group = 1 and group = 2) both have exponential survival, then the group variable satisfies the proportional hazards property. Also show that the two groups satisfy the accelerated failure time assumption.

Chapter 2   Nonparametric Survival Function Estimation

2.1 The Kaplan-Meier Estimate of the Survival Function 17
2.2 Exercise 20
2.3 The Actuarial Life Table 20
2.4 The Variance of the Kaplan-Meier Estimator 23
2.5 Hypothesis Tests 24
2.6 Confidence Intervals 25
2.7 Some Problems with the Kaplan-Meier Estimator of S(t) 25
2.8 Using PROC LIFETEST 27
2.9 Two Macros as Alternatives to PROC LIFETEST 32
2.10 Planning a Study to Control the Standard Error 37
2.11 Example 39
2.12 The KMPLAN Macro 39
2.13 Exercise 42
2.14 Interval-Censored Data 42
2.15 Macros 48

2.1 The Kaplan-Meier Estimate of the Survival Function

This chapter discusses the estimation of a survival function, S(t), for various values of *t* from data of the form $(t_1, d_1), \ldots, (t_n, d_n)$ as described previously. For now, let's assume that the times are ordered and that there are no ties, so that $t_1 < t_2 < \ldots < t_n$. In Chapter 5 you will learn about estimation methods that assume a survival distribution of a given form.

2.1.1 Example

Suppose that you follow ten patients for survival and observe the following times (in months):

5, 12, 25, 26, 27, 28, 37, 39, 40+, 42+.

You would like to estimate the 36-month survival rate, i.e., S(36), from these data. Since four of the ten survived more than 36 months, it is reasonable to estimate S(36), the probability of surviving at least 36 months by 4/10 or 0.40. Now suppose, however, that there are an additional three patients who were censored at 32, 33, and 34 months respectively, so that now the data look like this:

5, 12, 25, 26, 27, 28, 32+, 33+, 34+, 37, 39, 40+, 42+.

What do you do now? On the one hand, you don't know whether any of these patients with censored times survived more than 36 months or not, so you might be inclined to omit them and still estimate S(36) by 0.40. On the other hand, these three patients, known to have survived for more than 32, 33, and 34 months, respectively, had better prospects of surviving at least 36 months than a patient who had just been entered. The fact that they have survived as long as they have should be taken into consideration. The problem is how to use these censored times. The following method, first presented by Kaplan and Meier(1958), allows us to use such censored data correctly in estimating S(t).

Consider the data set. Since the first death occurs at five months, it is reasonable to estimate S(t) by 1.00 for $0 \leq t < 5$. Of the 13 patients at risk just prior to five months, 12 survived past that time. Thus you would estimate S(t) by 12/13 for $t = 5$ or slightly more than 5. There's no reason to reduce that estimate prior to 12 months, since there are no additional deaths until $t = 12$. Now, 11 of the 12 patients who survived past $t = 5$ survived past $t = 12$. Thus, the probability of surviving past 12 months, *for those who survived past 5 months*, is estimated to be 11/12. In order to survive past $t = 12$, the patient must first survive past $t = 5$ and then survive from $t = 5$ past $t = 12$. The probability of doing both is the product of the probabilities of each and is, therefore, estimated by (12/13)(11/12). Continuing in this fashion, we see that the probability of surviving past 25 is estimated by (12/13)(11/12)(10/11), and the probability of surviving past 28 is estimated by (12/13)(11/12)(10/11)(9/10)(8/9)(7/8). Here's where the censored times play a role. The next death is at $t = 37$. But because of the three censored times at times prior to 37, there were only four patients who were at risk at $t = 37$ (not seven). Three of these four survived past 37 months. So you should estimate the probability of surviving past 37 months, for those surviving past 28 months, to be 3/4. The probability of surviving past 37 months is, therefore, estimated by (12/13)(11/12)(10/11)(9/10)(8/9)(7/8)(3/4).

Do you see the pattern in this? At each death time t_i the probability of surviving past $t = t_i$ is reduced by being multiplied by $(r_i - 1)/r_i$ where r_i is the number at risk just prior to the ith time. Censored times do not alter that probability, but reduce the number at risk at succeeding death times. The calculations for the estimated values of S(t), denoted $\hat{S}(t)$, are illustrated in Table 2.1:

Table 2.1 Calculation of Kaplan-Meier Estimates of S(t)

i	t_i	d_i	r_i	$\hat{S}(t) \; t_i \leq t < t_{i+1}$
0	0	-	-	1.00
1	5	1	13	12/13 = 0.92
2	12	1	12	0.92(11/12) = 0.85
3	25	1	11	0.85(10/11) = 0.77
4	26	1	10	0.77(9/10) = 0.69
5	27	1	9	0.69(7/8) = 0.62
6	28	1	8	0.62(7/8) = 0.54
7	32	0	7	0.54
8	33	0	6	0.54
9	34	0	5	0.54
10	37	1	4	0.54(3/4) = 0.40
11	39	1	3	0.40(2/3) = 0.27
12	40	0	2	0.27
13	42	0	1	0.27

The table is called a Kaplan-Meier, or product-limit, life table. In this table, each r_i is the number of patients at risk at time t_i, i.e., the number whose times are greater than or equal to t_i. Each d_i is 0 or 1 depending upon whether the time is a censored or a death time. The graphical representation of the calculated survival probabilities, shown in Figure 2.1, is often called a Kaplan-Meier survival curve. The values of $\hat{S}(t)$, are called Kaplan-Meier, or product-limit, survival estimates.

Figure 2.1

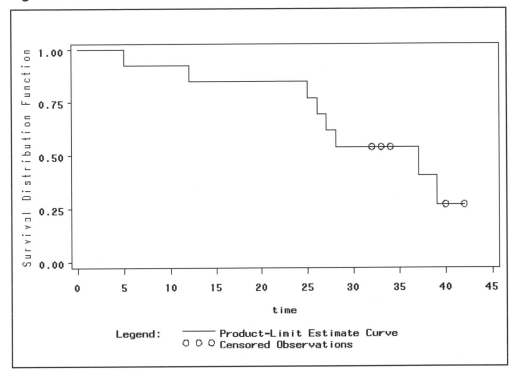

Notice that the Kaplan-Meier survival function is a step function that is decreased at each death time. You may be tempted to draw a smooth curve connecting the upper right-hand corner of the steps or to connect them with straight-line segments, reasoning that the "true" survival curve is not really flat over intervals of time. You should resist that temptation. If there are no deaths in our sample over a time interval, the only consistent way to estimate the survival probabilities during that interval is with a horizontal line segment. In this graph, the censored survival times are indicated with small circles. That step is not necessary, but it is often done to provide additional information. Later in this chapter you will learn how to produce tables and graphs like these.

Some writers prefer to plot $1 - \hat{S}(t)$ (the estimated distribution function) rather than $\hat{S}(t)$. This simply plots the estimated proportion of those who died over time instead of the estimated proportion surviving. A recent article (Pocock et al., 2002) argues that such graphs make comparisons of survival functions more apparent.

2.1.2 The Kaplan-Meier Estimation Formula

While in theory there should not be tied observation times, in actual practice ties are possible. This can be accounted for by letting the t_i be the observation times and, for any i, allowing for the possibility that there is more than one patient whose observation time is t_i. Let d_i be the number of deaths at time t_i. Then if there is only one patient whose time is t_i, this corresponds to the previous notation.

Examine the table in order to confirm the following formula

$$\hat{S}(t) = \prod_{t_i \le t} \left[\frac{r_i - d_i}{r_i} \right]$$

(2.1)

The popularity of the Kaplan-Meier method is due to several desirable properties possessed by the resultant estimator of S(t). The most important is that, under rather mild assumptions regarding the censoring distribution, $\hat{S}$ (t) is asymptotically normally distributed with mean S(t). This means that as the sample size gets larger and larger, the random variable $\hat{S}$ (t) gets close to having a normal distribution and the mean value of that distribution is the true, unknown, value of S(t). Thus by calculating an estimate of the variance of $\hat{S}$ (t_0), we can construct confidence intervals for S(t_0) and perform hypothesis tests concerning it. This will be explored more fully in Section 2.6.

2.2 Exercise

Calculate the Kaplan-Meier survival function for the following data. Times are in months. 1.2, 4.5, 7.3+, 9.0, 11.4, 12.3+, 14.8, 17.6, 21.6+, 31.1.

2.3 The Actuarial Life Table

Long before the now-classic Kaplan and Meier paper, demographers and actuaries were using a method called the actuarial life table to study the longevity of natural populations. Their motivation came from commercial needs. With the development of the insurance industry, it became important to be able to calculate the probability that someone of a given age would survive to various ages in order to price insurance policies and annuities. Although demographers and actuaries were dealing with mortality rates in natural populations rather that the survivorship of patients with a disease or subject to a particular treatment regimen, their methods can be applied to these situations as well. The actuarial life table is particularly suitable when, instead of knowing the actual survival and censoring times, you know only that they are in particular time intervals, such as 0 to 3 months, 3 months to 6 months, etc.

2.3.1 The Actuarial Estimates

To construct the actuarial life table, start by partitioning the time axis into subintervals by the numbers $0 = \tau_0 < \tau_1 < \tau_2 < \ldots$ The partitions are usually taken to be of equal length (e.g., three months, six months, or one year), but that is not necessary. Suppose at time 0 we have N individuals at risk and that during the first interval, $[\tau_0, \tau_1)$, there are c_1 individuals censored. Then the number of patients at risk during that interval went from N at time τ_0 to $N - c_1$ at time τ_1. It is reasonable to assume that it would not be introducing much error to consider the number at risk during this interval to be constant and equal to the average of these two values, $N - c_1/2$. This is called *the effective number at risk* in this interval. Suppose there were e_1 deaths in this interval. Then the probability of dying in this interval is estimated to be e_1 divided by the effective number at risk in the interval, i.e., $e_1/(N - c_1/2)$. Likewise, the probability of surviving this interval is estimated to be $p_1 = 1 - e_1/(N - c_1/2)$. More generally, if r_i represents the number at risk at the beginning of the ith interval, e_i the number who die in this interval, and c_i the number censored in this interval, then $r_i - c_i/2$ will be thought of as the average (or effective) number at risk in the ith interval, and $p_i = 1 - e_i/(r_i - c_i/2)$ can be the estimated probability of surviving the ith interval for those surviving all previous intervals. This is called the conditional survival for that interval. $S(\tau_i)$ would then be estimated by the product of the p_j's for $j \le i$. The actuarial method is somewhat dependent on the choice of the τ_i's. It is sometimes preferred when the sample size and the number of deaths is quite large. In that case the Kaplan-Meier life table can be lengthy, while the actuarial table is more compact. Also, the Kaplan-Meier method requires some calculation at each death time, while the actuarial method requires only one calculation for each interval. Since we do this with computers, this is not as important a consideration as it once was. In medical research, the Kaplan-Meier method is generally preferred and discussions that follow focus on that method. Actually, if we were to apply the actuarial method with smaller and smaller subinterval lengths, we would be approaching the Kaplan-Meier results as a limit. This is why the Kaplan-Meier method is often called the product limit method. The actuarial life table for the data presented earlier in this chapter is given in Table 2.2. A graph of this estimated survival function produced by this method is given in Figure 2.2. Interval widths were chosen to be six months, although other choices are possible.

Table 2.2 Calculation of Actuarial Estimates of S(t)

Interval (months)	Number Entering Interval	Number Censored	Effective Number in Interval	Deaths in Interval	Conditional Survival	Cumulative Survival
[0, 6)	13	0	13.0	1	0.92	1.00
[6, 12)	12	0	12.0	0	1.00	0.92
[12, 18)	12	0	12.0	1	1.00	0.92
[18, 24)	11	0	11.0	0	1.00	0.85
[24, 30)	11	0	11.0	4	0.64	0.85
[30, 36)	7	3	5.5	0	1.00	0.54
[36, 42)	4	1	3.5	2	0.43	0.54
[42, ∞)	1	1	0.5	0	1.00	0.23

Figure 2.2

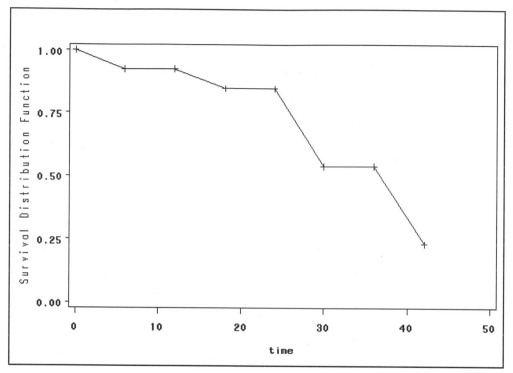

2.3.2 Estimates of Other Functions

The actuarial method is also called the life table method in the documentation for PROC LIFETEST. This method can also produce estimates of the density and hazard functions at the midpoint of each subinterval. Such estimates are not readily derived from the Kaplan-Meier method. Using τ_{mi} to represent the midpoint of the ith interval, and approximating the derivative by the fraction used in defining that derivative, we can estimate the density $f(\tau_{mi})$ by

$$\hat{f}(\tau_{m_i}) = [\hat{S}_a(\tau_{i-1}) - \hat{S}_a(\tau_i)] / (\tau_i - \tau_{i-1}) \tag{2.2}$$

where τ_{mi} is the midpoint of the ith interval and $\hat{S}(.)$ represents actuarial survival estimates. Furthermore, we can estimate the hazard $h(\tau_{mi})$ by $\hat{h}(t_{mi}) = \hat{f}(\tau_{mi})/\hat{S}_a(\tau_{mi})$, where $\hat{S}_a(\tau_{mi})$ is estimated by $[\hat{S}_a(\tau_{i-1}) + \hat{S}_a(\tau_i)]/2$. A little algebra shows that this hazard estimate for the midpoint of the interval (τ_{i-1}, τ_i) can be written as

$$\hat{h}(\tau_{m_i}) = \frac{e_i}{[r_i - (c_i + e_i)/2](\tau_i - \tau_{i-1})} \tag{2.3}$$

Note that this estimate can be thought of as the estimated probability of dying in an interval in which there were e_i deaths and an "average" of $r_i - (c_i + e_i)/2$ at risk divided by the length of the interval. These estimates may not be very good for small samples. In fact, any interval with no deaths would have an estimated hazard of zero at its midpoint. This is not surprising, but it could be rather unrealistic.

2.3.3 Exercise

For the data in Exercise 2.2, calculate the actuarial life table. Take intervals of width six months. Find the estimated hazard at the midpoint of each interval.

2.4 The Variance of the Kaplan-Meier Estimator

There are two formulas that have been advocated and used for estimating the variance of the Kaplan-Meier estimate of the survival function. The most popular one is Greenwood's formula (Greenwood, 1926). It is the method used by PROC LIFETEST, which will be discussed in Section 2.8.

2.4.1 Greenwood's Formula

The most commonly used estimate of the variance of $\hat{S}(t)$ was originally described by Greenwood (1926) for the actuarial estimate of the survival function. It can be shown, however, that it is appropriate for the Kaplan-Meier estimate as well. I will give a rough derivation of it that treats certain quantities that are actually random as being constant and ignores the dependence of the factors in (2.1). Miller (1981) gives a more complete argument.

We begin by considering the variance of $\log \hat{S}(t)$. Taking the natural logarithm of both sides of (4.1) we obtain

$$\log[\hat{S}(t)] = \sum_{t_i \leq t} \log \frac{r_i - d_i}{r_i} \tag{2.4}$$

Now each $(r_i - d_i)/r_i$ can be thought of as an estimate of a proportion. Specifically, it is the proportion of those at risk at time t_i who do not die at that time. Hence its variance is estimated by.

$$\frac{\dfrac{r_i - d_i}{r_i} \dfrac{d_i}{r_i}}{r_i} = \frac{(r_i - d_i)d_i}{r_i^3}$$

Using the delta method, (see Appendix B) and the fact that the derivative of $\log(x)$ is $1/x$, the variance of $\log[(r_i - d_i)/r_i]$ can be estimated by $\{(r_i - d_i)/r_i\}^{-2}\{[(r_i - d_i)d_i]/r_i^3\}$ which reduces to $d_i/[(r_i - d_i)r_i]$. Thus we have

$$\text{var}[\log \hat{S}(t)] \approx \sum_{t_i \leq t} \frac{d_i}{(r_i - d_i)r_i} \tag{2.5}$$

Again, we apply the delta method, this time to estimate $\text{var}[\hat{S}(t)]$ as $\text{var}\{\exp[\log(\hat{S}(t)]\}$. Recalling that the derivative of $\exp(x)$ is $\exp(x)$, and that $\exp[\log(x)] = x$, the final result is

$$\text{var}[\hat{S}(t)] \approx [\hat{S}(t)]^2 \sum_{t_i \leq t} \frac{d_i}{(r_i - d_i)r_i} \tag{2.6}$$

Formula (2.6) is known as Greenwood's formula for estimating the variance of $\hat{S}(t)$.

2.4.2 Peto's Formula

Another simpler formula has been proposed by Peto (Peto et al., 1977). Let $R(t)$ be the number of patients at risk at time t. That is, $R(t)$ is the number of patients who have not died or been censored with times less than t. Peto's formula is given by

$$\text{var}[\hat{S}(t)] \approx \frac{[\hat{S}(t)]^2[1 - \hat{S}(t)]}{R(t)} \tag{2.7}$$

The justification for this formula for estimating the variance of $\hat{S}(t)$ is quite simple. If no patients had censored times less than t, then $\hat{S}(t)$ would be an estimate of a binomial proportion and its variance would be $\hat{S}(t)[1 - \hat{S}(t)]/N$ where N is the number of patients in the study. In that case, $R(t) = N\hat{S}(t)$ and (2.7) is exact. If some patients are censored at times less than t, then $R(t) < N\hat{S}(t)$. Thus, (2.7) overestimates the variance but, it is claimed, not by much. Also, note that (2.7) produces variance estimates that are appropriately increased as the number at risk is diminished either by death or censoring. The Greenwood formula produces variance estimates that change only at death times. Shuster (1992) provides an excellent discussion of the comparative merits of these two estimates.

2.4.3 Exercise

For the data in Exercise 2.2, find the estimated variance of the Kaplan-Meier estimate at each death time using both Greenwood's formula and Peto's formula.

2.5 Hypothesis Tests

From the fact that $\hat{S}(t)$ is asymptotically normal with mean $S(t)$ we can take $[\hat{S}(t) - S(t)]/[\text{var}(\hat{S}(t)]^{1/2}$ to be distributed, approximately, as a normal random variable with mean zero and variance one for reasonably large sample sizes. This, in turn, leads to hypothesis tests involving $S(t)$. For example, for a specific value, t_0, of t we would reject the null hypothesis of H_0: $S(t_0) = p$ in favor of the alternative H_A: $S(t_0) \neq p$ at the 0.05 significance level if and only if $|\hat{S}(t_0) - p| \geq 1.96\{\text{Var}[\hat{S}(t_0)]\}^{1/2}$. Also, if $S_1(t)$ and $S_2(t)$ are survival functions for two independent groups and $\hat{S}_1(t)$ and $\hat{S}_2(t)$ are their Kaplan-Meier estimates then, for any value, t_0, of t we would reject the null hypothesis H_0: $S_1(t_0) = S_2(t_0)$ in favor of the alternative H_A: $S_1(t_0) \neq S_2(t_0)$ at the 0.05 significance level if and only if $|\hat{S}_1(t_0) - \hat{S}_2(t_0)| > 1.96\{\text{Var}[\hat{S}_1(t_0)] + \text{Var}[\hat{S}_2(t_0)]\}^{1/2}$. Generally, however, it is preferable to compare survival curves using methods, such as those to be introduced in the next chapter, which take the entire survival curve into consideration.

2.6   Confidence Intervals

We can, of course, write a $(1 - \alpha)100\%$ confidence interval for S(t) as $\hat{S}(t_0) \pm z_{\alpha/2}\{\text{Var}[\hat{S}(t_0)]\}^{1/2}$. A problem with this approach is that it sometimes leads to confidence limits outside the permissible range (0 to 1) of S(t). One solution to this is to simply replace any computed limit that is out of this range by 0 or 1. Kalbfleisch and Prentice (1980) suggest another approach.

Let $V(t) = \log\{-\log[S(t)]\}$ and $\hat{V}(t) = \log\{-\log[\hat{S}(t)]\}$. Then using the delta method, we have

$$\text{Var}\left[\hat{V}(t)\right] \approx \frac{\text{Var}\left[\hat{S}(t)\right]}{\left[S(t)\log S(t)\right]^2} \tag{2.8}$$

Denote this approximation of $\text{Var}[\hat{V}(t)]$ by $s^2(t)$. Then $\hat{V}(t) \pm z_{\alpha/2}s(t)$ is an approximate $(1-\alpha)100\%$ confidence interval for V(t). Applying the exponential function twice produces $\hat{S}(t)^{\exp(\mp x)}$ as an approximate $(1-\alpha)100\%$ confidence interval for S(t) where $x = z_{\alpha/2}s(t)$. The endpoints of any such interval are always between 0 and 1. In this formula, either the Greenwood or Peto formula can be used for $\text{Var}[\hat{S}(t)]$. The latter gives more conservative (wider) confidence intervals.

Keep in mind that both confidence interval methods refer to pointwise confidence intervals for specified values, t_0, of t. That is, for a value of t, we are calculating values of random variables L and U such that the interval (L, U) has a probability of $(1 - \alpha)100\%$ of containing S(t). This is not the same as constructing functions L(t) and U(t) such that the probability that L(t) < S(t) < U(t) *for all values of t* is $(1 - \alpha)100\%$. Such a pair of functions is called a $(1 - \alpha)100\%$ confidence band for S(t). Two methods of producing confidence bands, developed by Hall and Wellner (1980) and Nair (1984), are implemented in Version 9 of SAS and are discussed in Section 2.8.

2.6.1 Exercise

For the data in Exercise 2.2, find 95% confidence intervals for S(t) at each observed time using a) Greenwood's formula and both methods discussed in 2.6 b) Peto's formula and both methods discussed in Section 2.6.

2.7.   Some Problems with the Kaplan-Meier Estimator of S(t)

There are other nonparametric estimators of S(t). Nelson (1969), Reid (1981), and Sander (1975) have proposed alternatives, but none has approached the popularity of the Kaplan-Meier estimator. Thus they will not be discussed further here. We should, however, point out some shortcomings of the Kaplan-Meier estimator. One problem, discussed in detail by Miller (1983), is the low efficiency of the estimates relative to the estimators that are associated with parametric models. That is, for a given sample, the variance of $\hat{S}(t)$ will be greater than the corresponding variance of the estimator based on a parametric model. Such behavior is not unexpected. The Kaplan-Meier method produces estimates that are valid while freeing us from any parametric assumptions. We always pay a price for this freedom. That price is increased variance. This problem is most severe for larger values of t– precisely those values we are likely to be most interested in. Another problem with the Kaplan-Meier estimator is the counter-intuitive property that later deaths tend to lower the estimated survival curve more than earlier deaths. This phenomenon has been reported and described by Cantor and Shuster (1992) and by Oakes (1993), although others probably have noticed it as well. To see how this happens, consider the set of survival data given as an example in Section 2.1.1. Now suppose we were to learn that the death that was recorded as happening at $t = 5$ actually did not occur until $t = 41$. This will change the Kaplan-Meier life table. It will now be as follows.

Table 2.3 Revised Kaplan-Meier Estimates of S(t)

i	t_i	d_i	r_i	$\hat{S}(t)\, t_i \leq t < t_{i+1}$
0	0	-	-	1.00
1	12	1	13	12/13 = 0.92
2	25	1	12	0.92(11/12) = 0.85
3	26	1	11	0.85(10/110 = 0.77
4	27	1	10	0.77(9/10) = 0.69
5	28	1	9	0.69(7/8) = 0.62
6	32	0	8	0.62
7	33	0	7	0.62
8	34	0	6	0.62
9	37	1	5	0.62(4/5) = 0.49
10	39	1	4	0.49(3/4) = 0.37
11	40	0	3	0.37
12	41	1	2	0.37(1/2) = 18
13	42	0	1	0.18

Compare this table to Table 2.1. In the right hand tail, the revised table actually has smaller estimated survival probabilities. Since later survival probabilities tend to be of greater interest, we would consider the revised table, with everything the same except that one death had a later time, to indicate worse survival. This seems to contradict the fact that the revised data, with one death delayed from 5 months to 41 months, apparently indicates better survival. Closer scrutiny of the calculations shows us how this happened arithmetically. In the earlier table, the death at time $t = 5$ when there were 13 patients at risk diminished the survival probability by multiplying it by 12/13. In the later table, this factor no longer appears, but the death when there were only two patients at risk reduces the survival probability by a factor of 1/2. An even more extreme example would be created if the patient who had been observed longest had died. In that case, the final survival probability estimate would be zero. This is not simply an arithmetical oddity that rarely happens in real life. Consider a study in which patients with cancer are followed for both disease-free survival and survival. An event for the disease-free survival analysis would be death from any cause or recurrence of tumor. By definition, the true survival curve for disease-free survival must be below the corresponding curve for survival. After all, for any time t, one has greater probability of dying or having disease recurrence by time *t* than of dying by that time. If, however, patients tend to die after their tumor recurs, then, as in the example, the Kaplan-Meier survival curve for survival can be below the Kaplan-Meier curve for disease-free survival.

Incidentally, sometimes a Kaplan-Meier survival curve ends at zero. Upon seeing such a curve, many will mistakenly conclude that all of the patients died. That is not the case. If the longest observed time represents a death, then that death will multiply the previous Kaplan-Meier estimate by $(1 - 1)/1$, which is zero. Thus a Kaplan-Meier curve that ends at zero means that the patient with the longest observation time died – not that all patients died.

2.8 Using PROC LIFETEST

2.8.1 Introduction to PROC LIFETEST

PROC LIFETEST produces Kaplan-Meier and actuarial life tables and graphs. Specifically, this procedure produces output that includes the survival distribution estimates as well as the Greenwood estimates of their standard errors. It can also produce comparisons of survival distributions, but this is discussed in the next chapter. To use this procedure you must have a SAS data set with a time variable. Generally you will have a variable that indicates whether the time is complete or censored as well, although that is not necessary if no times are censored. Although here this variable is taken to have the values zero and one depending on whether the time is censored or complete, respectively, PROC LIFETEST does not require that these values be used. You can specify any set of values that can indicate that the time is censored. This will be true of the macros that will be introduced later as well. This can be handy if the data contain values that indicate different reasons for censoring.

2.8.2 The Syntax for PROC LIFETEST

The basic syntax for PROC LIFETEST looks like this:

proc lifetest <*options*>;
time *timevar*<**eventvar*(*list of values*)>;

Here Timevar is the name of the variable that gives the amount of time a patient was followed and Eventvar is the name of the variable that tells whether or not the event was observed. If there are no censored times, then you can specify the TIME statement with only the time variable. The list in parentheses gives the values that indicate that the time is censored. As with other SAS procedures, the data set to be used is the last one created if it is not specified as one of the options in the procedure statement. Of course, as with many other SAS procedures, PROC LIFETEST can do analyses for distinct subgroups of the sample with a BY statement and you can use the subsetting WHERE to restrict the analysis to a subset of the data. The following is a list of the most common options that you might want to use. Many other options are available. See the PROC LIFETEST documentation in the *SAS/STAT User's Guide*.

- PLOTS = (*type*) produces graphs of some useful functions. The values for *type* can be chosen from

SURVIVAL or S	for a graph of the estimated survival function versus time
HAZARD or H	for a graph of the hazard function versus time
PDF or P	for a graph of the density function versus time

LOGSURV or LS	for a graph log $\hat{S}$ (t) versus time
LOGLOGS or LLS	for a graph of log[–log $\hat{S}$ (t)] versus log(t).

The requests for the hazard and density graphs are valid only if the actuarial method is used. The graphs of log $\hat{S}$ (t) versus time and log[–log $\hat{S}$ (t)] versus log(t) can be helpful in deciding on a parametric model. This will be discussed in Chapter 5. Starting with Version 7, the default is to print graphs in high resolution. This is what you would probably want if you are using an inkjet or laser printer, but it will work only if you have SAS/GRAPH installed. You can use the GOPTIONS statement and the SYMBOL statement to customize the graphs. The SYMBOL statement can also be used to control the lines. The default is to use different colors for the graphs. You might want to alter that if you plan to print the graph in black and white.

- METHOD = *type* specifies the type of survival estimate calculated. Using PL or KM for type produces Kaplan-Meier estimates. (PL stands for "product-limit", another name for the Kaplan-Meier estimate.) ACT or LIFE or LT produces actuarial estimates. If the METHOD option is not used, Kaplan-Meier estimates are produced by default. If the actuarial method is chosen, the output includes hazard and density function estimates at the interval midpoints as well as their standard errors. If you choose actuarial estimates, you can specify that the intervals be used in several ways. You can give the endpoints explicitly by a statement like `intervals = 2, 4, 6, 8, 10, 12` or `intervals = 2 to 12 by 2`. Note that the first interval will start with 0 even if that value is not given. Instead, you can specify the width of each interval with a statement of the form WIDTH = *value*. A third choice is to specify the number of intervals with a statement of the form NINTERVAL = *value*. PROC LIFETEST will then divide the entire range of the times by the number chosen. It may alter that number slightly to produce endpoints that are round numbers. Finally, you can choose to use none of these choices. In that case PROC LIFETEST will proceed as if you had specified `ninterval = 10`.

- If you want to produce a SAS data set which contains the survival function estimates as well as lower and upper bounds of a confidence interval for the survival function, you can specify OUTSURV = *dataset name* or OUTS = *dataset name*. You might want to do this in order to use the values in this data set for further calculations or analyses. If you use the actuarial method, you will also get confidence intervals for the density function and hazard function. The default is to get 95% confidence intervals. You can override that with the option ALPHA = *value*. This will produce (1 – *value*)100% confidence intervals. Note that the confidence intervals are symmetric of the form *estimator* $\pm\ z_{\alpha/2}$se. For the survival estimate confidence interval, *se* is the square root of the Greenwood variance. Bounds below 0.0 or above 1.0 are replaced by 0.0 and 1.0, respectively.

- You can use an option of the form TIMELIST = *number-list* where *number-list* is a list of time values. This option can be used to produce a Kaplan-Meier table that contains rows for only those times in the list. By using this option, you can produce more compact printouts. For example, suppose you have survival data for 500 patients with follow-up of up to 10 years. Without this option, the Kaplan-Meier life table could contain up to 501 lines, one for each distinct time and one for time zero. If you use the TIMELIST option as follows: `timelist = 1 2 3 4 5 6 7 8 9 10`, you would produce a life table with only 11 lines.

Starting with Version 9, PROC LIFETEST can produce a data set containing more information about the estimated survival function. The SURVIVAL statement produces a data set containing the survival estimates and, optionally, several other useful values as well. Adding the option OUT = *dataset name* allows you to specify the name of this data set. CONFTYPE = *type* will produce confidence intervals based on a transformation that ensures that the endpoints are between 0 and 1. One of these transformations, CLOGLOG, produces confidence intervals based on the transformation $g(x) = \log[-\log(x)]$ discussed earlier. Three other transformations are available. CONFBAND = *type* causes confidence bands to be produced. Values for *type* can be EP for the method of Nair (called equal precision confidence bands), HW for the method of Hall and Wellner, or ALL for both. The option ALPHA = *value* allows you to specify the precision of the confidence intervals and confidence bands. The default value is 0.05 for 95% confidence intervals and confidence bands. This option can be used only with product limit estimates.

2.8.3 *Example of the Use of PROC LIFETEST*

The following program uses data generated in a clinical trial for the treatment of pediatric leukemia. The trial was conducted by the Southwest Oncology Group. The event of interest was death, and the time is in years. The data from this study continue to be maintained by the Children's Oncology Group, which graciously provided, through its statistician, Jonathan Shuster, permission for its use. Output 2.1 is produced.

```
data leuk;
input time d @@;
   datalines;
0.0493 1   0.2849 1   0.4082 1   0.8767 1   0.8877 1   1.1233 1 1.2247
0   1.3753 1   1.5425 1   1.5836 1   1.7397 1   1.7589 1  1.7726 1
1.9233 1   1.9562 0   2.0493 1   2.2986 1   2.3425 1   3.7315 1   4.0548
1   4.0685 0   4.5863 1   4.9534 1   5.1534 0  5.7315 0   5.8493 1
5.8685 1   6.0712 0   6.1151 0   7.3781 0   7.6630 0   8.0438 0   8.1890
0   8.2055 0   8.2548 0   8.4274 0  8.4521 0   8.7589 0   9.0356 0
9.8959 0   9.9151 0   9.9178 0  10.1151 0  10.4027 0  10.6000 0
10.6603 1  10.6685 0  10.7260 0 10.9260 0  10.9370 0  11.2027 0
11.4548 0  11.4712 0  11.5589 0 11.6082 0  11.6164 0  11.6521 0
11.7123 0  11.7671 0  11.8466 0 11.8575 0  11.8685 0  11.9863 0
12.0082 0
;

proc lifetest plots=(s);
time time*d(0);
run;
```

Output 2.1

```
                       The LIFETEST Procedure

                   Product-Limit Survival Estimates

                             Survival

                          Standard   Number   Number
   TIME    Survival   Failure   Error     Failed    Left

  0.0000    1.0000    0        0           0        64
  0.0493    0.9844    0.0156   0.0155      1        63
  0.2849    0.9688    0.0313   0.0217      2        62
  0.4082    0.9531    0.0469   0.0264      3        61
  0.8767    0.9375    0.0625   0.0303      4        60
  0.8877    0.9219    0.0781   0.0335      5        59
  1.1233    0.9063    0.0938   0.0364      6        58
  1.2247*   .         .        .           6        57
  1.3753    0.8904    0.1096   0.0391      7        56
  1.5425    0.8745    0.1255   0.0415      8        55
  1.5836    0.8586    0.1414   0.0437      9        54
  1.7397    0.8427    0.1573   0.0457     10        53
  1.7589    0.8268    0.1732   0.0475     11        52
  1.7726    0.8109    0.1891   0.0492     12        51
  1.9233    0.7950    0.2050   0.0507     13        50
  1.9562*   .         .        .          13        49
  2.0493    0.7787    0.2213   0.0522     14        48
  2.2986    0.7625    0.2375   0.0536     15        47
  2.3425    0.7463    0.2537   0.0549     16        46
  3.7315    0.7301    0.2699   0.0560     17        45
  4.0548    0.7138    0.2862   0.0571     18        44
  4.0685*   .         .        .          18        43
  4.5863    0.6972    0.3028   0.0581     19        42
  4.9534    0.6806    0.3194   0.0590     20        41
  5.1534*   .         .        .          20        40
  5.7315*   .         .        .          20        39
  5.8493    0.6632    0.3368   0.0601     21        38
  5.8685    0.6457    0.3543   0.0610     22        37
  6.0712*   .         .        .          22        36
  6.1151*   .         .        .          22        35
  7.3781*   .         .        .          22        34
  7.6630*   .         .        .          22        33
  8.0438*   .         .        .          22        32
  8.1890*   .         .        .          22        31
  8.2055*   .         .        .          22        30
  8.2548*   .         .        .          22        29
  8.4274*   .         .        .          22        28
  8.4521*   .         .        .          22        27
  8.7589*   .         .        .          22        26
  9.0356*   .         .        .          22        25
  9.8959*   .         .        .          22        24
  9.9151*   .         .        .          22        23
  9.9178*   .         .        .          22        22
 10.1151*   .         .        .          22        21
 10.4027*   .         .        .          22        20
 10.6000*   .         .        .          22        19
 10.6603    0.6117    0.3883   0.0666     23        18
 10.6685*   .         .        .          23        17
 10.7260*   .         .        .          23        16
 10.9260*   .         .        .          23        15
 10.9370*   .         .        .          23        14
```

Output 2.1 (continued)

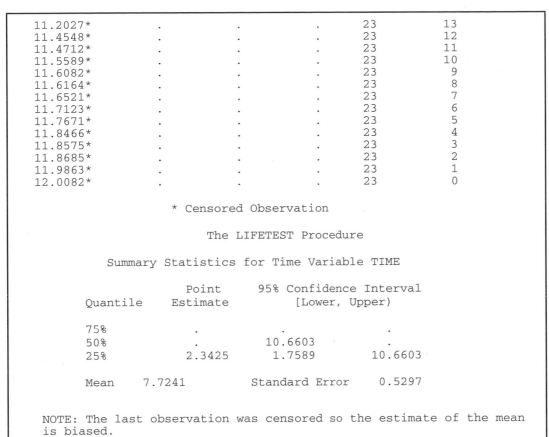

```
11.2027*          .          .          .          23        13
11.4548*          .          .          .          23        12
11.4712*          .          .          .          23        11
11.5589*          .          .          .          23        10
11.6082*          .          .          .          23         9
11.6164*          .          .          .          23         8
11.6521*          .          .          .          23         7
11.7123*          .          .          .          23         6
11.7671*          .          .          .          23         5
11.8466*          .          .          .          23         4
11.8575*          .          .          .          23         3
11.8685*          .          .          .          23         2
11.9863*          .          .          .          23         1
12.0082*          .          .          .          23         0

                    * Censored Observation

                    The LIFETEST Procedure

         Summary Statistics for Time Variable TIME

                     Point       95% Confidence Interval
         Quantile   Estimate        [Lower, Upper)

            75%         .             .                  .
            50%         .          10.6603               .
            25%      2.3425        1.7589            10.6603

         Mean   7.7241      Standard Error    0.5297


NOTE: The last observation was censored so the estimate of the mean
is biased.
```

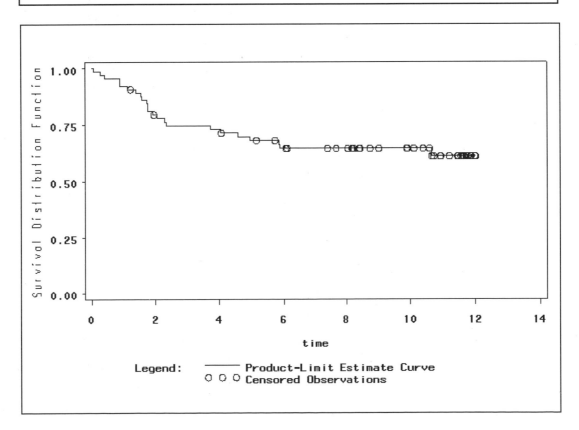

Output 2.1 (continued)

```
Summary of the Number of Censored and Uncensored Values

         Total    Failed   Censored   %Censored
          64        23        41       64.0625
```

For each uncensored time in the data set, the Kaplan-Meier estimates of the survival and death probabilities and their (Greenwood) standard errors are printed. An asterisk indicates a censored survival time. Although survival and death probabilities are not printed for censored observations, they should be taken as the same values as those for the preceding uncensored observation. The number of subjects who failed up to (and including) that time and the number remaining at risk is also printed.

PROC LIFETEST also produces certain useful summary statistics: estimates of the 25th, 50th, and 75th percentiles, when they are defined, as well as the mean. Note that the 25th percentile is the time at which the 16th patient (out of 64) died. In this example, no estimate of the 50th and 75th are printed because these percentiles are not reached. When the largest survival time is censored, the estimated mean is biased. It is underestimated in such cases. Finally, the number of observations and the number censored and uncensored are printed.

2.8.4 Exercise

Use PROC LIFETEST to analyze the data given in Exercise 2.2. Produce 95% confidence intervals (any method) and confidence bands (any method). Compare their width.

2.9 Two Macros as Alternatives to PROC LIFETEST

This section describes two macros that offer some features not available in PROC LIFETEST. They are printed in Section 2.15, but you don't need to retype them. You can download them as well as the examples from the companion Web site for this book. The first is the macro, KMTABLE. It allows you to specify either the Greenwood or Peto formula for the variance of $\hat{S}(t)$ and either $\hat{S}(t) \pm z_{\alpha/2}[\text{Var}\,\hat{S}(t)]^{1/2}$ or the alternative method described in Section 2.6 for $(1-\alpha)100\%$ confidence intervals.

The following template makes it easier to use this macro. You can simply insert it into your program after you have included a file containing the macro KMTABLE and defined the data set to be used.

```
%kmtable(dataset=              /* default is _last_ */
        ,pct=                 /* default is 95for 95% CI */
        ,time=                /* time variable */
        ,cens=                /* variable indicating censored
                                 or complete times */
        ,censval=             /* value(s) that indicate
                                 censored observation */
        ,method=              /* 1 for method used in Proc
                                 Lifetest, 2 for other methods*/
        ,variance=            /* G or g for Greenwood's
                                 formula, P or p for Peto's formula */
        ,byvar=               /* optional variable for
                                 separate tables */
        ,print=               /* yes (default) to print  table, no to
                                 suppress printing */
        )
```

Consider the data set to which we applied PROC LIFETEST earlier in this chapter. After defining this data set, you can simply insert the template with the parameters filled in as follows

```
%kmtable(
        dataset= leuk      /* default is _last_ */
                           /* default is 95 for 95% CI */
        ,time= time        /* time variable */
        ,cens=d            /* variable indicating
                              censored or complete times */
        ,censval= 0        /* value(s) that indicate
                              censored observation */
        ,method= 2         /* 1 for method used in Proc
                              Lifetest 2 for method yields limits in
                              (0,1) */
        ,variance=p        /* G or g for Greenwood's
                              formula, P or p for Peto's formula */
                           /* optional variable for
                              separate tables  */
                           /* yes (default) to print
                              table, no to suppress printing */
        )
```

or equivalently

```
%kmtable(dataset=leuk, time=time, cens=d, censval=0,
method=2, variance=p)
```

This invocation of the macro KMTABLE produces Output 2.2

Output 2.2

```
                    The SAS System


                  Survival
                  Distribution
                  Function      Peto      Method 2     Method 2
   OBS   TIME   D  Estimate     stderr    95 pct lcl   95 pct ucl

    1   0.0000  1  1.00000     0.00000    1.00000      1.00000
    2   0.0493  1  0.98438     0.01550    0.89422      0.99778
    3   0.2849  1  0.96875     0.02175    0.88078      0.99209
    4   0.4082  1  0.95313     0.02642    0.86168      0.98464
    5   0.8767  1  0.93750     0.03026    0.84199      0.97607
    6   0.8877  1  0.92188     0.03355    0.82244      0.96672
    7   1.1233  1  0.90625     0.03644    0.80317      0.95675
    8   1.2247  0  0.90625     0.03675    0.80194      0.95705
    9   1.3753  1  0.89035     0.03940    0.78265      0.94645
   10   1.5425  1  0.87445     0.04178    0.76367      0.93542
   11   1.5836  1  0.85855     0.04394    0.74497      0.92404
   12   1.7397  1  0.84265     0.04591    0.72654      0.91234
   13   1.7589  1  0.82675     0.04772    0.70836      0.90035
   14   1.7726  1  0.81086     0.04938    0.69040      0.88811
   15   1.9233  1  0.79496     0.05091    0.67265      0.87565
   16   1.9562  0  0.79496     0.05142    0.67117      0.87629
   17   2.0493  1  0.77873     0.05287    0.65326      0.86339
   18   2.2986  1  0.76251     0.05420    0.63555      0.85028
   19   2.3425  1  0.74629     0.05542    0.61802      0.83697
   20   3.7315  1  0.73006     0.05654    0.60066      0.82349
   21   4.0548  1  0.71384     0.05757    0.58347      0.80984
   22   4.0685  0  0.71384     0.05823    0.58177      0.81076
   23   4.5863  1  0.69724     0.05920    0.56435      0.79666
   24   4.9534  1  0.68064     0.06007    0.54709      0.78239
   25   5.1534  0  0.68064     0.06082    0.54524      0.78346
   26   5.7315  0  0.68064     0.06159    0.54332      0.78456
   27   5.8493  1  0.66318     0.06244    0.52537      0.76946
   28   5.8685  1  0.64573     0.06319    0.50759      0.75419
   29   6.0712  0  0.64573     0.06406    0.50550      0.75548
   30   6.1151  0  0.64573     0.06497    0.50333      0.75681
   31   7.3781  0  0.64573     0.06591    0.50105      0.75819
   32   7.6630  0  0.64573     0.06691    0.49867      0.75963
   33   8.0438  0  0.64573     0.06794    0.49616      0.76113
   34   8.1890  0  0.64573     0.06903    0.49354      0.76270
   35   8.2055  0  0.64573     0.07017    0.49078      0.76433
   36   8.2548  0  0.64573     0.07137    0.48786      0.76603
   37   8.4274  0  0.64573     0.07263    0.48479      0.76782
   38   8.4521  0  0.64573     0.07397    0.48154      0.76969
   39   8.7589  0  0.64573     0.07538    0.47809      0.77165
   40   9.0356  0  0.64573     0.07687    0.47443      0.77371
   41   9.8959  0  0.64573     0.07845    0.47054      0.77589
   42   9.9151  0  0.64573     0.08014    0.46638      0.77818
   43   9.9178  0  0.64573     0.08194    0.46192      0.78061
   44  10.1151  0  0.64573     0.08387    0.45714      0.78319
   45  10.4027  0  0.64573     0.08594    0.45199      0.78592
   46  10.6000  0  0.64573     0.08817    0.44642      0.78884
   47  10.6603  1  0.61175     0.08984    0.41363      0.76065
   48  10.6685  0  0.61175     0.09245    0.40743      0.76416
   49  10.7260  0  0.61175     0.09529    0.40063      0.76795
   50  10.9260  0  0.61175     0.09842    0.39316      0.77205
   51  10.9370  0  0.61175     0.10187    0.38489      0.77651
   52  11.2027  0  0.61175     0.10572    0.37567      0.78139
   53  11.4548  0  0.61175     0.11004    0.36532      0.78676
   54  11.4712  0  0.61175     0.11493    0.35359      0.79270
   55  11.5589  0  0.61175     0.12054    0.34016      0.79934
```

Output 2.2 (continued)

56	11.6082	0	0.61175	0.12706	0.32460	0.80683
57	11.6164	0	0.61175	0.13477	0.30631	0.81536
58	11.6521	0	0.61175	0.14407	0.28446	0.82522
59	11.7123	0	0.61175	0.15562	0.25784	0.83679
60	11.7671	0	0.61175	0.17047	0.22465	0.85066
61	11.8466	0	0.61175	0.19059	0.18222	0.86775
62	11.8575	0	0.61175	0.22007	0.12703	0.88954
63	11.8685	0	0.61175	0.26953	0.05793	0.91871
64	11.9863	0	0.61175	0.38118	0.00274	0.95988
65	12.0082	0	0.61175	.	.	.

The macro KMPLOT is designed to be invoked immediately after KMTABLE. It allows you to produce high-resolution graphs of the survival curves. Of course, you can use it only if you have licensed SAS/GRAPH. KMPLOT offers the following choices:

- The confidence intervals calculated by KMTABLE may be plotted on the same graph as the survival curve.

- The censored or complete times can be marked.

- Multiple plots for distinct values of a BY variable specified in KMPLOT can be printed either separately or on the same graph. In the latter case, confidence intervals cannot also be produced, since placing multiple curves and their confidence intervals on the same graph would be confusing.

- A cutoff condition such as t < *timeval* or r > *n at risk* can be specified to omit the extreme right-hand tails from the curve(s) plotted. See Section 2.15 for the macro.

The following template below makes it easier to use KMPLOT. See Section 2.15 for the macro.

```
%macro kmplot(
mark=                  /* yes to mark times on curve,
                          no (default) to not mark times */
,ci=                   /* yes for confidence intervals,
                          no (default) for no ci's */
,combine=              /* yes to produce multiple plots
                          on the same graph, no (default)
                          for separate plots */
,xlabel=               /* label for the horizontal axis,
                          default is time */
,ylabel=               /* label for the vertical axis,
                          default is Pct Survival */
,title=                /* default is Kaplan-Meier Survival Curve */
,cutoff=               /* clause to restrict curve(s), usually of form
                          time < value or r < value (for n at risk)*/
);
```

The following example shows how the macro KMPLOT can be invoked. It is assumed that you have previously invoked KMTABLE. Figure 2.3 is produced.

```
%kmplot(
        mark= yes          /* yes to mark times on curve,
                              no (default) to not mark times */
        ,ci= yes           /* yes for confidence intervals, no (default)
                              for no ci's */
                           /* yes to produce multiple plots on the same
                              graph, no default)for separate plots */
                           /* label for the horizontal axis, default is
                              time */
                           /* label for the vertical axis,
                              default is Pct Survival */

        ,title= Figure 2.3 /* default is Kaplan-Meier
                              Survival Curve */
                           /* clause to restrict curve(s), usually of
                              form time < value or r > value (for n at
                              risk)*/
)
```

or equivalently

```
%kmplot(mark=yes, ci=yes, title=Figure 2.3)
```

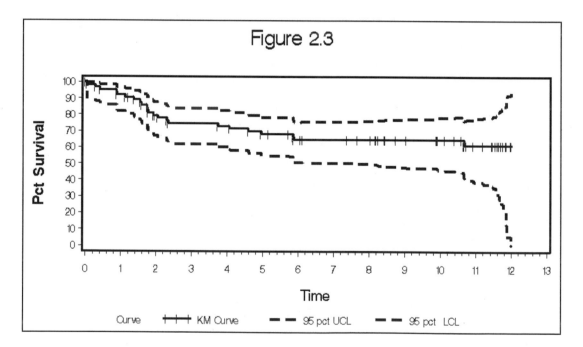

2.9.1 Exercise

Use KMTABLE and KMPLOT on the data of Exercise 2.2. Try several different options.

2.10 Planning a Study to Control the Standard Error

2.10.1 General Considerations

When estimating parameters from sample data, you would generally present not only those estimates, but also information that provides some idea as to their precision. This is usually done by reporting the standard error of the estimates or confidence intervals for the parameters being studied. If you are working with data that have previously been collected, you have no control over that precision. On the other hand, when asked to plan a study whose purpose is estimation, you can recommend study characteristics that can be expected to provide a desired level of precision for the estimates obtained. In many situations, the only relevant study characteristic is the sample size. For example, biostatisticians are constantly asked to calculate the sample size needed to produce an estimator of a mean or proportion that will have sufficiently small standard error.

If p is the usual estimate of a population proportion, π, based on a sample of size n, its standard error can be estimated as $[p(1-p)/n]^{1/2}$. Thus, if we want that standard error to be less than or equal to s, we need $n \geq p(1-p)/s^2$. The only remaining problem is that we cannot know in advance what p will be. However, if we have some idea of what π is, we can use that value. As an alternative, we note that $p(1-p)$ is at its maximum of .25 when $p = .5$. Thus a conservative estimate of the sample size needed $s^2/4$.

2.10.2 The Survival Analysis Situation

When estimating survival probabilities, however, the situation is a bit more complicated. The standard error of such estimates will, in general, depend not only on the sample size, but also on the rate and pattern of the patients' entry onto the study. This section shows how to predict, based on these characteristics, the Peto and Greenwood standard errors of Kaplan-Meier estimates of the survival distribution and presents a macro to perform the necessary calculations. To simplify matters a bit, we will assume that patients are accrued unto a study uniformly over A units of time and then followed for an additional time, τ, after which the analysis is done. While on study their survival function is given by S(t) and their hazard by h(t). The only reason for censoring will be that a patient is still alive at the end of that follow-up time. More complex situations can be accommodated, if that is desired (Cantor, 2001).

2.10.3 Projecting the Peto Standard Error

The estimated variance of $\hat{S}(t)$ as given by Peto's formula is $[\hat{S}(t)]^2[1 - \hat{S}(t)]/R(t)$ where R(t) is the number at risk at time t. Predicting that variance in advance, based on specific study characteristics, requires some prediction of $\hat{S}(t)$, the proportion surviving at least to time t, and R(t), the number whose time on study is at least t. The prediction of $\hat{S}(t)$ is not as critical as it may appear, and we will return to it later. Let's focus now on R(t). Let N be the sample size and $P_R(t)$ be the probability that a subject is at risk, i.e., alive and on study, t units of time after entry. Then a reasonable prediction for R(t) is N times $P_R(t)$. Now a person is at risk at time t if and only if both of the following conditions are true:

1. The subject's survival time is at least t.

2. The subject entered the study early enough to be followed for time t.

Since these can be thought of as independent events, their joint probability is the product of their individual probabilities. The first of these is estimated by $\hat{S}(t)$. The second will depend on when the patient entered the study. If t is less than or equal to τ, then the probability of entering early enough to be at risk for time t is 1. Otherwise, to be at risk for time t, a subject would have had to enter prior to time $A + \tau - t$. Assuming uniform patient entry, that probability is $(A + \tau - t)/A$. Putting all of this together, we have

$$
\begin{aligned}
P_R(t) &= \frac{\hat{S}(t)(A + \tau - t)}{A} \quad \text{if } t > \tau \\
&= \hat{S}(t) \quad \text{if } t \le \tau
\end{aligned}
\tag{2.9}
$$

Thus the projected standard error of $\hat{S}(t)$ is given (approximately) by

$$
\begin{aligned}
&\sqrt{\frac{A\,\hat{S}(t)[1 - \hat{S}(t)]}{N(A + \tau - t)}} \quad \text{if } t > \tau \\
&\sqrt{\frac{\hat{S}(t)[1 - \hat{S}(t)]}{N}} \quad \text{if } t \ge \tau
\end{aligned}
\tag{2.10}
$$

2.10.4 Dealing with $\hat{S}$ (t)

Now consider the factor $\hat{S}(t)[1 - \hat{S}(t)]$. Like the proportion p it takes on its largest possible value of 0.25 when $\hat{S}(t)$ is 0.5. Also it is larger for values of $\hat{S}(t)$ closer to 0.5. This fact enables us to replace the $\hat{S}(t)$ in the formula by 0.5, a value that provides a conservative estimate. The potential error in using 0.5 for $\hat{S}(t)$ is not too bad if $\hat{S}(t)$ turns out to be reasonably close to that value. For $\hat{S}(t) = 0.5$, $\sqrt{\hat{S}(t)[1 - \hat{S}(t)]}$ is 0.5. For $\hat{S}(t) = 0.7$ or 0.3, $\sqrt{\hat{S}(t)[1 - \hat{S}(t)]}$ is about 0.46.

2.10.5 Projecting the Greenwood Variance

In order to project the value of (2.6), we begin by replacing the observed times, t_i, that are less than or equal to t in (2.6) by a partition of the interval $[0, t]$ given by $0 = x_0 < x_1 < \ldots < x_n = t$ where each $x_i - x_{i-1} = \Delta x$. The d_i can now be thought of as the number of deaths in the interval $[x_{i-1}, x_i)$ and r_i as the number at risk at time x_i. We next replace each of these by approximations of their expected value. The expected value of d_i is approximated by $h(x_i)r_i\Delta x$. The expected value of r_i is $NS(x_i)$ if $x_i < \tau$ and $NS(x_i)(A + \tau - x_i)/A$ if $x_i \ge \tau$. Thus the projected value of the right side of (2.6) is given by

$$
S^2(t)\left\{ \frac{1}{N}\sum_{x_i < t^*} \frac{h(x_i)\Delta x}{S(x_i)[1 - h(x_i)\Delta x]} + \frac{A}{N}\sum_{\tau \le x_i \le t} \frac{h(x_i)\Delta x}{S(x_i)(A + \tau - x_i)[1 - h(x_i)\Delta x]} \right\}
$$
$$
\tag{2.9}
$$

where $t^* = \min\{t, \tau\}$ and the second summation is taken as zero if $t \le \tau$.

Taking limits as $\Delta x \to 0$, we get as the projected variance estimate

$$S^2(t)\left\{\frac{1}{N}\int_0^\tau \frac{h(u)du}{S(u)} + \frac{A}{N}\int_\tau^t \frac{h(u)du}{S(u)(A+\tau-u)}\right\} \text{ if } t > \tau$$

$$S^2(t)\frac{1}{N}\int_0^t \frac{h(u)du}{S(u)} \quad \text{if } t \le \tau \tag{2.11}$$

2.11 Example

Suppose that one of the primary objectives of a study you are planning is to estimate survival probabilities over time for patients with advanced Hodgkin's disease who are given an experimental treatment regimen. You expect to be able to accrue 30 patients per year for four years and that the five-year survival rate will be about 80%. You would like to predict the standard error of $\hat{S}(5)$ if you accrue for four years and follow patients for three years more before performing the analysis. Then $\hat{S}(5) = 0.8$, $N = 120$, $A = 4$, $\tau = 3$, and $t = 5$. If we assume that the true survival function is exponential with $S(5) = 0.8$, we get $\lambda = \log(0.8)/5 = 0.045$. Thus we need to do the calculation given by the first part of (2.11) with $S(u) = \exp(-0.045u)$, $h(u) = .045$, $S(5) = 0.8$ and N, A, τ, and t as above. Since the second integral cannot be expressed exactly, you would have to rely on numerical approximation. Of course, the Quad subroutine from PROC IML, as described in Appendix C can be used. As an alternative, you can use a macro, KMPLAN.

2.12 The KMPLAN Macro

KMPLAN calculates the Peto and Greenwood predicted standard error of $\hat{S}(t)$ for assumed functions $S(u)$ and $h(u)$ a given sample size, accrual time, follow-up time, and a value of t. This macro appears in Section 2.15.

To use this macro you can fill in the parameters in the template.

```
%kmplan(
          s =                    /* expression for S(u) */
          ,h =                   /* expression for h(u) */
          ,N =                   /* Sample size */
          ,A =                   /* Accrual time */
          ,tau =                 /* follow-up time */
          , t =                  /* time for which projected
                                    se is wanted */
          )
```

2.12.1 *Example of the Use of KMPLAN*

Consider the scenario described in Section 2.11. If we use KMPLAN by entering and running the macro followed by

```
%kmplan(s = exp(-.045*u) , h = .0455 ,N = 120 , A = 4, tau = 3, t = 5);
```

we get the following output:

Output 2.4

```
                        The SAS System
                      Greenwood Formula


                         VARG    STDERRG

      time = 5      0.001566 0.039574


                        Peto Formula


                         VARP    STDERRP

       time = 5      0.002681 0.051783
```

If we consider a standard error of about 4% (based on the Greenwood formula) for the five-year survival estimate to be too large, we might consider planning for longer follow-up or a larger sample. To facilitate doing several runs of the KMPLAN macro, you can submit something like the following:

```
%macro doit;
%do nn = 120 %to 260 %by 20;
title "Sample Size = &nn";
%kmplan(s = exp(-.045*u), h = .045 ,N = &nn , A = 4 , tau = 3 ,
t = 5);
%end;
%mend;
%doit;
```

Do you see how this works? We've created a macro called DOIT that contains a macro loop delimited by the %DO and %END statements. While a DATA step loop allows you to perform a set of statements in a DATA step several times, a macro loop allows you to run any segment of SAS code, including DATA steps, procs, and macros, several times. Within this macro loop, the macro KMPLAN is run repeatedly with the value of the macro variable *N*, which represents the sample size, replaced first by 160, then by 180, then by 200, etc., up to 260. The results are given in Output 2.5. To save space, I left out the results for several of the sample sizes.

Output 2.5

```
                    Sample Size = 160
                    Greenwood Formula

                       VARG    STDERRG

        time = 5    0.001175 0.034272


                     Peto Formula


                       VARP    STDERRP

        time = 5    0.002011 0.044845



                    Sample Size = 200
                      Greenwood Formula

                       VARG    STDERRG

          time = 5     0.000940 0.030654

                       Peto Formula

                       VARP    STDERRP

          time = 5     0.001609 0.040111

                     Sample Size = 220

                     Greenwood Formula

                       VARG    STDERRG

          time = 5    0.000854 0.029227

                       Peto Formula

                       VARP    STDERRP

        time = 5     0.001463 0.038244
```

It looks like a sample size of about 200 to 220 will be needed if a Greenwood standard error of about 3% for the estimate of S(5) is desired.

You are probably wondering which formula, Greenwood's or Peto's, to use for the variance and standard error of Kaplan-Meier survival estimates. Peto's formula is certainly easier to compute. This is not too important if we have good computational resources. In fact, it is Greenwood's formula that is usually used by statistical software such as SAS. Perhaps the best way to compare the two is through simulations. Consider a scenario in which 250 patients enter a study over four years and are followed for five additional years. Assume that survival is exponential with constant hazard equal to 0.35. Table 2.4 presents results for 1,000 simulations of such a study. These simulations allow for 3% annual loss to follow-up – an additional complexity not discussed earlier. More detail can be found in Cantor (2001).

Table 2.4: Accuracy of Projected Standard Errors

t (years)	Projected Peto SE	Sample Mean of Peto SE's	Projected Greenwood SE	Sample Mean of Greenwood SE's	Sample SE
1	0.0327	0.0325	0.0325	0.0324	0.0334
2	0.0364	0.0362	0.0360	0.0359	0.0366
3	0.0353	0.0349	0.0346	0.0346	0.0346
4	0.0324	0.0319	0.0316	0.0315	0.0309
5	0.0289	0.0283	0.0281	0.0283	0.0278
6	0.0293	0.0285	0.0253	0.0252	0.0241
7	0.0312	0.0295	0.0239	0.0237	0.0237
8	0.0381	0.0337	0.0246	0.0237	0.0254

The last column provides the best estimate of the "true" standard error of the Kaplan-Meier estimate. Notice that both the Peto formula and the Greenwood formula give results which, on the average, are quite close to the sample standard errors for smaller values of t. As the time increases, however, the conservatism of the Peto formula becomes greater, while the Greenwood results show little bias. For both the Peto and Greenwood formulas, the projected standard errors remain fairly close to their sample means.

2.13 Exercise

Use the KMPLAN macro to find the projected Greenwood standard error of the Kaplan-Meier estimate of the survival function at $t = 5$ years if 50 patients are accrued over three years with three years of follow-up. Assume that survival is exponential with a median survival time of five years. Use a modification of the %DOIT macro above to explore the effect of increasing the follow-up time to four and five years.

2.14 Interval-Censored Data

2.14.1 The Nature of Interval Censoring

Sometimes, when dealing with survival data, you want to assess patients only sporadically for the endpoint under study. Thus you may know only that the ith patient achieved the endpoint at a time in the interval $(L_i, R_i]$. Here L_i can be 0, and R_i can be infinite. If these intervals were not too wide, most analysts would simply treat such an observation as if it occurred at time R_i. For example, if a cancer patient was free of disease at time 3.4 and was found to have relapsed when evaluated at time 3.9, that patient would be assigned an event time of 3.9. A consequence of this is that reported survival results can be influenced by the frequency with which patients are evaluated for the endpoint being studied. In fact, if we were really being "fussy," much of survival data probably should be considered to be interval censored. However, we prefer not to introduce the complications that this would require.

2.14.2 The ICE Macro

Peto (1973) and Turnbull (1976) discuss a method of dealing with interval-censored data such as this. The method is quite complicated and produces estimates that may not be defined in certain intervals. A macro ICE performs the required computations. It can be found on the SAS Web site at http://www.sas.com/techsup/download/stat. The ICE macro uses some utilities that are contained in the file Xmacro.sas, so you will need it as well. It is found in the same location.

2.14.3 Using the ICE Macro

In order to use the ICE macro you need to have two time variables in your data. For (right, left, or interval) censored data these two variables give the left and right endpoints of the interval in which the event is known to have occurred. If these variable names are, for example, L and R, then L can be zero for a left-censored observation. For a right-censored observation, you can take R to be some arbitrary large number that is larger than the largest observed time. If an event time is known, you take L and R both equal to that time. The macro permits the use of several optional arguments. Many are rather technical and allow you to control the method and details of the likelihood maximization. The defaults will usually work fine, so these arguments won't be discussed here. The following arguments may be useful:

DATA =   The name of the SAS data set to be used. The default is to use the last data set defined.

BY *varlist*   An optional list of BY variables. If this is used, then the ICE macro produces separate analyses for each combination of BY variable values.

TIME =   This is the only argument that is required. It gives the names of the variable representing the left and right endpoints of the time interval. They may be enclosed in parentheses, brackets, or braces, but that is not necessary.

FREQ *varname* A numeric variable indicating the number of subjects represented by an observation.

OPTIONS *list* This is a list of display options that you may use. If you use PLOT you get a graph of the survival curve.

Here are a couple of suggestions.

The file Macro.sas contains a statement of the form

%INCLUDE *filename*   where *filename* is the path and name of the file Xmacro.sas. You may need to change this statement to conform to the path of Xmacro.sas on your computer.

Also the Ice.sas program contains the statement

```
call gdrawl(xy1,xy2)color="cyan";
```

This produces a graph with light blue lines that look fine on a color monitor or when printed by a color printer. With a black and white printer, however, they are difficult to see. If you intend to print the graph on such a printer, you might want to change it to

```
call gdrawl(xy1,xy2);
```

The default color will be black. By the way, this statement is part of the graphics capability of PROC IML.

2.14.4 Example

The following example is the one given in the documentation provided with Ice.sas. The only change I made was to use the `options=plot` argument to get the graph of the survival function and to change the color as described above.

```
data ex1;
input l r f;
datalines;
0 2  1
1 3  1
2 10 4
4 10 4
;
run;
%ice(data=ex1, time=(l r), freq=f, options=plot);
```

The data indicate that one patient died in less than two units of time and one died between times one and three. Four patients lived past time = 2 and four lived past Time = 4. We cannot tell whether their times are right censored (i.e., known only to be greater than 2 and 4) or interval censored (i.e. between 2 or 4 and 10). The results are given in Output 2.6 and Figure 2.4.

Output 2.6

```
                         The SAS System

              Nonparametric Survival Curve for Interval Censoring



Number of Observations: 4
Number of Parameters: 3
Optimization Technique: Newton Raphson Ridge


                          Parameter Estimates
                    Q          P        THETA
                    1          2        0.1999995
                    2          3        0.0000010
                    4          10       0.7999995
```

Output 2.6 (continued)

```
      Survival Curve Estimates and 95% Confidence Intervals

      LEFT     RIGHT     ESTIMATE        LOWER        UPPER
       0         1       1.0000            .            .
       2         2       0.8000         0.4494       1.0000
       3         4       0.8000         0.4494       1.0000
      10        10       0.0000            .            .
```

Figure 2.4

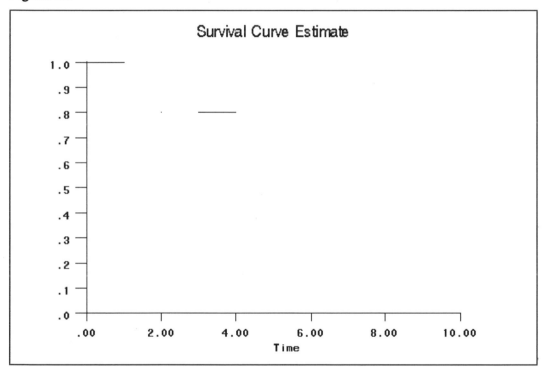

2.14.5 Discussion of the Results

The results give the estimated survival function as 1.0 for t between 0 and 1, as 0.8 for $t = 2$ and for t between 3 and 4, and as 0.0 for $t = 10$. Note that survival estimates are not defined for t between 1 and 2 or t between 2 and 3. This illustrates the fact that the method of Peto and Turnbull may result in an estimated survival function that excludes certain intervals.

2.14.6 A More Realistic Example

For a more realistic example, let us reconsider the leukemia survival data discussed in Section 2.8.3. Let's pretend that we have learned that the death dates recorded were actually the dates that the deaths were reported and that the actual dates of death are unknown except that they are between some known earlier date and the date given in the original data. Applying this new information, we can change the data so that each patient is associated with an interval in which the death occurred. For the right-censored death times, we will take the upper endpoint to be 15 years. The data set now looks like this:

Output 2.7

```
                    The SAS System

        Obs           l              r

          1         0.0000         0.0493
          2         0.0000         0.2849
          3         0.0000         0.4082
          4         0.0517         0.8767
          5         0.0627         0.8877
          6         0.2983         1.1233
          7         1.2247        15.0000
          8         0.5503         1.3753
          9         0.7175         1.5425
         10         0.7586         1.5836
         11         0.9147         1.7397
         12         0.9339         1.7589
         13         0.9476         1.7726
         14         1.0983         1.9233
         15         1.9562        15.0000
         16         1.2243         2.0493
         17         1.4736         2.2986
         18         1.5175         2.3425
         19         2.9065         3.7315
         20         3.2298         4.0548
         21         4.0685        15.0000
         22         3.7613         4.5863
         23         4.1284         4.9534
         24         5.1534        15.0000
         25         5.7315        15.0000
         26         5.0243         5.8493
         27         5.0435         5.8685
         28         6.0712        15.0000
         29         6.1151        15.0000
         30         7.3781        15.0000
         31         7.6630        15.0000
         32         8.0438        15.0000
         33         8.1890        15.0000
         34         8.2055        15.0000
         35         8.2548        15.0000
         36         8.4274        15.0000
         37         8.4521        15.0000
         38         8.7589        15.0000
         39         9.0356        15.0000
         40         9.8959        15.0000
         41         9.9151        15.0000
         42         9.9178        15.0000
         43        10.1151        15.0000
         44        10.4027        15.0000
         45        10.6000        15.0000
         46         9.8353        10.6603
         47        10.6685        15.0000
         48        10.7260        15.0000
         49        10.9260        15.0000
         50        10.9370        15.0000
         51        11.2027        15.0000
         52        11.4548        15.0000
         53        11.4712        15.0000
         54        11.5589        15.0000
         55        11.6082        15.0000
         56        11.6164        15.0000
         57        11.6521        15.0000
         58        11.7123        15.0000
         59        11.7671        15.0000
         60        11.8466        15.0000
         61        11.8575        15.0000
         62        11.8685        15.0000
         63        11.9863        15.0000
         64        12.0082        15.0000
```

If we use the ICE macro on this data set we get the following results:

Output 2.8

```
   Nonparametric Survival Curve for Interval Censoring

Number of Observations: 64


Number of Parameters: 14


Optimization Technique: Newton Raphson Ridge


                 Parameter Estimates


              Q         P       THETA

              0     0.0493   0.0360236
         0.0627     0.2849   0.0191629
         0.2983     0.4082   0.0000010
         0.7586     0.8767   0.0528832
         1.0983     1.1233   0.0237823
         1.2247     1.3753   0.0000010
         1.5175     1.5425   0.1203109
         1.9562     2.0493   0.0000010
         3.2298     3.7315   0.0325140
         3.7613     4.0548   0.0000010
         4.1284     4.5863   0.0332702
         5.7315     5.8493   0.0349769
           10.6    10.6603   0.0340564
        12.0082        15    0.6130156


Survival Curve Estimates and 95% Confidence Intervals


       LEFT      RIGHT    ESTIMATE     LOWER      UPPER

          0          0     1.0000       .          .
     0.0493     0.0627     0.9640     0.8949     1.0000
     0.2849     0.2983     0.9448     0.8423     1.0000
     0.4082     0.7586     0.9448     0.8481     1.0000
     0.8767     1.0983     0.8919     0.7778     1.0000
     1.1233     1.2247     0.8681     0.7133     1.0000
     1.3753     1.5175     0.8681     0.7227     1.0000
     1.5425     1.9562     0.7478     0.5915     0.9042
     2.0493     3.2298     0.7478     0.6050     0.8907
     3.7315     3.7613     0.7153     0.5681     0.8625
     4.0548     4.1284     0.7153     0.5682     0.8624
     4.5863     5.7315     0.6820     0.5379     0.8262
     5.8493      10.6      0.6471     0.5024     0.7917
    10.6603    12.0082     0.6130     0.4614     0.7647
        15         15      0.0000       .          .
```

Output 2.8 (continued)

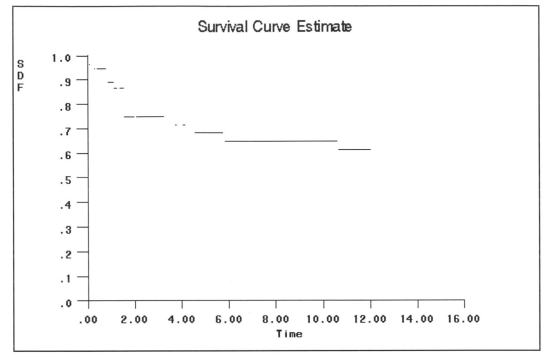

You might want to compare the table and graph to the results obtained in Section 2.8.3 when the data were not considered interval censored.

2.14.7 Exercise

Make up a data set containing at least ten interval-censored survival observations. Use the ICE macro to estimate the survival function.

2.15 Macros

2.15.1 The KMTABLE Macro

```
%macro kmtable(dataset=_last_     /* dataset used by macro */
              ,pct=95             /* for conf. int. */
              ,time=              /* time variable  */
              ,cens=              /* variable that indicates
                                     censored or complete time */
              ,censval=           /* value(s) that indicate
                                     censored time */
              ,method=            /* 1 for conf. int. method used
                                      in Proc Lifetest, 2 for other*/
              ,variance=          /* G or g for Greenwoods
                                      formula, P or p for Petos */

              ,byvar=none         /* Optional by variable(s) */
              ,print=yes          /* no to suppress printing */
);
%global byvari perc ttime;
%let byvari=&byvar;
%let perc=&pct;
%let ttime=&time;
```

```
 data &dataset;
set &dataset;
none=1;
run;
proc sort data=&dataset;
by &byvar;
run;
/*  Create dataset, x, with survival estimates */
proc lifetest noprint outs=x data=&dataset;
by &byvar;
time &time*&cens(&censval);
run;
data x; set x; retain temp;
if survival ne . then temp = survival;
if survival = . then survival = temp;
proc sort out=y;
by &byvar &time;
run;
/* Add number at risk, r, to dataset */
data y;
set y;
by &byvar;
if first.&byvar then r=0;
else r+1;
keep r &byvar;

run;
/* Merge number at risk with survival estimates */
proc sort;
by &byvar descending r;
run;
data table;
merge x y;
run;
proc sort;
by &byvar descending r;
run;
/* Create Life Table */
data table;
set table;
by &byvar;
                /* Allow for G or P, check for valid values,
                   if mis-specified, set values and put
                   warning in log.                        */
if _n_ = 1 then do;
        %if &variance = G %then %let variance=g;
        %if &variance = P %then %let variance=p;
        if "&variance" not in ('g', 'p') then do;
                put;
                put '**********************************';
                put '*Note: Invalid value of variance used*';
                put '*for choice of variance formula.  g *';
                put '*for Greenwood will be used.        *';
                put '**********************************';
                put;
        end;
         if &method not in (1, 2) then do;
                put;
                put '**********************************';
                put '*Note:  Invalid value of method used*';
                put '*for choice of CI. Method 1 (as in  *';
                put '*Proc Lifetest) will be used.       *';
                put '**********************************';
                put;
        end;
end;
                    /* defaults for variance and conf int method */
%if &variance ne g and &variance ne p %then
%let variance = g;
%if &method ne 1 and &method ne 2 %then
%let method = 1;
                    /* normal critical value for conf. int. */
```

```
z=-probit((100-&pct)/200);
d=1-_censor_;
                        /* Peto s.e. */
sp=survival*sqrt((1-survival)/r);
                        /* Greenwood s.e. */
if first.&byvar then do;
        sum=0;
        stderr=0;
 end;
 else do;
        sum+d/(r*(r-d));
        sg=survival*sqrt(sum);
end;
if "&variance"='g'
then stderr=sg;
if "&variance"='p'
then stderr=sp;
  /*  Confidence interval limits */
if &method=1 then do;
        lcl=survival-z*stderr;
        lcl=max(0,lcl);
        ucl=survival+z*stderr;
        ucl=min(1.00, ucl);
end;
if &method=2 then do;
        s=-stderr/log(survival)/survival;
        lcl=survival**(exp(z*s));
        ucl=survival**(exp(-z*s));
end;
if first.&byvar then do;
        stderr=0;
        lcl=1;
        ucl=1;
end;
  /*  Create column label for table */
%if &variance=g %then
label stderr = 'Greenwood*stderr';;
 %if &variance = p %then
label stderr = 'Peto*stderr';;
%if &method = 1 %then %do;
        label lcl= "Method 1*&pct pct lcl";;
        label ucl="Method 1*&pct pct ucl";;
%end;
%if &method = 2 %then %do;
        label lcl = "Method 2*&pct pct lcl";;
        label ucl = "Method 2*&pct pct ucl";;
%end;
run;
proc sort;
  by &byvar;

run;
/* Print life table  */
%if &print = yes %then %do;
        proc print l split='*';
var  &time d survival stderr lcl ucl;
  %if &byvar ne none %then by &byvar;;
%end;
run;
%mend kmtable;
```

2.15.2 The KMPLOT Macro

```
%macro kmplot(mark=no                      /* yes to mark times
                                              on curve */
              ,ci=no                       /* yes for conf. intervals */
              ,ylabel= Pct Survival        /* label for y axis */
              ,xlabel=Time                 /* label for x axis */
              ,combine=no                  /* yes to put multiple plots on
                                              same graph */
              ,cutoff=none                 /* clause to restrict curve(s),
                                              usually of form time<value or
                                              r<value (for n at risk) */
              ,title= Kaplan-Meier Survival Curve
);
/* no conf. interval if multiple plots on graph */
%if &combine=yes %then %let ci=no;;
/* Define symbol statements */
%if &combine&mark=yesno %then %do;
   symbol1 l=1 f- , v=none  i=stepjl w=3 c=black;
        symbol2 l=3 f= ,v=none i=stepjl w=3 c=black;
        symbol3 l=5 f= ,v=none i=stepjl w=3 c=black;
        symbol4 l=33 f= ,v=none i=stepjl w=3 c=black;
        %end;
%if &combine&mark=yesyes %then %do;
        symbol1 l=1 f=swiss v="|" i=stepjl w=3 c=black;
        symbol2 l=3 f=swiss v="|" i=stepjl w=3 c=black;
        symbol3 l=5 f=swiss v="|" i=stepjl w=3 c=black;
        symbol4 l=33 f=swiss v="|" i=stepjl w=3 c=black;
        %end;
%if &combine&mark=noyes %then %do;
        symbol1 l=1 f=swiss v="|" i=stepjl w=3 c=black;
        symbol2 l=3 f= ,v=none i=stepjl w=3 c=black;
        symbol3 l=3 f= ,v=none i=stepjl w=3 c=black;
        %end;
%if &combine&mark=nono %then %do;
        symbol1 l=1 f= , v=none i=stepjl w=3 c=black;
        symbol2 l=3 f= , v=none i=stepjl w=3 c=black;
        symbol3 l=3 f= , v=none i=stepjl w=3 c=black;
        %end;
/* White out by if no by variables */
%if &byvari=none %then goptions cby=white;;
/* Create dataset for plot(s) */
data;
set table;
survival=survival*100;
lcl=100*lcl;
ucl=100*ucl;
y=survival;
curve=1;
output;
y=ucl;
curve=2;
%if &ci=yes %then output;;
y=lcl;
curve=3;
%if &ci=yes %then output;;
run;
proc sort;
  by &byvari curve &ttime;
run;
proc format;
  value curve 1='KM curve' 2='UCL' 3='LCL';
run;
/* Define axes and legends */
axis1 width=3 minor=none
      label=(h=1.5 f=swissb a=90 j=center
      "&ylabel")
      value = ( h=1.0 f=swiss) order=(0 to 100 by 10);
axis2 width=3
      label=(h=1.5 f=swiss  "&xlabel")
      value=(h=1.0 f=swiss);
```

```
%if &combine=no %then
legend1 label= (f=swiss h=1.0  'Curve')
value=(f=swiss h=1.0 j=1 'KM Curve' "&perc pct UCL" "&perc pct LCL");;
legend2 label=(f=swiss h=1.0)
         value=(f=swiss h=1.0 j=1);
 %if &combine=no %then %do;

/* gplot for separate curves */
        proc gplot;
%if &cutoff ne none %then where &cutoff;;
        plot y*time= curve /
        legend=legend1
        vaxis=axis1 haxis=axis2
        %if &ci=no %then nolegend;;
        ;
           format curve curve.;
        by &byvari;
%end;
run;
 %if &combine=yes %then %do;
/* gplot for combined curves */
        proc gplot;
%if &cutoff ne none %then where &cutoff;;
        plot y*time=&byvari/ legend=legend2
        vaxis=axis1 haxis=axis2;
      %end;
title &title;
run;
%mend kmplot;


Kmplan

%macro kmplan(s = , h = ,N = , A = , tau = , t = );
proc iml;
  start f1(u);
      v = &h/&s;
       return(v);
  finish;

  start f2(u);
      v = &h/(&s*(&A + &tau - u));
      return(v);
  finish;

  start surv(u);
      v = &s;
       return(v);
  finish;

  if &t < &tau then a = {0 &t};
  else a= {0 &tau};
  b = {&tau &t};
  call quad(z1, "f1", a);
  call quad(z2, "f2", b);
  if &t > &tau then varg = (surv(&t))**2*(z1/&n + &a/&n*z2);
  else varg = (surv(&t))**2*z1/&n;
  stderrg = sqrt(varg);
  print 'Greenwood Formula';
  print  "time = &t   " varg[format=8.6] stderrg[format=8.6];
  varp = surv(&t)*(1 - surv(&t))/&n;
  if &t > &tau then varp = varp*&a/(&a + &tau - &t);
  stderrp = sqrt(varp);
  print 'Peto Formula';
  print "time = &t   " varp[format=8.6] stderrp[format=8.6];
  run;
%mend;
```

Chapter 3   Nonparametric Comparison of Survival Distributions

3.1   Notation 53
3.2   The Log Rank Statistic 54
3.3   More Than Two Groups 56
3.4   Other Linear Rank Tests..57
3.5   Using PROC LIFETEST 59
3.6   Exercises 64
3.7   A Test for Trend 64
3.8   Stratified Analyses..65
3.9   The Macro LINRANK...66
3.10 Permutation Tests and Randomization Tests..73
3.11 The Mantel-Byar Method 79
3.12 Power Analysis 84
3.13 Early Stopping Based on Conditional Power...92
3.14 Listings of Macros 95

3.1 Notation

In this chapter you will learn how to compare two or more groups with respect to survival. Although it would be possible to jump right into the more general discussion of K groups for any integer $K > 1$, the exposition will be clearer if the initial presentation is for $K = 2$ groups. The generalization to $K > 2$ will then be straightforward.

First some slight modifications to previous notation are needed. Let's begin by labeling the groups being compared by 1 and 2 and assuming that they have unknown survival functions $S_1(t)$, and $S_2(t)$ respectively. Suppose you have samples of sizes N_1 and N_2 from these groups. Let $N = N_1 + N_2$ and let $t_1 < t_2 < \ldots < t_M$ be the distinct ordered censored or complete times for the combined sample. There may be ties so that $M \le N$. For each i from 1 to M and for $j = 1$ and 2, let d_{ij} be the number of deaths in group j at time t_i and let $d_i = d_{i1} + d_{i2}$. That is, d_{i1} is the number of deaths among those in group 1, d_{i2} is the number of deaths among those in group 2, and d_i is the total number of deaths at time t_i. Since we are allowing ties, d_{i1}, d_{i2}, and d_i may be greater than 1. Let R_{ij} be the number at risk in group j just prior to time t_i and let $R_i = R_{i1} + R_{i2}$. As an example, suppose that in group 1 we have times 3, 5, 8+, 10, and 15 and in group 2 we have times 2, 5, 11+, 13+, 14, and 16 where times followed by a plus sign are censored. We can then represent these data in the following table:

Table 3.1

i	t_i	d_{i1}	d_{i2}	d_i	R_{i1}	R_{i2}	R_i
1	2	0	1	1	5	6	11
2	3	1	0	1	5	5	10
3	5	1	1	2	4	5	9
4	8	0	0	0	3	4	7
5	10	1	0	1	2	4	6
6	11	0	0	1	1	4	5
7	13	0	0	0	1	3	4
8	14	0	1	1	1	2	3
9	15	1	0	1	1	1	2
10	16	0	1	1	0	1	1

The shading in the table shows the group(s) for each observation time as indicated in this legend:

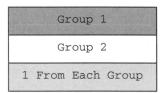

Group 1
Group 2
1 From Each Group

3.2 The Log Rank Statistic

3.2.1 Background

The log rank statistic is a straightforward extension of concepts introduced in the classic paper by Mantel and Haenszel (1959). That paper shows how independent two-by-two contingency tables can be combined to generate one overall statistic. For this reason, the log rank statistic is often referred to as the Mantel-Haenszel statistic. The use of this idea to compare survival distributions was first presented by Nathan Mantel (1966). The term *log rank* comes from a paper by Peto and Peto (1972) in which they develop the statistic by considering an estimate of the logarithms of survival functions.

3.2.2 A Heuristic Development of the Statistic

At each time t_i, where *i* goes from 1 to *M*, we have d_i deaths of which d_{i1} are from group 1 and d_{i2} are from group 2. These deaths occur among the R_i patients at risk at time t_i. Of these R_i patients, R_{i1} are in group 1 and R_{i2} are in group 2. If the two groups were equivalent with respect to survival, we would expect these deaths to be apportioned between those groups according to each group's proportion of the number at risk at that time. That is, the expected values of d_{i1} and d_{i2}, under the null hypothesis that $S_1(t)$ is equivalent to $S_2(t)$ conditional on the fact their total is d_i, are $d_i R_{i1}/R_i$ and $d_i R_{i2}/R_i$, respectively. We will denote these quantities by E_{i1} and E_{i2}. Then $d_{i1} - E_{i1}$ is a measure of how well or poorly group 1 did at time t_i compared to group 2. If $d_{i1} - E_{i1} > 0$ then group 1 experienced more deaths than expected at this time and if $d_{i1} - E_{i1} < 0$ then group 1 experienced fewer deaths than expected at this time. Similar statements can be made about $d_{i2} - E_{i2}$. Now let $d_{.1} = \Sigma d_{i1}$, $d_{.2} = \Sigma d_{i2}$, $E_1 = \Sigma E_{i1}$, and $E_2 = \Sigma E_{i2}$, where all of these sums are taken over $i = 1, 2, \ldots, M$. Then $d_{.1} - E_1$, which equals $\Sigma(d_{i1} - E_{i1})$, is a statistic that measures how well or poorly group 1 did compared to group 2 over the entire course of the study. A positive value would indicate that group 1 had more mortality than expected under the null hypothesis and, thus, that the sample represented by group 2 has better survival. The remaining problem, of course, is to be able to say something about the distribution of this statistic so that we can determine whether it offers strong evidence that one group has better survival than the other. This will be discussed in the next section.

3.2.3. Two Alternatives

One way to evaluate the significance of the statistic $d_{.1} - E_1$ is to note that, following general principles for statistics of this kind, $(d_{.1} - E_1)^2/E_1 + (d_{.2} - E_2)^2/E_2$ has, asymptotically (that is, approximately for large samples), a χ^2 distribution with one degree of freedom under the null hypothesis of equivalent survival distributions. Since the numerators of this statistic must be equal, this can be written as $(d_{.1} - E_1)^2(1/E_1 + 1/E_2)$. Another approach is to note that each of the $d_{i1} - E_{i1}$ have, under the null hypothesis, zero means as does their sum, $d_{.1} - E_1$. The variances of each of the $d_{i1} - E_{i1}$ are equal to $v_i = [R_{i1}R_{i2}d_i(R_i - d_i)]/[R_i^2(R_i - 1)]$. This is a consequence of the fact that, conditional on d_i, d_{i1} has a hypergeometric distribution. Although the $d_{i1} - E_{i1}$ are not independent, it can be shown that the variance of $\Sigma(d_{i1} - E_{i1}) = d_{.1} - E_1$ is approximately equal to the sum of the v_i's. Furthermore, $d_{.1} - E_1$ has, for reasonably large sample sizes, a distribution that is approximately normal. Thus we can compare $(d_{.1} - E_1)/(\Sigma v_i)^{1/2}$ to a standard normal distribution. These two approaches to testing the equivalence of two survival distributions can, therefore, be described as follows:

- Calculate $(d_{.1} - E_1)^2(1/E_1 + 1/E_2)$. Reject the null hypothesis of equivalent survival distributions at the α significance level if its value exceeds the $(1 - \alpha)100$th percentile of a χ^2 distribution with one degree of freedom. For $\alpha = 0.05$, that value is 3.84.
- Calculate $(d_{.1} - E_1)/(\Sigma v_i)^{1/2}$. Reject the null hypothesis of equivalent survival distributions at the α significance level if its absolute value exceeds the $(1 - \alpha/2)100$th percentile of a standard normal distribution. For $\alpha = 0.05$, that value is 1.96.

The fact that $1.96^2 = 3.84$ is not a coincidence. In fact, the $(1 - \alpha)100$th percentile of a χ^2 distribution with one degree of freedom equals the square of the $(1 - \alpha/2)100$th percentile of a standard normal distribution. Thus the second approach is equivalent to comparing $(d_{.1} - E_1)^2/(\Sigma v_i)$ to the same critical value as the statistic in the first approach. Looking at both approaches, it is clear they differ only in that $(d_{.1} - E_1)^2$ is divided by $(1/E_1 + 1/E_2)^{-1}$ in the first case, and Σv_i in the second. Since it can be shown that $(1/E_1 + 1/E_2)^{-1} \geq \Sigma v_i$, the first approach will produce a smaller statistic and hence a more conservative test. Both approaches can be found in the literature on the subject. In fact, the statistic $(d_{.1} - E_1)^2(1/E_1 + 1/E_2)$ was used in the predecessor of PROC LIFETEST. PROC LIFETEST uses the statistic $(d_{.1} - E_1)/(\Sigma v_i)^{1/2}$. That formula will be used here and as a basis for generalizations that follow.

3.2.4 Example

Table 3.2 illustrates the calculation of the log rank statistic for the small sample discussed earlier in this chapter. However, note that, since the approximations of the distribution of both statistics described earlier are approximately valid only for reasonably large samples, it would not be appropriate to use them with such a small sample. Later, we will see an approach that is valid for small samples.

Table 3.2

i	t_i	d_{i1}	d_{i2}	d_i	R_{i1}	R_{i2}	R_i	E_{i1}	v_i
1	2	0	1	1	5	6	11	0.455	0.248
2	3	1	0	1	5	5	10	0.500	0.250
3	5	1	1	2	4	5	9	0.889	0.432
4	8	0	0	0	3	4	7	0.000	0.000
5	10	1	0	1	2	4	6	0.333	0.222
6	11	0	0	0	1	4	5	0.000	0.000
7	13	0	0	0	1	3	4	0.000	0.000
8	14	0	1	1	1	2	3	0.333	0.222
9	15	1	0	1	1	1	2	0.500	0.250
10	16	0	1	1	0	1	1	0.000	0.000
Totals		4	4	8				3.010	1.624

From Table 3.2, we have $d_{.1} - E_1 = 0.990$ and $\Sigma v_i = 1.624$. The log rank statistic has the value of $0.990/1.624^{1/2} = 0.777$. Referring to a table of the standard normal distribution we find a p-value for a two-sided test to be 0.437. As an alternative, you could refer the value of $0.990^2/1.624$ to a χ^2 distribution with one degree of freedom, obtaining the same p-value. The conservative formula, $(d_{.1} - E_1)^2(1/E_1 + 1/E_2)$, leads to a p-value of 0.522.

Such values of the test statistic would not provide evidence to reject the null hypothesis that these two samples come from populations with equivalent survival. Recall, however, what was said earlier about the inadequacy of these sample sizes.

Notice that values of i for which $d_i = 0$ do not really enter into the calculation. For those lines of the table, d_{i1}, E_{i1}, and v_i are all 0. Thus, these sums are often taken over only the times at which there is at least one death.

3.3 More Than Two Groups

3.3.1 Some New Notation

The generalization of this result to more than two groups requires some new notation. This notation will involve vectors and matrices, so you might want to review the discussion of this topic in Appendix A. Suppose we have K groups whose unknown survival distributions are $S_1(t)$, $S_2(t)$, . . ., $S_K(t)$. Let N_j be the sample size in group j and $N = \Sigma N_j$. Again, let $t_1 < t_2 < . . . < t_M$ be the distinct ordered times in the combined sample. Extending the notation for two groups, R_{ij} will be the number at risk among those in group j and R_i will be the total number at risk just prior to time t_i. Also d_{ij} will be the number of deaths among those in group j, d_i will be the total number of deaths, and $E_{ij} = d_i R_{ij}/R_i$ will be the expected number of deaths in group j at time t_i. Then denote by $\mathbf{d}_i$ the column vector $(d_{i1}, d_{i2}, . . . d_{iK})'$ and by $\mathbf{E}_i$ the column vector $(E_{i1}, E_{i2}, . . . E_{iK})'$. Let $\mathbf{d}$ and $\mathbf{E}$ be the vector sums of the $\mathbf{d}_i$ and $\mathbf{E}_i$, respectively, over i. The vector $\mathbf{d} - \mathbf{E}$ is the generalization for $K > 2$ of the $d_{.1} - E_1$ that was used above for $K = 2$.

3.3.2 The Log Rank Statistic for K > 2

It is often the case in statistics that a univariate statistic of the form x^2/s^2 has, under the null hypothesis that the expected value of x is 0, a χ^2 distribution with one degree of freedom. The log rank statistic (or at least one form of it) is of that type. When such a statistic is generalized to a column vector $\mathbf{x}$, the usual generalization of the test statistic is of the form $\mathbf{x}'\mathbf{V}^{-1}\mathbf{x}$, where $\mathbf{V}$ is the covariance matrix of $\mathbf{x}$. This will be the case here. Thus, in order to give the log rank statistic for any $K > 2$, the estimated covariance matrix of the vector $\mathbf{d} - \mathbf{E}$ is needed. Let's start with the variances and covariances for each time t_i and for groups j and l. For each time t_i, the variance of $d_{ij} - E_{ij}$ can be estimated by

$$\text{var}_{ij} = \frac{d_i (R_i R_{ij} - R_{ij}^2)(R_i - d_i)}{R_i^2 (R_i - 1)} \tag{3.1}$$

and the covariance of $d_{ij} - E_{ij}$ and $d_{il} - E_{il}$ can be estimated by

$$\text{cov}_{ijl} = \frac{- R_{ij} R_{il} d_i (R_i - d_i)}{R_i^2 (R_i - 1)} \tag{3.2}$$

The required variances and covariances for each entry of the covariance matrix of $\mathbf{d} - \mathbf{E}$ can then be estimated by summing these expressions over i.

Now there is something else we must do. Recall that in the $K = 2$ case, we did not deal with the binary vector for the two groups and the 2-by-2 covariance matrix of that vector. Since the two components of that vector must be negatives of each other, we dealt only with one component. In fact, it's not hard to see that the two-dimensional covariance matrix would be singular, i.e., it would not have an inverse. Dealing with just one of the components and its variance works fine. We used the first component, although we could just as well have used the second. In the $K > 2$ case, the components of $\mathbf{d} - \mathbf{E}$ must sum to zero, and its covariance matrix will again be singular. So we let $\mathbf{S}$ be $\mathbf{d} - \mathbf{E}$ with one component removed and let $\mathbf{V}$ be the covariance matrix of $\mathbf{S}$. Then if the jth component is the one missing from $\mathbf{S}$, $\mathbf{V}$ is simply the covariance matrix of $\mathbf{d} - \mathbf{E}$ with the jth row and j^{th} column removed. $\mathbf{S}'\mathbf{V}^{-1}\mathbf{S}$ has, under the null hypothesis that all of the groups have equivalent survival, an asymptotic χ^2 distribution with $K - 1$ degrees of freedom. It can be shown that the value of this statistic is the same regardless of which component of $\mathbf{d} - \mathbf{E}$ is omitted from $\mathbf{S}$.

As in the two-sample case, you can instead base the test on the fact that the statistic $(d_{.1} - E_1)^2/E_1 + (d_{.2} - E_2)^2/E_2 + \ldots + (d_{.K} - E_K)^2/E_K$ has, asymptotically, a χ^2 distribution with $K - 1$ degrees of freedom under the null hypothesis. The resultant test will, as in the two-sample case, be conservative. It does not require matrix inversion, however. PROC LIFETEST uses the test statistic $\mathbf{S}'\mathbf{V}^{-1}\mathbf{S}$, as do the macros we will discuss later.

3.4 Other Linear Rank Tests

3.4.1 Weighted Sums

The log rank, or Mantel-Haenszel, test described earlier is actually just one realization of a general class of tests. Suppose we have, for each time, t_i, a weight, w_i. (We will have something to say later about how those weights might be defined.) Instead of the statistic $\mathbf{d} - \mathbf{E}$ that is the sum, over i, of the differences $\mathbf{d}_i - \mathbf{E}_i$, we can consider the weighted sum, $\Sigma w_i (\mathbf{d}_i - \mathbf{E}_i)$. Each component of that weighted sum is still a measure of the extent to which that group has survival that differs from its expectation under the null hypothesis. However, the log rank test (all $w_i = 1$) assigns the same weight to every death time. Other choices for the w_i will assign differing weights to different death times. For example, if the w_i increase as i increases, then later death times will affect the statistic more than earlier ones. To calculate the covariance matrix of this weighted sum, simply multiply each component of the covariance matrix in the previous section by w_i^2. Thus, we now have

$$var_{ij} = \frac{w_i^2 d_i (R_i R_{ij} - R_{ij}^2)(R_i - d_i)}{R_i^2 (R_i - 1)} \qquad (3.3)$$

and

$$cov_{ijl} = \frac{- w_i^2 R_{ij} R_{il} d_i (R_i - d_i)}{R_i^2 (R_i - 1)} \qquad (3.4)$$

As before, summing over i gives the variances and covariances of $\Sigma w_i (\mathbf{d}_i - \mathbf{E}_i)$. Letting $\mathbf{S}_w$ be the vector obtained by deleting one component from $\Sigma w_i (\mathbf{d}_i - \mathbf{E}_i)$ and $\mathbf{V}_w$ the covariance matrix formed by omitting the corresponding row and column from the covariance matrix of $\Sigma w_i (\mathbf{d}_i - \mathbf{E}_i)$, once again you can obtain the statistic $\mathbf{S}_w' \mathbf{V}_w^{-1} \mathbf{S}_w$. That statistic, under the null hypothesis, has an asymptotic χ^2 distribution with K - 1 degrees of freedom. In addition to the log rank test, several other tests, derived from other ways of defining the w_i's, have been presented by various authors. Such tests are known as linear rank tests.

3.4.2 Some Choices for Weights

Defining $w_i = R_i$ for all i gives us the Gehan test (1965). Gehan originally described this test for two groups, prior to Mantel's article introducing the log rank test, as a generalization of the Wilcoxon rank sum test. For this reason it is often known as the generalized Wilcoxon, or simply Wilcoxon, test. Breslow (1970) extended this test to K groups, and thus it is sometimes known as the Breslow test. Since the w_i's are decreasing, this test will give greater weight to earlier deaths than the log rank test. Tarone and Ware (1977) discuss weights defined by $w_i = R_i 1/2$. Still another choice, suggested by Harrington and Fleming (1982), is to assign weights equal to $[\hat{S}(t_i)]\rho$ where the Kaplan-Meier estimate is based on the combined sample and ρ is a fixed nonnegative constant. This is a generalization of a test discussed by Prentice (1978) in which $\rho = 1$. Gray and Tsiatis (1989) discuss the interesting case of K = 2 and when the main interest is in comparing the cure rates of groups 1 and 2 assuming that survival among the non-cures is the same for both groups. In this case they show that the asymptotically optimal weights w_i are the reciprocals of the Kaplan-Meier estimates at t_i. To avoid zero values of this estimate, they use what is often called the left-continuous version of this Kaplan-Meier estimator. In this version, the "step" in the estimated survival curve is defined to take place immediately after each death time, instead of at that time.

Of course the preceding paragraph raises the important question of which test, i.e., which set of weights, to use. Although all are valid, you should not compute more than one statistic and choose the one "most significant." You may, however, specify the test to be done based upon the way you expect the survival distributions to differ from the null hypothesis. For two groups, if the ratio of the hazards is constant over time (recall that we called this the proportional hazards assumption in Chapter 2) and the censoring distributions are the same, then the log rank test will have maximal power in the class of all linear rank tests (Peto and Peto, 1972). Perhaps for this reason, this test is the most frequently used. You may recall from Chapter 2 that PROC LIFETEST provides a plot of the censoring times for each group. This plot provides a visual check of the assumption that the censoring distributions are the same. Lee et al. (1975) and Tarone and Ware (1977) show that when the proportional hazards assumption does not hold, other tests may have greater power. Only the Gehan and log rank tests are available in SAS. If the proportional hazards assumption seems tenable, then the log rank test is probably the best choice. Otherwise, we might perform power calculations for the type of alternative considered likely using a variety of test statistics and choose the statistic that provides the greatest power or the desired power most efficiently. This will be discussed later in this chapter.

3.4.3 Summarizing

Summarizing the discussion up to this point, we see that if t_1, t_2, . . ., t_M are the distinct death times, in ascending order, for patients in K groups and if w_1, w_2, . . . , w_M are a set of weights, then the linear rank test, determined by these weights, at significance level α is performed as follows:

1. Form a table like the one in Section 3.2.4. There should be a line for each time, t_i, at which a death occurred. The ith line should contain, for each group, j, the number of deaths, d_{ij}, in group j at time t_i, and R_{ij}, the number still at risk in group j just prior to time t_i. This line should also contain, for each group, j, $E_{ij} = d_i R_{ij}/R_i$ where d_i and R_i are the sums of the d_{ij} and R_{ij} in the ith row, and var$_{ij}$ as defined by (3.3).

2. Let $\mathbf{d}_i$ be the vector $(d_{i1}, d_{i2}, \ldots d_{iK})'$ and $\mathbf{E}_i$ be the vector $(E_{i1}, E_{i2}, \ldots E_{ik})'$. Form the vector sum, $\Sigma w_i(\mathbf{d}_i - \mathbf{E}_i)$ and the K sums (over i), Σvar$_{ij}$, where var$_{ij}$ is the variance of $w_i(d_{ij} - E_{ij})$.

3. For each pair of distinct groups, j and l, and each row, i, calculate cov$_{ijl}$, the covariance of $w_i(d_{ij} - E_{ij})$ and $w_i(d_{il} - E_{il})$. For each pair, j and l, form the sums (over i) Σcov$_{ijl}$.

4. Form the K by K matrix in which the jth main diagonal element is given by the jth sum, Σvar$_{ij}$ and the j,l off-diagonal entry is given by the sum Σcov$_{ijl}$.

5. Form the vector $\mathbf{S}_w$ by removing one component from the vector $\Sigma w_i(\mathbf{d}_i - \mathbf{E}_i)$. Form the (K–1) by (K–1) matrix $\mathbf{V}_w$ by removing from the matrix formed in Step 4 the row and column corresponding to that same component.

6. Calculate $\mathbf{S}_w' \mathbf{V}_w^{-1} \mathbf{S}_w$ and compare it to the $(1-\alpha)$100th percentile of a χ^2 distribution with K–1 degrees of freedom. If $\mathbf{S}_w' \mathbf{V}_w^{-1} \mathbf{S}_w$ exceeds that value, then reject the null hypothesis of equivalent survival in the K groups in favor of the alternative that their survival distributions differ. As an alternative, find the probability that a random variable having a χ^2 distribution with K–1 degrees of freedom has a value that exceeds $\mathbf{S}_w' \mathbf{V}_w^{-1} \mathbf{S}_w$. That is the p-value of the test statistic. Reject the null hypothesis if that p-value is less than α.

Of course, if you have access to SAS and a computer to run it on, you will not actually be doing these steps. Nevertheless, it is useful to know how PROC LIFETEST and the following macro work.

3.5 Using PROC LIFETEST

3.5.1 The STRATA Statement and the Output It Generates

PROC LIFETEST can perform the log rank test and the Gehan test (referred to in the output and documentation as the Wilcoxon test) to compare two or more groups with respect to time to death. To get these results, simply add to the statements that invoke PROC LIFETEST a statement like this one:

```
STRATA varname(s);
```

where each *varname* is the name of a grouping variable. More than one grouping variable may be specified. If a numeric variable is used, it may be followed by a list of the form $(a_1, a_2, \ldots, a_m)$.

Such a list creates strata of the form $x < a_1$, $a_1 \leq x < a_2$, . . . , $a_{m-1} \leq x < a_m$, and $a_m \leq x$. The output of PROC LIFETEST will then contain

- Life tables as described in Chapter 2 for each combination of strata defined by *varname(s)* and for the combined sample.

- Plots requested for each combination of strata.

- The vector $\Sigma(\mathbf{d}_i - \mathbf{E}_i)$ of log rank scores and $\Sigma R_i(\mathbf{d}_i - \mathbf{E}_i)$ of Gehan (Wilcoxon) scores as well as their covariance matrices.

- The resultant $\chi 2$ statistics and their *p*-values.

- The asymptotic likelihood ratio test statistic for testing the equality of the hazards of exponential distributions. The test is valid only if the survival distributions of each of the groups being compared are exponential. By contrast, the other two statistics and their *p*-values require no distributional assumptions. This third statistic and other parametric methods will be discussed in Chapter 5.

3.5.2 *Example*

For an example of the use of PROC LIFETEST to compare survival distributions, we look at some breast cancer data collected and maintained by the Cancer Registry of the H. Lee Moffitt Cancer Center and Research Institute. The data set contains, for each patient treated at the Cancer Center, the number of years followed, Years, another variable, Cens, which takes on the value 0 for a censored time and 1 for a death, the disease stage 0, I, II, III, or IV, and the age as $0 - 59$, $60 - 69$, $70 - 79$ and 80+. For this analysis, we dichotomized age as LT 60 and GE 60 and compared these two groups.

Here is the program:

```
data; set tmp1.breastdata;
if agegrp = '0-59' then age = 'LT 60';
else age = 'GE 60';
run;
symbol1 c=black l = 1 w = 3;
symbol2 c=black l = 3 w = 3;
proc lifetest censoredsymbol = none plots = (s) timelist = 1 to 8;
time years*cens(0);
strata age;
run;
```

Notice the use of the SYMBOL statement to cause the graphs to be black, to use different style lines (l = 1 and l = 3), and to make the lines thicker (w = 3). The default would cause the lines to be the same style, but different colors. Since we are printing this book in black and white that was not desirable. PROC LIFETEST produced Output 3.1.

Output 3.1

```
                        The LIFETEST Procedure

                     Stratum 1: age = GE 60

                  Product-Limit Survival Estimates

                                          Survival
                                          Standard   Number  Number
   Timelist      years     Survival   Failure    Error     Failed    Left

    1.00000     0.99932     0.9688     0.0312    0.00707      19      549
    2.00000     1.96030     0.9271     0.0729    0.0112       40      431
    3.00000     2.89665     0.9013     0.0987    0.0133       51      335
    4.00000     3.93703     0.8570     0.1430    0.0171       65      247
    5.00000     4.93361     0.8013     0.1987    0.0216       79      177
    6.00000     5.75770     0.7835     0.2165    0.0234       82      114
    7.00000     6.84736     0.7330     0.2670    0.0312       87       54
    8.00000     7.89870     0.6498     0.3502    0.0512       91       16


              Summary Statistics for Time Variable years

                          Quartile Estimates

                          Point      95% Confidence Interval
              Percent   Estimate      [Lower       Upper)

                  75        .            .            .
                  50        .            .            .
                  25     6.79261      5.60164         .


                   Mean     Standard Error

                 6.74275           0.10923
```

NOTE: The mean survival time and its standard error were underestimated because the largest observation was censored and the estimation was restricted to the largest event time.

Output 3.1 (continued)

```
                        The LIFETEST Procedure

                      Stratum 2: age = LT 60

                  Product-Limit Survival Estimates

                                        Survival
                                        Standard    Number    Number
  Timelist      years     Survival    Failure    Error      Failed     Left

  1.00000      0.99384    0.9645     0.0355    0.00660      28       709
  2.00000      1.99863    0.8831     0.1169    0.0123       81       521
  3.00000      2.98152    0.8189     0.1811    0.0157      114       365
  4.00000      3.88775    0.7736     0.2264    0.0181      132       272
  5.00000      4.99932    0.7268     0.2732    0.0212      145       179
  6.00000      5.59069    0.6876     0.3124    0.0242      153        93
  7.00000      6.94593    0.6472     0.3528    0.0305      157        41
  8.00000      6.94593    0.6472     0.3528    0.0305      157        14


              Summary Statistics for Time Variable years

                       Quartile Estimates

                           Point      95% Confidence Interval
             Percent     Estimate      [Lower       Upper)

               75           .             .            .
               50           .             .            .
               25        4.70089       3.57837      5.34976


                   Mean      Standard Error

                  5.64828         0.09014
```

NOTE: The mean survival time and its standard error were underestimated because the largest observation was censored and the estimation was restricted to the largest event time.

```
           Summary of the Number of Censored and Uncensored Values

                                                    Percent
       Stratum    age      Total   Failed   Censored   Censored

           1     GE 60      692      91       601      86.85
           2     LT 60      891     157       734      82.38
       -----------------------------------------------------------
           Total           1583     248      1335      84.33


                        The LIFETEST Procedure

          Testing Homogeneity of Survival Curves for years over Strata


                          Rank Statistics

             age        Log-Rank      Wilcoxon

            GE 60     ❶ -23.532     ❷  -22538
            LT 60        23.532         22538
```

Output 3.1 (continued)

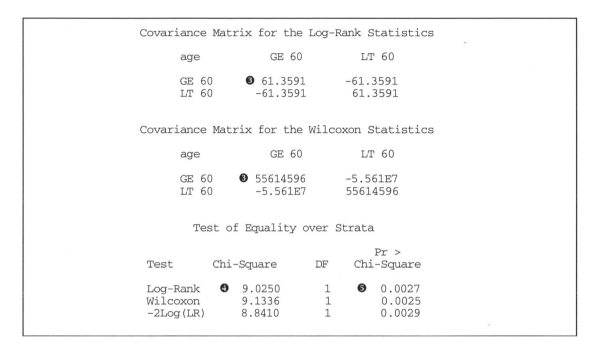

```
           Covariance Matrix for the Log-Rank Statistics

            age            GE 60           LT 60

            GE 60     ❸ 61.3591        -61.3591
            LT 60      -61.3591         61.3591


           Covariance Matrix for the Wilcoxon Statistics

            age            GE 60           LT 60

            GE 60     ❸ 55614596       -5.561E7
            LT 60      -5.561E7         55614596


                Test of Equality over Strata

                                          Pr >
            Test      Chi-Square    DF   Chi-Square

            Log-Rank   ❹ 9.0250      1    ❺ 0.0027
            Wilcoxon     9.1336      1      0.0025
            -2Log(LR)    8.8410      1      0.0029
```

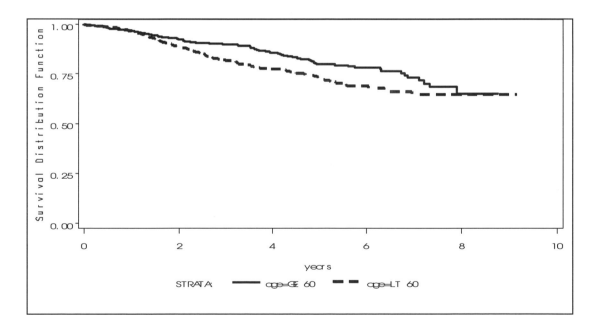

The rank statistics shown in the output are the sums of the (weighted) O – E's for each group. They must sum to zero over the groups. The main diagonal elements of the covariance matrices are the variances of the statistics for each group. From this output we can surmise the following:

❶ There were more than 23 more deaths than expected under the null hypothesis among the younger patients and, of course, the same number fewer than expected among the older patients. Thus these data offer evidence that younger breast cancer patients tend to have worse survival rates than older patients.

❷ When the differences of the numbers of deaths at each time from that expected are weighted by the numbers at risk and summed over all death times, those weighted sums are –22538 and 22538 for older patients and younger patients, respectively.

❸ The variances of these sums are 61.3591 and 55614596 for the log rank and Gehan sums, respectively.

❹ The values of the χ^2 statistics for these two tests are $23.532^2/61.3591$ for the log rank test and $22538^2/55614596$ for the Gehan test.

❺ Both tests conclude that the two age groups differ. The p-values are 0.0027 for the log rank test and 0.0025 for the Gehan test.

We will return to these data later for a more informative analysis.

3.5.3 A Word of Caution

While in this case both tests yield the same conclusion, you should realize that this may not always be true. In fact, Prentice and Marek (1979) give an interesting example, based on real data, in which the p-value for the log rank test was 0.01, but the p-value for the Gehan test was 0.76! *It is important that the statistical test to be used is specified in advance and that choice be honored when the analyses are done.* Later in this chapter, you will learn how power considerations may provide a reason for a preference. Unless you have such a reason for a preference, you should probably use the log rank test, however.

3.6 Exercises

3.6.1 Use PROC LIFETEST to compare the groups defined by stage of disease with respect to survival in the breast cancer data set.

3.6.2 Create an artificial set of survival data for two groups so that the Gehan test will be significant, but the log rank test will not. Check this with PROC LIFETEST.

3.7 A Test for Trend

Consider the general situation in which we are comparing K groups labeled 1, 2, . . . , K. Suppose u_1, u_2, . . . u_k. are values of some test statistic from samples taken from these groups. As we just noted, one common approach is to consider $\mathbf{u'Vu}$ where $\mathbf{u}$ is the vector $(u_1, u_2, . . . u_k)'$ and $\mathbf{V}$ is its covariance matrix. But now suppose we suspect that the groups do not just differ, but differ in the same order as their numeric labels. In other words, we might want to test the alternate hypothesis that the values in group i tend to be greater than the values in group i – 1 for i = 2, 3, . . . , K. If that is true, we would expect a test for this trend to have greater power than the "omnibus test" that there is some difference between the groups. One approach to this is to consider the sum $1u_1 + 2u_2 + . . . + Ku_K$. If the u_i's were increasing, this sum would be greater than if they were not increasing. Similarly, if the u_i's were decreasing, this sum would be less than if they were not decreasing. Thus a test for trend can be performed by considering the statistic $(1u_1 + 2u_2 + \ldots + Ku_K)^2/V^{1/2}$ where V is the variance of $1u_1 + 2u_2 + \ldots + Ku_K$. This statistic will have an asymptotic χ^2 distribution with 1 degree of freedom under the null hypothesis. Of course, we prefer to write the statistic $1u_1 + 2u_2 + \ldots + Ku_K$ as the vector product $\mathbf{x'u}$ where $\mathbf{x} = (1, 2, \ldots, K)'$ and $\mathbf{u} = (u_1, u_2, \ldots u_k)$. The variance of $\mathbf{x'u}$ can be shown to be $\mathbf{x'Vx}$ where $\mathbf{V}$ is the covariance matrix of $\mathbf{u}$. The vector $(1, 2, \ldots, K)'$ could, of course, be replaced by any vector of increasing values.

In some cases you might find it reasonable to assume, for three or more groups, that the differences in survival, if any, should be in the form of a trend in one direction or the other. For example, the groups might be determined by the extent of disease with group 1, 2, and 3 representing increasing extents. Then, if these groups do differ in survival, you would expect to find not simply a difference in the components of $\Sigma w_i(\mathbf{d_i - E_i})$ but that those components are in ascending order. Similarly, if higher numbered groups are defined by increasing doses of a drug that you believe is beneficial, then, if increasing doses are associated with increased benefit, you would expect the components of $\Sigma w_i(\mathbf{d_i - E_i})$ to be decreasing. If each group j is associated with a quantitative variable such as drug dose, x_j, let $\mathbf{x}$ be the column vector $(x_1, x_2, \ldots, x_K)'$ where $x_1 < x_2 < \ldots < x_K$. As discussed earlier, we can compare $[\mathbf{x'}\Sigma w_i(\mathbf{d_i - E_i})]^2/[\mathbf{x'Cx}]$, where $\mathbf{C}$ is the covariance matrix of $\Sigma w_i(\mathbf{d_i - E_i})$, to the appropriate critical value from a χ^2 distribution with one degree of freedom . Note that we don't have to deal with matrix inversion here. Both the numerator and denominator are scalars. If the groups have a natural ordering that is not associated with a quantity, you can replace the vector $\mathbf{x}$ by $(1, 2, \ldots, K)'$. You might do this, for example, to compare groups with stage II, III, and IV breast cancer.

3.8 Stratified Analyses

3.8.1 The Idea of Stratification

If the groups you are comparing are created by randomizing patients to different treatment regimens, then they probably will be roughly equivalent with respect to other factors which might influence survival such as age, sex, and severity of disease. Factors that influence survival are said to be prognostic for survival. You might force the treatment groups to be equivalent with respect to some prognostic factor by the manner in which you set up the treatment assignment. For example, if you want to compare two treatments with a randomized study and you feel that males and females have different survival, you might randomize males and females separately in blocks of four so that each block of four patients of the same sex has two on each treatment. Thus both treatment groups will have about the same proportion of males.

Although a randomized study is the gold standard for medical research, sometimes this ideal cannot be attained. This can happen when a large segment of the medical community becomes convinced of the superiority of a new treatment without the benefit of randomized studies to support that conviction while others are equally certain of the superiority of the older treatment. In such a case, it may be impossible to conduct a randomized study. Anyone wanting to compare these two treatments will be forced to resort to comparing groups determined by physician choice, not randomization. Of course, such groups may, and probably will, differ with respect to several important prognostic variables.

Sometimes we are interested in comparing patients in naturally occurring groups, such as race, sex, and tumor histology. These groups may very well differ in the distribution of some other factor that is prognostic for survival.

For example, in a study of neuroblastoma, a type of cancer found in young children, investigators with the Pediatric Oncology Group (POG) noticed that children with diploid tumors seemed to have worse survival than those whose tumors were hyperdiploid (Look et al., 1991). It was also noticed that those with diploid tumors tended to have more advanced disease (described by POG staging criteria as stage A, B, C, or D) than those with hyperdiploid tumors. Thus it was possible that the effect of ploidy was due to the association of ploidy with stage of disease. The investigators were interested in whether the prognostic effect of diploid tumors was due to its association with more advanced disease or whether ploidy is prognostic for survival independently of disease stage. By doing log rank tests comparing those with diploid tumors to those with hyperdiploid tumors stratified by other known prognostic factors such as stage and age, they were able to establish that tumor ploidy is an important prognostic factor independent of these other prognostic factors. As a result of these analyses, in future treatment studies of this disease by the POG, those with diploid tumors were given more intensive treatment (Bowman et al., 1997).

In order to compare two or more groups with respect to survival, while taking into consideration a prognostic variable for which these groups may differ, we can perform a stratified analysis.

3.8.2 The Stratified Statistic

To perform any of the linear rank tests described in Section 3.4 with stratification by a variable that takes on Q values, say 1, 2, . . . , Q, begin by computing the vector of weighted differences and the covariance matrix of that difference for each of the Q strata. Denote by S_{wq} and V_{wq} the vector of differences and its covariance matrix for stratum q. As before, each S_{wq} must have one component deleted, and each V_{wq} must have that corresponding row and column deleted. Then $(\Sigma S_{wq})'(\Sigma V_{wq})^{-1}(\Sigma S_{wq})$ has, under the null hypothesis, a χ^2 distribution. Here the indicated sums are over q = 1, 2, . . . Q. The number of degrees of freedom is the dimension of each S_{wq}, namely one fewer than the number of groups being compared. Of course, for each q, $S'_{wq}V_{wq}^{-1}S_{wq}$ provides a test statistic for the comparison of the groups in stratum q.

3.9 The Macro LINRANK

3.9.1 LINRANK's Capabilities

The macro LINRANK provides several capabilities not present in PROC LIFETEST. For one thing, it makes it possible to specify any one of a broader range of linear rank tests. In addition to the log rank and Gehan (Wilcoxon) tests, those proposed by Tarone and Ware and by Harrington and Fleming can also be performed. Recall that the Harrington and Fleming weights are formed by raising an estimated survival function to a power, ρ. In this case, the left-continuous Kaplan-Meier estimator (discussed in Section 3.4.2) is used and the exponent, ρ, can also be specified. A value of -1 gives the statistic of Gray and Tsiatis. If the Harrington and Fleming weights are chosen, the default value of ρ is one. The default is the log rank test. Stratification is permitted and the test for trend is done if there are more than two groups being compared. If there are K > 2 groups, then the default group weights are (1, 2, . . . , K) where the jth group in the natural ordering of the group names is assigned weight j. Optionally, if the group names are numeric, drug dosage for example, it is possible to specify that the group names are to be the group weights in the trend test. Finally, the output includes the numbers and expected numbers of deaths in each group as well as the value of χ^2 and the associated p-value. If a stratified analysis is requested, then each of the stratum results as well as pooled results are given. Since matrix operations are needed in the calculation of the test statistics, PROC IML is used. The macro listing is given at the end of this chapter and can be found on the companion SAS Web site for this book.

You can use this macro by filling in values for the parameters in the following template:

```
%linrank(dataset=            /* default is _last_   */
        time=                /* name of time variable,
                                default is time */
        ,cens=               /* name of censoring
                                variable */
        ,censval=            /* value(s) of censoring
                                variable */
        ,groupvar=           /* name of grouping variable */
        ,method=             /* test to be done - choices are
                                log rank (default)
                                gehan
                                tarone
                                harrington  */
        ,rho=                /* exponent used with
                                harrington test -
                                default is 1, -1 gives
                                the Gray/Tsiatis
                                statistic */
        ,stratvar=           /* name of stratification
                                variable -  default
                                is _none_ */
        ,stratmis=           /* use yes to consider
                                missing value for stratvar as
                                a stratum - default is no */
        ,trend=              /* use order (default) to
                                cause group weights for
                                trend test to be determined
                                by natural order of the
                                group names - values for
                                group names (numeric) to be
                                weights */

)
```

3.9.2 Example (Unstratified)

As an example of the use of this macro, consider once again the breast cancer data from the Cancer Registry maintained by the H. Lee Moffitt Cancer Center and Research Institute. In Chapters 4 and 5 you will learn about methods to analyze the effect of continuous variables such as age on survival. First, we do an unstratified analysis comparing the age groups. For this analysis the default log rank test was used. The following code invokes the macro LINRANK:

```
data x; set breastdata;
if agegrp = '0-59' then age = 'LT 60';
else age = 'GE 60';
%include 'c:\linrank.sas';
%linrank( time=years, cens= cens ,
            censval=0   ,groupvar= age )
```

The results are given below as Output 3.2.

Output 3.2

```
                          Summary of Events vs Expected
                                 Method = logrank

                       Percent of
            Frequency     Total                                   Weighted
   age        Count     Frequency    Events    Expected    Diff     Dif

  GE 60        692      43.7145        91       114.532   -23.5322  -23.5322
  LT 60        891      56.2855       157       133.468    23.5322   23.5322
             =========                        ======
               1583                            248

                              Covariance Matrix
                               Method = logrank

                 age          GE 60          LT 60

                GE 60        61.3591       -61.3591
                LT 60       -61.3591        61.3591

                           Method = logrank

                              RESULTS
                   CHISQUARE        DF    P_VALUE

                   9.0249536         1  0.0026632
```

The results, which duplicate the PROC LIFETEST results presented earlier, offer strong evidence that the patient's age is an important factor in survival and that younger patients have worse survival rates than older ones.

Because these results are rather counter-intuitive, we might want to explore our data further. Let's look at the stage distribution of these patients using PROC FREQ. Here are the results:

Output 3.3

```
                            The FREQ Procedure

                           Table of age by stage

        age         stage

        Frequency
        Percent
        Row Pct
        Col Pct    0        I        II       III      IV      Total

        GE 60          2       11       26        7        9        55
                    0.87     4.76    11.26     3.03     3.90     23.81
                    3.64    20.00    47.27    12.73    16.36
                   28.57    50.00    26.53    11.67    20.45

        LT 60          5       11       72       53       35       176
                    2.16     4.76    31.17    22.94    15.15     76.19
                    2.84     6.25    40.91  , 30.11    19.89
                   71.43    50.00    73.47    88.33    79.55

        Total          7       22       98       60       44       231
                    3.03     9.52    42.42    25.97    19.05    100.00
```

This is interesting. The younger patients tend to have higher stage disease than the older ones. About 9% of the younger patients have stage 0 or I disease compared to almost 24% of the older ones. Fifty percent of the younger patients have stage III or IV disease compared to about 30% of the older patients. If you did Exercise 3.6.1, you saw that patients of higher stage have a worse survival rate. Could it be that the poorer survival of the younger women is associated with their advanced stage of disease? To answer that question, we can use the Linrank macro once again. This time we will compare the older and younger patients, stratifying on stage. The call to the LINRANK macro looks like this:

```
%linrank(time=years, cens= cens,
         censval=0, groupvar= age, stratvar = stage)
```

Here are the results.

Output 3.4

❶ Deleted Observations

Obs	obsnumb	years	cens	age	stage
1	1	0.04654	0	GE 60	
2	2	8.30938	0	LT 60	
3	3	7.04997	0	LT 60	
4	4	2.26146	0	LT 60	
5	5	0.34497	0	LT 60	
6	6	0.42163	0	LT 60	
7	7	0.02738	0	GE 60	
8	8	2.20945	0	GE 60	
9	9	3.58385	0	GE 60	
10	10	0.00000	0	GE 60	
11	11	0.01643	0	GE 60	
12	12	0.15332	0	GE 60	
13	13	4.30664	0	GE 60	
14	14	2.36277	0	GE 60	
15	15	1.49760	1	GE 60	
16	16	0.45175	1	GE 60	

❷ Summary of Events vs Expected
stage = 0
Method = logrank

age	Frequency Count	Percent of Total Frequency	Events	Expected	Diff	Weighted Diff
GE 60	96	51.3369	3	2.08414	0.91586	0.91586
LT 60	91	48.6631	1	1.91586	-0.91586	-0.91586
	=========		======			
	187		4			

Output 3.4 (continued)

```
                              Covariance Matrix
                                 stage = 0
                             Method = logrank


                  age          GE 60          LT 60

               GE 60          0.99356        -0.99356
               LT 60         -0.99356         0.99356

                             stage = 0
                         Method = logrank

                              RESULTS
               CHISQUARE          DF    P_VALUE

               0.8442392           1  0.3581872

                    Summary of Events vs Expected
                              stage = I
                          Method = logrank

                      Percent of
              Frequency   Total
        age     Count    Frequency    Events    Expected    Diff       Diff

       GE 60     305     52.3156        22       18.8211    3.17887    3.17887
       LT 60     278     47.6844        13       16.1789   -3.17887   -3.17887
              =========                ======
                 583                     35

                              Covariance Matrix
                                 stage = I
                             Method = logrank

                  age          GE 60          LT 60

               GE 60          8.67900        -8.67900
               LT 60         -8.67900         8.67900

                             stage = I
                         Method = logrank

                              RESULTS
               CHISQUARE          DF    P_VALUE

                1.16433            1  0.2805693
```

Output 3.4 (continued)

```
                       Summary of Events vs Expected
                               stage = II
                             Method = logrank

                  Percent of
       Frequency   Total                                        Weighted
 age    Count      Frequency    Events    Expected     Diff       Diff

GE 60    219       38.8988        38      44.7536    -6.75360   -6.75360
LT 60    344       61.1012        63      56.2464     6.75360    6.75360
       =========               ======
         563                     101

                        Covariance Matrix
                            stage = II
                          Method = logrank

               age         GE 60          LT 60

             GE 60        24.5870       -24.5870
             LT 60       -24.5870        24.5870

                            stage = II
                          Method = logrank

                              RESULTS
             CHISQUARE            DF    P_VALUE

             1.8550914            1  0.1731924

                       Summary of Events vs Expected
                               stage = III
                             Method = logrank

                  Percent of
       Frequency   Total                                        Weighted
 age    Count      Frequency    Events    Expected     Diff       Diff

GE 60     28       19.0476         7       9.6698    -2.66980   -2.66980
LT 60    119       80.9524        47      44.3302     2.66980    2.66980
       =========               ======
         147                      54

                        Covariance Matrix
                            stage = III
                          Method = logrank

               age         GE 60          LT 60

             GE 60         7.91722       -7.91722
             LT 60        -7.91722        7.91722

                            stage =III
                          Method = logrank

                              RESULTS
             CHISQUARE            DF    P_VALUE

             0.9002966            1  0.3427022
```

Output 3.4 (continued)

```
                         Summary of Events vs Expected
                                 stage = IV
                            Method = logrank

                   Percent of
           Frequency    Total                                       Weighted
  age        Count    Frequency    Events    Expected     Diff        Diff

GE 60         33       37.9310       19       21.8344    -2.83445   -2.83445
LT 60         54       62.0690       33       30.1656     2.83445    2.83445
           =========                ======
              87                       52

                           Covariance Matrix
                              stage = IV
                          Method = logrank

                     age        GE 60       LT 60
                    GE 60      12.5412    -12.5412
                    LT 60     -12.5412     12.5412

                           stage = IV
                        Method = logrank

                              RESULTS
                    CHISQUARE         DF    P_VALUE

                    0.6406144          1   0.4234884

                     Summary of Events vs Expected
                                ❸
                     Pooled Over All Values of stage

                   Percent of
           Frequency    Total                                       Weighted
  age        Count    Frequency    Events    Expected     Diff        Diff

GE 60        681      43.4588       89        97.163    -8.16312   -8.16312
LT 60        886      56.5412      157       148.837     8.16312    8.16312
           =========                ======
             1567                     246

                           Covariance Matrix
                     Pooled Over All Values of stage

                     age        GE 60       LT 60

                    GE 60      54.7180    -54.7180
                    LT 60     -54.7180     54.7180

                        Pooled Results
                        Method = logrank

                              RESULTS
                    CHISQUARE         DF    P_VALUE

                    1.2178164          1   0.2697896
```

Note the following features of the output:

❶ For 16 patients, Stage was missing from the data set. Since we used the default that does not count missing values as stratum values, those patients are excluded from the analysis and a list of them is printed. If we had specified STRATMISS = YES, these 16 patients would have been used as another stratum. For the previous, unstratified analysis, all patients had valid values for all needed variables, so no such listing was printed.

❷ The macro then performs the log rank tests for each value of the stratification variable, Stage. In each case, the results are not statistically significant. In fact, for two of the five values of Stage, those younger than 60 years old have better, although not significantly better, survival rates.

❸ Finally, the macro pools all of the stages to provide one overall test for the effect of age while stratifying by stage. The results do not approach significance. Our conclusion is that, while younger women with breast cancer seem to have worse survival rates than older women, the difference may be due to the fact that younger women tend to be diagnosed with more advanced disease.

3.9.3 Exercise

Use the LINRANK macro to perform a comparison of the stages stratifying on age. Can the effect of stage on survival be accounted for by the fact that those of advanced stage tend to be younger?

3.10 Permutation Tests and Randomization Tests

3.10.1 Motivation

Let us now revisit the issue of our test statistic's distribution. We said earlier that the test statistics we are dealing with in this chapter have, *asymptotically*, a χ^2 distribution. The question of when a sample is large enough for us to have confidence in the asymptotic behavior of our test statistic is a difficult one that we won't try to address here. But certainly, we would be concerned about using a χ^2 distribution with sample sizes of less than ten in a group. What do we do then?

3.10.2 Permutation Tests – The General Idea

You have probably already seen an approach to this problem when comparing proportions. When using PROC FREQ it is not unusual to get an output like this.

Output 3.5

```
                        The FREQ Procedure

                     Table of group by response

            group       response

            Frequency|
            Percent
            Row Pct
            Col Pct        Yes       No    Total
            ─────────┼────────┼────────┼
                1   |    3    |    7    |    10
                    |  15.00  |  35.00  |  50.00
                    |  30.00  |  70.00  |
                    |  27.27  |  77.78  |
            ─────────┼────────┼────────┼
                2   |    8    |    2    |    10
                    |  40.00  |  10.00  |  50.00
                    |  80.00  |  20.00  |
                    |  72.73  |  22.22  |
            ─────────┼────────┼────────┼
            Total         11        9        20
                        55.00    45.00   100.00
```

Output 3.5 (continued)

```
                    Statistics for Table of group by response

      Statistic                        DF      Value      Prob

      Chi-Square                        1      5.0505     0.0246
      Likelihood Ratio Chi-Square       1      5.3002     0.0213
      Continuity Adj. Chi-Square        1      3.2323     0.0722
      Mantel-Haenszel Chi-Square        1      4.7980     0.0285
                   Phi Coefficient                       -0.5025
                   Contingency Coefficient               0.4490
                   Cramer's V                            -0.5025

      WARNING: 50% of the cells have expected counts less
           than 5. Chi-Square may not be a valid test.


                        Fisher's Exact Test

              Cell (1,1) Frequency (F)           3
              Left-sided Pr <= F              0.0349
              Right-sided Pr >= F             0.9973

              Table Probability (P)           0.0322
              Two-sided Pr <= P               0.0698

                     Sample Size = 20
```

PROC FREQ warns us that, because of small cell counts, the χ^2 test may not be valid. It also provides as an alternative, Fisher's Exact Test, and its *p*-value. This test can be thought of as the earliest example of an important type of statistical test—the permutation test.

In order to perform the permutation test indicated in the output, we consider all of the ways in which the twenty subjects in this study could be assigned to the two treatment groups with ten in each group. Then we compute the χ^2 statistic for each of those assignments of the subjects to the two groups and count the number of these χ^2 statistics that are greater than or equal to the χ^2 statistic for the actual data. Dividing that number by the total number of possible assignments gives the desired *p*-value. That *p*-value does not require any assumptions about the asymptotic distribution of a test statistic.

In the previous example, there are $20!/(10!)^2 = 184,756$ ways to assign twenty subjects to two groups with ten in each group. Apparently (although for obvious reasons I haven't checked) 6.98% of them produced χ^2 statistics equal to or greater than the χ^2 statistic, associated with the actual observed table. Thus the *p*-value for Fisher's Exact Test is .0698. This same idea can be applied to other hypothesis testing situations as well. It requires the following steps:

1. Decide on a test statistic and calculate its value for the actual data.

2. If the sample sizes in the two groups are N_1 and N_2, calculate the values of the same statistic for each of the $(N_1 + N_2)!/(N_1!N_2!)$ possible assignments of the $N_1 + N_2$ observations into two groups with sample sizes N_1 and N_2.

3. The proportion of these values that are equal to or greater than the value of the statistic for the actual data is the desired *p*-value.

3.10.3 *Randomization Tests*

Now suppose we need to compare groups with respect to survival based on samples for which use of the χ^2 approximation might be questionable and yet the sample is too large for the permutation test to be feasible. This can happen if the number of deaths is small. Consider, for example, two samples, each of size 20. If half or more in each sample died, the asymptotic test would probably be reasonable. But if there were only a total of five or six deaths it might not be. Yet the permutation test described above would have over $40!/20!^2$ (which is about 1.38×10^{11}) log rank tests to consider. In such cases, a randomization test can offer an alternative. A randomization test does not attempt to look at all possible ways of assigning the subjects to the two groups. Instead, it considers a random sample of such assignments and looks at the proportion of these assignments that lead to a test statistic at least as large as the observed value. The p-value obtained is then an estimate of the true permutation test p-value. By controlling the size of the sample of assignments, we can control the precision of that estimate. For example, a sample of 1000 such assignments with 40 providing test statistics as least as large as the one observed would result in an estimated p-value of 0.04 with a standard deviation of $[(0.04)(0.96)/1000]^{1/2} = 0.006$.

It should be obvious that methods based on this principle require a great deal of computation, although an algorithm introduced by Mehta and Patel (1983) does reduce the amount considerably. A product called Proc-StatXact, sold by a company they formed, can be added to SAS. It can do randomization tests as well as a large variety of permutation tests, including those based on the log rank test and the Gehan test.

3.10.4 *Macros for Permutation and Randomization Tests*

For readers of this book who do not have Proc-StatXact, I provide here a set of macros to perform permutation and randomization log rank and Gehan tests. The technique used is based on the idea of a *randomization test wrapper* described by Cassell (2002). The basic idea is to break the problem into three parts.

1. Starting with the original data set, create a data set consisting of a large number of replicates of the original data set. Each replicate has its group assignments permuted. Add a variable to represent the replicate number. For a permutation test on groups with sizes n_1 and n_2 you will have $(n_1 + n_2)!/(n_1!n_2!)$ replicates, one for each way of choosing n_1 of the $n_1 + n_2$ observations to be in one of the two groups. For a randomization test, you will choose some large number of replicates, in which the group memberships are randomly determined, perhaps 1000 – 5000.

2. Run PROC LIFETEST to perform the log rank or Gehan test, by replicate. Use the OUTPUT statement to produce a data set containing the values of the test statistic for each replicate in the data set described earlier. You will also want to suppress the normal output, which would otherwise be quite voluminous.

3. Use a DATA step on the data set produced in step 2 to calculate the proportion of replicates for which the value of the test statistic is at least as large as the value of the test statistic for the original data. That proportion is the p-value for a permutation test or an estimate of the p-value for a randomization test. For a randomization test, you might want to compute the standard error of the estimate or a confidence interval for the true value.

3.10.4.1 The RAND_GEN Macro

The macro RAND_GEN, which can be used to generate a large number of replicates of a data set with the group assignments permuted, is a slight variation of the macro of the same name discussed by David Cassell. I appreciate his allowing me to use it. Here is the syntax.

```
%RAND_GEN(INDATA =         ,
   TIME =        ,
   CENS =     ,
   NUMREPS=    ,
   GROUP =         ,
   SEED=        );
```

where

INDATA is the name of the data set being used.

TIME is the name of the time variable.

CENS is the name of the censoring variable.

NUMREPS is the number of replications desired. The default is 1000.

GROUP is the name of the grouping variable. The grouping variable must have the values 1 and 2.

SEED is the value of the seed for the random number generator. The default is 0. This value will creates a different stream of random numbers, and hence a different result, each time. If you use a positive number as the value of SEED, the stream of random numbers, and hence the result, will be the same each time.

3.10.4.2 The PERM_GEN Macro

The macro PERM_GEN, can be used to create a data set containing a replicate of the original data set for each possible reassignment of the groups. Here is the syntax.

```
%PERM_GEN(INDATA =    ,
TIME =    ,
CENS =    ,
GROUP =    ,
N1 =    ,
N2 =    )
```

where

INDATA is the name of the data set to be used.

TIME is the name of the time variable.

CENS is name of the censoring variable.

GROUP is the name of the grouping variable. The grouping variable must have values 1 and 2.

N1 and N2 are the sample sizes in groups 1 and 2, respectively.

3.10.4.3 The TEST Macro

After invoking either the RAND_GEN macro or the PERM_GEN macro, you can invoke the TEST macro. This macro performs either the log rank or Gehan test by replicate, creates a data set containing the values of the chi-square statistics, and counts the number of these values that exceed the chi-square value for the original data to compute a *p*-value. Here is the syntax.

```
%TEST(TIME =   ,
CENS =      ,
CENSVAL =   ,
TEST =      ,
GROUP =     ,
TYPE =      );
```

Here TIME, CENS, and GROUP are the same as in the RAND_GEN or PERM_GEN macros. In addition,

CENSVAL   is a list of values of the censoring variable that indicate a censored time.

TEST   is the name of the test desired. It should be logrank or gehan.

TYPE   should be rand or perm depending upon whether RAND_GEN or PERM_GEN is used.

3.10.5 Example

Consider the same data set as in Section 3.1. The following SAS code would need to be preceded by either the text of the macros being used or statements that follow this syntax:

```
%INCLUDE path\PERM_GEN;
%INCLUDE path\test;
```

where PERM_GEN and TEST are files containing the macros of those names. You can then use the following statements to perform the permutation log rank test:

```
data x; input time cens group;
datalines;
3 1 1
5 1 1
8 0 1
10 1 1
15 1 1
2 1 2
5 1 2
11 0 2
13 0 2
14 1 2
16 1 2
;

%perm_gen( indata = x, time = time, cens = cens, n1 = 5, n2 = 6, group
= group);

%test(time = time  , cens = cens, censval = 0  , test = logrank, group
= group, type = perm);
```

The output is simply as follows:

Output 3.6

```
                        Permutation
                        logrank Test
                          P-Value
                         (2-sided)
                           0.465


                        Asymptotic
                         P-Value
                         0.44587
```

The macro PERM_GEN uses PROC PLAN to produce the permuted data sets. This creates some extraneous output that is not needed and thus is not included here.

The PERMTEST macro needed to do 11!/(5!6!) = 462 log rank tests. Apparently, for 215 of them (46.5% of 462), the chi-square statistic had a value at least as great as the value for the original data. If you prefer to do a randomization test, the PERM_GEN invocation could be replaced by this statement:

```
%rand_gen(indata = x, time = time, cens = cens, numreps =  1000, group
= group);
```

The value of the parameter type in the test macro should then be changed from PERM to RAND. The results are as follows:

Output 3.7

```
        Randomization
        logrank Test
          Estimated                Lower     Upper
           P-Value                 95 Pct    95 Pct    Number of
          (2-sided)     stderr     Bound     Bound     Replicates

            0.479      0.015797    0.44804   0.50996      1000

                             The SAS System
                               Asymptotic
                                P-Value

                                0.44587
```

3.10.6 Exercises

3.10.6.1 Explain why a permutation test comparing two samples with both sample sizes equal to 3 cannot possibly get a *p*-value less than 0.05 and with samples of sizes 3 and 4 cannot get a *p*-value less than .01.

3.10.6.2 Consider the following data:

```
time    d    group
1.2     1      1
3.1     0      1
4.5     1      1
7.6     1      1
8.0     1      1
9.1     1      1
3.5     0      2
4.2     0      2
9.3     1      2
9.4     0      2
```

Use the macros PERM_GEN and TEST to compare group 1 and group 2 using both the permutation log rank test and the permutation Gehan test. How many permutations need to be considered for the permutation test? Now suppose you learn that the group 1 death that you thought was at time 9.1 was actually at time 8.3. Re-do these analyses with the data corrected and note the effect on the results. Explain. Would the results be different if this time were changed to 9.5? Explain.

3.10.6.3 Although Exercise 3.10.6.2 does not require too many permutations, reanalyze these data with a randomization test. Take a sample of 100 permutations. Note that we would usually use this method for larger samples and would use more than 100 permutations.

3.11 The Mantel-Byar Method

Let's turn now to a slightly different situation. Consider a cohort of patients who will each, on a certain date, be considered candidates for an organ transplant. In general they will have some waiting time until they can get their transplants. Some will die and some will be censored without ever receiving the transplant. Some will die and some will be censored after receiving the transplant. You would like to analyze the effect of the transplant on survival. Clearly it will not be correct to simply compare the transplanted patients to those not transplanted using the methods described earlier in this chapter. For example, those who died early would likely have been poor prognosis patients. Since they died early, they probably would have been in the untransplanted group. Those who got transplanted had to survive long enough to get it, and thus might have had a better prognosis.

Previously, we compared groups defined by a variable that remained constant for all time. Now we are dealing with a variable whose value can change over time. Transplant status can change from untransplanted to transplanted during the course of the study. There is, however a simple modification of the log rank test, first presented by Mantel and Byar (1974) that addresses questions of this sort in an appropriate manner. An alternative method of dealing with data of this type will be discussed in Chapter 4.

Think of each patient as originally being in the pretransplant state. He may die or be censored while still in this state, or he may receive his transplant, thus changing from the untransplanted to the transplanted state. In that state he may die or be censored. The question then becomes whether the data provide evidence that the two states differ in their impact on survival. Although in this example, which was the motivation for the paper by Mantel and Byar, there are only two states and only one possible state change, from untransplanted to transplanted, it's not any more difficult to allow much greater generality. Suppose there are K states. For convenience, label them 1, 2, . . . , K. The ordering isn't important here. Patients enter the study in one of these states. They can each make any number of state changes, from any of the states to any of the others, at any time. Each patient is finally censored or dies in one of the states. This more general formulation of their method was suggested by Mantel and Byar in their paper. Cantor (1994) describes this in greater detail and presents a SAS macro for its implementation.

The essential idea of the Mantel-Byar method is to have a table similar to the one used in the log rank test to keep track of the number at risk and number who die *in each state* at the time of each death. The departure from the log rank test is due to the fact that, in addition to diminishing the number at risk in each state when a patient in that state dies or is censored, you also diminish the number in state j_1 and increase the number in state j_2 when a patient goes from state j_1 to state j_2. Once you change the way the R_{ij} is calculated, all of the other formulas in Section 3.4 remain unchanged. Remember that R_{ij} is the number at risk in state j at the time of the ith death. Crowley (1974) has shown that the statistic $\mathbf{S'V^{-1}S}$, which is defined just as it is in that section has, asymptotically, a χ^2 distribution with K–1 degrees of freedom under the null hypothesis of equivalent survival in each state, just as the log rank statistic does.

3.11.1 The MANTBYAR Macro

In order to permit the flexibility of state changes described earlier, it is necessary to use a slightly more complex method of describing the data to be analyzed. First of all, there must be a variable that serves as a unique identifier for each patient. The name of this variable is specified in the macro call, but will be Id in this description. Two other variables that will be called State and Time here are also used. Each observation tells the macro that patient identified by Id entered the state identified by State at time Time. Time is 0 for an observation that indicates a patient entry onto the study. If there are K states, they will be labeled 1, 2, . . . , K. A patient who is censored will be thought of as entering state 0. A patient who dies will be thought of entering state K + 1. For example, suppose a patient with Id = 1 starts in a study by entering in state 3. He changes to state 1 at time 34, to state 4 at time 40, and back to state 3 at time 51. Finally he is censored while in state 3 at time 65. The part of the data set based on this patient will look like this:

Id	State	Time
1	3	0
1	1	34
1	4	40
1	3	51
1	0	65

Of course, there will be similar observations for each of the other patients. The observations do not have to be sorted by Id or Time.

The MANTBYAR macro is invoked by a macro call which sets values for the macro variables that give the name of the SAS data set to be used, the names of the Id, State, and Time variables, the number of states, and, optionally, a format for the State variable. The default data set is the last data set defined, the default Id variable is Id, the default time variable is Time, and the default number of states is two. The default format for the state variable is to associate the format State1 with 1, State2 with 2, and so on. The macro can be invoked by filling the spaces in the following template.

```
%macro mantbyar(dataset =      /* default is last */
              ,state =         /* name of the state
                                  variable */
              ,time =          /* name of time
                                  variable, default is
                                  time */
              ,nstates =       /* the number states,
                                  default is 2 */
   ,format =       /* format for state
                      variable, default is
                      STATE1, STATE2, etc
                      */
   ,id =           /* the unique patient
                      identifier, default
                      is id */
   )
```

The output produced by this macro contains the covariance matrix for testing the O – E's for each state and a table of observed and expected number of events in each state with a p-value for the association of each state with the event. Each of these p-values is based on referring the O – E divided by its standard deviation to the standard normal distribution. Finally, an overall test of the homogeneity of the states is given. This is based on referring the statistic $S'V^{-1}S$ to a χ^2 distribution with $K - 1$ degrees of freedom.

3.11.2 Example: Artificial

Consider the following data set representing three patients and the macro invocation that follows:

```
data; input patid state time; datalines;
1 1 0
1 2 3.1
1 3 5.0
2 2 0
2 1 3.2
2 0 5.0
3 1 0
3 2 4.2
3 3 5.1
;
%mantbyar(dataset= _last_ , state=state , time=time, nstates=2 ,
format= default.,id=patid);
```

The first variable is a patient identifier. The second is a state variable. There are two states represented by the values 1 and 2. Recall that zero represents a patient who is censored and three represents a patient who is dead. The third variable represents time. Thus, in this data set, the patient whose identifier equals 1 started in state 1, changed to state 2 at time 3.1, and died at time 5.0. Of course we would not really use this method for such a small sample. The approximation of the test statistic by a χ^2 random variable would not be valid. Nevertheless, let's look at it as a simple example of the method we are discussing and the use of the MANTBYAR macro. The results are given in the following output.

Output 3.8

```
                          The SAS System

                        Covariance Matrix


                              COV
                           STATE1        STATE2

                  STATE1    0.2222       -0.2222
                  STATE2   -0.2222        0.2222

                Summary of Results for Each State
          Observed      Expected       O/E           O-E      P-value

STATE1  0.000000     0.333333      0.000000     -0.333333 0.479500
STATE2  2.000000     1.666667      1.200000      0.333333 0.479500




                Test of Homogeneity of States


                    CHISQ     DF            P

                   0.5000      1     0.4795001
```

The output gives the observed and expected number of deaths in each state. The ratio of observed to expected and their difference are both used to express the effect of the state on survival, so both are given. Finally the *p*-value for each state is given. These must be the same if there are only two states. In this case the overall *p*-value will also be equal to this common value.

3.11.3 Example: Real

The Natural History of Insulin Dependent Diabetes Mellitus (IDDM) is a study that created and maintains a data base of siblings of children with IDDM (Riley et al., 1990). At the time of the analysis, there were 1354 children in the data base. All were nondiabetic upon entry. One of the study's objectives was to follow these children for conversion to IDDM and to look for factors related to conversion. One of the factors studied was the level of insulin antibodies as measured in JDF units. At any time a patient is classified into one of five states as follows:

Antibody Level (JDF units)	State
< 20	1
≥ 20, < 40	2
≥ 40, < 80	3
≥ 80, < 160	4
≥ 160	5

The results of running the macro are given in Output 3.9.

Output 3.9

```
                        Covariance Matrix

COV          STATE1     STATE2     STATE3     STATE4     STATE5

STATE1       1.0016    -0.2645    -0.2063    -0.2879    -0.2429
STATE2      -0.2645     0.2704    -0.0018    -0.0025    -0.0016
STATE3      -0.2063    -0.0018     0.2113    -0.0021    -0.0011
STATE4      -.02879    -0.0025    -0.0021     0.2941    -0.0016
STATE5      -0.2429    -0.0016    -0.0011    -0.0016     0.2472




                 Summary of Results for Each State

STATE       Observed    Expected        O/E        O-E     P-Value

STATE1      11.0000     32.9656      0.3337    -21.965    < 0.0001
STATE2       3.0000      0.2728     10.9990      2.7272   < 0.0001
STATE3       4.0000      0.2130     18.7820      3.7870   < 0.0001
STATE4      12.0000      0.2971     40.3921     11.7029   < 0.0001
STATE5       4.0000      0.2516     15.8984      3.7484   < 0.0001

          Test of Homogeneity of States

CHISQ              DF              P
626.7672            4           < 0.0001
```

The O-E column shows the impact of each state on the occurrence of the endpoint (in this case conversion to IDDM). The negative value for State1 and the positive values for the other states show that State 1 (antibody level < 20) had fewer conversions and the other states more conversions than would be expected if all states carried equivalent conversion risk. The P-Value column gives the *p*-value for the effect of each state. In this case, each one is highly significant. The heading Test for Homogeneity of States is a test of the null hypothesis that there is no difference in states versus the alternative that there is *some* difference. Not surprisingly, this is highly significant as well. A listing of the MANTBYAR macro is given at the end of this chapter. It can also be found on the companion Web site for this book.

3.11.4 Exercise

The data set created by stanford.sas, found on the companion Web site for this book, was derived from the Stanford heart transplant data. An observation in this data set represents the time since entering the transplant program that the patient identified by ID enters a state. State 1 is the pretransplant state and state 2 is posttransplant. State 0 is censored and state 3 is death. Perform the Mantel-Byar analysis to compare the two transplant states with respect to mortality.

3.12 Power Analysis

3.12.1 Introduction

In most areas of statistics, given a study design, significance level, and values for the population parameters, the power of the test to be done can be shown to be a function of the sample size. By "solving for the sample size," or perhaps by performing some crude iteration, you can determine the sample size that will produce the desired power (often 80% or 90%). Lachin (1981) provides an excellent introduction to this subject. In survival analysis, however, the situation is quite different. This is because the amount of information about survival conveyed by a sample is not determined by the sample size alone, but also by the *amount of time* those in the sample have been observed. Thus the following features of a study have to be considered in discussing its power:

- significance level of the test to be done.
- length of the accrual period.
- amount of post-accrual follow-up time.
- accrual rate. That is, the rate at which patients are entered into the study.
- distribution(s) of the loss to follow-up.
- survival distributions of the groups being compared.

The first three of these are under the control of the study planners. The last three are generally not subject to our control, although in some cases we can affect the accrual rate by the effort and resources devoted to accrual or by the number of institutions that are asked to participate in a multiinstitutional study. Similarly, loss to follow-up may be, in some cases, affected by the effort taken to reduce it. The survival distributions of the groups being compared must, of course, be hypothesized. They should have some basis in prior experience. They should be sufficiently different that such a difference would be clinically meaningful, but not so different as to be unrealistic.

While it would be preferable to discuss power for the comparison of any number of groups, no results have been published for more than two groups. In the next section the discussion will be restricted to that situation.

3.12.2 The Formula for Power Calculations

In the discussion that follows assume that the study planners have specified the six features we just listed. Assume also that you wish to estimate the power of certain linear rank tests (including the log rank test and the Gehan test) resulting from those specifications. By perturbing those specifications you can then, it is hoped, determine study parameters that are realistic and that will achieve the desired power. Many approaches to this problem assume that survival distributions of the two groups being compared are exponential (George and Desu, 1974 and Rubenstein, Gail, and Santner, 1981). Others allow for other distributions, but require that the proportional hazards assumption holds (Shuster,1992 and Cantor, 1992). In these cases the asymptotic efficiency of the log rank test can be shown to lead to a fairly simple result for the power of that test.

Experience with actual clinical trials suggests, however, that such assumptions are not necessarily realistic. For this reason, the method presented here, which is described by Lakatos (1988), requires no assumption concerning the survival distributions of the groups being compared. His formulation allows for rather complex designs and permits specifying the effects of crossovers and noncompliers. Shih (1995) discusses a program that implements the Lakatos method, maintaining the functionality described by Lakatos. The next section presents a SAS macro, SURVPOW, that also implements the Lakatos method. While SURVPOW does not allow for some of the complexity of the Lakatos approach as Shih does, it may be easier to invoke. It is usually easier to describe survival distributions of groups being compared in terms of survival probabilities at various times rather than by values of their hazard functions, and SURVPOW allows you to specify the alternative distributions in that way. Abandonment of the proportional hazards assumption allows for the possibility that an alternative linear rank test may have greater power than the log rank test. Thus you may specify a large class of such alternative test statistics.

Suppose you plan to accrue patients to a clinical trial designed to compare two groups for T units of time at rate r per time unit. You will then, after accrual ends, follow the study patients for an additional τ units of time before performing the final analyses. For definiteness, we denote the two groups by 1 and 2. To allow for unequal sample sizes, let p be the proportion that we plan to assign to group 1. Then the sample sizes, N_1 and N_2, are rTp and $rT(1-p)$, respectively. Let $h_j(t)$ be the hazard function and let $\psi_j(t)$ be the "hazard" function for patients' being lost to follow-up for group j where $j = 1, 2$.

Now suppose that the study period $[0, T + \tau]$ is partitioned into subintervals of equal length by $0 = t_0 < t_1 < t_2 < \ldots < t_M = T + \tau$ and let Δ be the common subinterval width. We need to discuss the expected number at risk in each group at each time t_i for the planned study, which will be denoted by $N_j(i)$ for $j = 1, 2$. For each subinterval, $[t_i, t_{i+1})$, the probability of death for a subject in group j can be approximated by $h_j(t_i)\Delta$. Similarly the probability that this subject will be lost to follow-up in this subinterval is approximately $\psi_j(t_i)\Delta$. This subject will also be censored in this subinterval if he or she entered the study between t_i and t_{i+1} time units prior to $T + \tau$. Assuming uniform accrual, that probability is approximately $\Delta/(T + \tau - t_i)$ for $t_i > \tau$ and 0 for $t_i \leq \tau$. These considerations lead to the recurrence relation

$$N_j(0) = N_j$$
$$N_j(i + 1) = N_j(i)[1 - h_j(t_i)\Delta - \psi_j(t_j)\Delta] \text{ for } t_i \leq \tau \qquad (3.5)$$
$$N_j(i + 1) = N_j(i)\left[1 - h_j(t_i)\Delta - \psi_j(t_j)\Delta - \frac{\Delta}{T + \tau - t_i}\right] \text{ for } t_i > \tau$$

Now let $\theta_i = h_1(t_i)/h_2(t_i)$ and $\varphi_i = N_1(i)/N_2(i)$. The test statistic given in Section 3.4.1, $S'_w V_w^{-1} S_w$, having a χ^2 distribution with one degree of freedom for two groups is a product of scalars in that case. The test is equivalent to comparing $S_w/V_w^{1/2}$ to a critical value of a standard normal distribution. Lakatos shows that this statistic has, in general, a normal distribution with unit variance and mean approximately equal to

$$E = \frac{\sum_{i=1}^{M} D_i w_i \left[\dfrac{\varphi_i \theta_i}{1 + \varphi_i \theta_i} - \dfrac{\varphi_i}{1 + \varphi_i}\right]}{\sqrt{\sum_{i=1}^{M} D_i w_i^2 \dfrac{\varphi_i}{(1 + \varphi_i)^2}}} \qquad (3.6)$$

where $D_i = [h_1(t_i)N_1(i) + h_2(t_i)N_2(i)] \Delta$, the expected number of deaths in the i_{th} subinterval. It follows that for a test being done with significance level α, the power is one minus the probability of a standard normal random variable being between $-E - z_{\alpha/2}$ and $-E + z_{\alpha/2}$ where $z_{\alpha/2}$ is the $(1 - \alpha/2)100$th percentile of a standard normal distribution.

3.12.3 The SURVPOW Macro

3.12.3.1 The Macro's Parameters

The macro SURVPOW takes the following parameters:

S1 and S2   These are the names of data sets that describe the survival distributions in groups 1 and 2, respectively. They must contain the two variables t (for time) and s (for survival probability at time t). If a data set contains only one observation, (t, s), the macro assumes that the group has exponential survival with S(t) = s. This equation determines the constant hazard for that group. If a data set contains exactly two observations and the variable t for the second observation is missing (i.e., has the value .), then the "cure" model $S(t) = \pi + (1 - \pi)e^{-\lambda t}$ is assumed with π equal to the value of s for the second observation and the first pair (t, s) being a point on the survival curve. Otherwise, it is assumed that the survival curve is given by the piecewise linear curve formed by connecting the points (t, s) for each observation. The values of t and s must satisfy the following conditions:

- For the first observation, t = 0 and s = 1.
  - The values of t must be increasing.
  - The values of s must be decreasing.
- The last value of t must be at least the total time of the study (the accrual time plus the follow-up time).

NSUB   This is the number of subintervals per time unit. The default is 365, which corresponds to subintervals of one day's duration when the time unit is years.

ACTIME   This is the number of time units of accrual. It is assumed that accrual occurs uniformly during this interval.

FUTIME   This is the number of time units for post-accrual follow-up.

RATE   This is the accrual rate per unit of time.

P   This is the proportion of patients assigned to group 1. The default is 0.5.

LOSS1   These are the rates for the assumed loss to follow-up. It is assumed that loss to
and LOSS2   follow-up is exponential. The defaults are 0.

W   This is the formula for the weights that define the linear rank test planned. The variable n, representing the total number at risk, may be used. Thus w = 1 gives the log rank test statistic (the default), w = n gives the Gehan test statistic, and w = (n**.5) gives the test statistic discussed by Tarone and Ware (1977). The parentheses are needed in the last example to assure that the expression w**2 is evaluated as intended. That's because SAS evaluates n**.5**2 as n**.25 instead of n.

SIGLEVEL   The (two-sided) significance level for the planned test. The default value is 0.05.

The macro is given in Section 3.14.5. This macro can be implemented by filling in values for the parameters in the following template:

```
%survpow(s1=      ,s2 =    /* data sets that define
                             alternative survival
                             distributions for groups 1
                             and 2*/
         ,nsub=              /* number of subintervals per
                             time unit. Default is 365 */
         ,actime=           /* accrual time */
         ,futime=           /* post-accrual follow-up
                             time */
         ,rate=             /* accrual rate */
         ,p=                /* proportion assigned to
                             group 1.Default is.5 */
         ,loss1=   ,loss2 =  /* exponential loss rates
                                in groups 1 and 2
                                Defaults are 0 */
         ,w=                /* weight function. Default
                             is 1 for log rank test. */
         ,siglevel=         /* significant level.
                             Default is 0.05    */
)
```

3.12.3.2 *Example*

Suppose that a clinical trial to compare a new treatment for stage IV prostate cancer to a standard treatment is being planned. Several hospitals, each able to place 10–20 per year on such a study, are potential participants. The hospitals' experience with the standard treatment can be summarized by a Kaplan-Meier survival curve. Although the entire life table produced by PROC LIFETEST or the Kmtable macro introduced in Chapter 2 could be used as one of the data sets, it is sufficient to use the following yearly survival probability estimates.

t	S(t)
0	1.00
1	0.86
2	0.68
3	0.60
4	0.51
5	0.39
6	0.25
7	0.24
8	0.23

Recall that the values of s must be strictly decreasing. Thus if there were no deaths after six years in the sample used to describe survival distribution in one of the study groups, so that s was constant after six years, we would need to create slight annual decreases to use this macro.

Now suppose that the planners don't expect the new treatment to produce much better long-term survival, but have reason to believe that it may delay death somewhat. Specifically, they feel that it might have a survival distribution similar to that summarized here.

t	S(t)
0	1.00
1	0.95
2	0.85
3	0.75
4	0.65
7	0.25
8	0.24

It is proposed to use the log rank test with a significance level of 0.05 to test the null hypothesis of equivalence of the survival distributions for the two treatment groups. Half will be assigned to each treatment. Suppose further that it is felt that there will be little or no loss to follow-up. To start, we will consider accruing 30 patients per year for four years followed by three years of additional follow-up. The power for this study is estimated by invoking the POWER macro as shown in the following code.

```
data group1;
    input t s;
    datalines;
0          1.00
1          0.86
2          0.68
3          0.60
4          0.51
5          0.39
6          0.25
7          0.24
8          0.23
;
data group2;
    input t s;
    datalines;
0          1.00
1          0.95
2          0.85
3          0.75
4          0.65
7          0.25
8          0.24
;
```

```
%survpow(s1=group1 ,s2=group2        /* data sets that
define the alternative survival distributions for groups 1 and 2*/
        ,actime=4     /* accrual time */
        ,futime=3     /* post-accrual followup time  */
        ,rate=30      /* accrual rate */
) ;
```

Note that default values are used for LOSS1 (Loss Rate 1), LOSS2 (Loss Rate 2), NSUB (number of subintervals), SIGLEVEL (Alpha), P (Prop in Grp1) , and W (Weights). The results are given in Output 3.10.

Output 3.10

Accrual Time	Followup Time	Accrual Rate	N	ALPHA	Prop in Grp 1
4	3	30	120	.05	.5

Loss Rate 1	Loss Rate 2	Weights	Power		
0	0	1	0.39087		

Clearly this power is inadequate. We would like to have at least an 80% probability of rejecting the null hypothesis if this alternative holds. Thus we need to increase the accrual time, follow-up time, or accrual rate. Of course the last of these requires getting more institutions to participate. Also, it is possible that, for the alternative above, another linear rank test may have greater power than the log rank test. If so, that test would be our choice. The following SAS program shows how the POWER macro may be embedded in a macro loop in order to consider the power of alternative tests over a range of study parameters. We will consider accrual rates of 40, 45, . . . , 70 per year and the log rank test, the Gehan test, and the Tarone-Ware statistic based on weights equal to the square root of the number at risk. The following code gives the necessary SAS statements. You will need to be familiar with the SAS macro language to understand it.

```
/* Create data set for weight functions.  n**.5 for the Tarone Ware
statistic, n for the Gehan statistic, and 1 for the log rank statistic
*/

data data;
    input w $;
    datalines;
(n**.5)
n
1
;

/* Create macro variables from weight functions */

data _null_;
    set data;
    i=_n_;
    call symput('w'||left(i), w);
run;
```

```
/* Create data sets for alternative */
data group1;
    input t s;
datalines;
0           1.00
1           0.86
2           0.68
3           0.60
4           0.51
5           0.39
6           0.25
7           0.24
8           0.23
;
data group2;
    input t s;
datalines;
0           1.00
1           0.95
2           0.85
3           0.75
4           0.65
7           0.25
8           0.24
;


/* loop on accrual rates and weight functions */

%macro loop;
%do arate=40 %to 70 %by 5;
    %do jj=1 %to 3;
    %survpow(s1=group1, s2= group2,   actime=4,futime=3
                    ,rate=&arate, w=&&w&jj ) ;
            %end;
    %end;
%mend;
%loop;
run;
```

Running this program produces the desired results for three sets of weights and over a range of accrual rates. Only the results for accrual rates of 60 and 65 patients per year are printed in the output.

Output 3.11

```
                        Power Analysis

Accrual      Followup      Accrual                   Prop in
  Time         Time          Rate     N     ALPHA    Grp 1

   4            3            60      240     .05       .5

      Loss         Loss
    Rate 1       Rate 2     Weights       Power

      0            0        (n**.5)      0.76418

                        Power Analysis

Accrual   Followup    Accrual                      Prop in
  Time      Time        Rate      N     ALPHA      Grp 1

   4         3          60       240     .05         .5
```

Output 3.11 (continued)

Loss Rate 1	Loss Rate 2	Weights	Power
0	0	n	0.80272

Power Analysis

Accrual Time	Followup Time	Accrual Rate	N	ALPHA	Prop in Grp 1
4	3	60	240	.05	.5

Loss Rate 1	Loss Rate 2	Weights	Power
0	0	1	0.66260

Power Analysis

Accrual Time	Followup Time	Accrual Rate	N	ALPHA	Prop in Grp 1
4	3	65	260	.05	.5

Loss Rate 1	Loss Rate 2	Weights	Power
0	0	(n**.5)	0.79652

Power Analysis

Accrual Time	Followup Time	Accrual Rate	N	ALPHA	Prop in Grp 1
4	3	65	260	.05	.5

Loss Rate 1	Loss Rate 2	Weights	Power
0	0	n	0.83303

Power Analysis

Accrual Time	Followup Time	Accrual Rate	N	ALPHA	Prop in Grp 1
4	3	65	260	.05	.5

Loss Rate 1	Loss Rate 2	Weights	Power
0	0	1	0.69732

The output shows that an accrual rate of 60/year with four years of accrual and three years of follow-up will be sufficient to achieve a power of 80%. That power is achieved for the Gehan test (W = n), but not the log rank test (W = 1). Recall that the Gehan test statistic puts greater weights on earlier deaths, when the number at risk is greater, while the log rank weights are constant. Therefore, for an alternative in which the difference between the two groups being compared is mostly in the early results, as in the previous example, we would expect the Gehan test to have greater power. It is interesting to note that the Tarone-Ware weights, $n^{1/2}$, which are intermediate between those of the Gehan and the log rank statistic, produce powers intermediate between them as well.

But let's carry this example a bit further to make another point. Suppose that, when planning this study, we did not consider the fact that the survival differences expected were in the early results. Instead we used only the information that the expected survival rates at three years were .6 and .75 and assumed, as is frequently done, that the survival in both groups would be exponential. In this case, the SAS program to find the power of the log rank test based on the original sample size of 120 might look like this:

```
data x1; input t s;
datalines;
3 .6
;
data x2; input t s;
datalines;
3 .75
;

  %survpow(s1=x1,s2=x2, actime=4, futime=3, rate = 30);
```

The resulting estimated power is 57%, considerably higher than the 39% found earlier. By ignoring the expected nature of the difference between the survival distributions of the treatments being compared, we have grossly overestimated the power. Looking at it from another point of view, by altering the rate parameter, we can see that a rate of 52 per year, for a total of 208 will produce an estimated power of 80% based on the exponential assumption. If that assumption is incorrect and the data sets Group1 and Group2 provide better descriptions of the survival distributions of the treatment groups being compared, then we will not have as large a sample as we really should. In fact the power will be 60% instead of 80%. Furthermore, we would be using the log rank test when, in fact, the Gehan test would have greater power.

In planning a clinical trial, it is quite common to use a method of power calculation based on the assumption of proportional hazards assuming that the log rank test (which is most powerful in that situation) is to be used to compare the groups. There is a considerable body of literature discussing ways to do this (George and Desu, 1974, Rubenstein, Gail, and Santner, 1981) and in many cases, such an approach may be appropriate. However, if the planners have some idea of the nature of the alternative that they expect, and if the alternative hazards do not have a constant ratio, then the method described here can be used. Remember that it is not statistically valid to perform a number of tests on a set of data and to choose for presentation the result that has the smallest p-value. It is, however, quite appropriate when planning a study, to consider the power of a variety of test statistics for the study parameters and alternative survival distributions being considered and to choose the test with the best power characteristics. Of course, the statistical test to be used should always be specified in the study protocol before the study is begun.

3.13 Early Stopping Based on Conditional Power

3.13.1 The Basic Problem

Let's turn now to a slightly different question. Suppose you are in the midst of a study designed to compare survival of patients under two treatment regimens. The study was designed to accrue 240 patients randomized between the two regimens over five years and to follow them for an additional year. The design parameters were determined by using the macro SURVPOW assuming exponential survival in both groups, a log rank test at the two-sided significance level of 0.05, and median survival times of one year and 1.5 years for the two groups. But three years into the study you use PROC LIFETEST to compare the groups. The following output are partial results:

Output 3.12

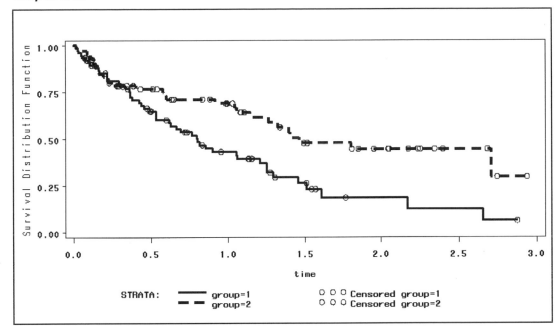

Test of Equality over Strata

Test	Chi-Square	DF	Pr > Chi-Square
Log-Rank	8.3460	1	0.0039
Wilcoxon	4.0357	1	0.0445
-2Log(LR)	9.4825	1	0.0021

Some investigators, seeing these results, might want to stop the study, declaring that group 2 has "significantly better" survival and reporting a *p*-value for that log rank test of 0.0039. That would be a mistake. If we allow ourselves the luxury of several looks at the data, the actual type I error probability will be much larger than the nominal significance level.

Nevertheless, it would seem reasonable to establish some criteria for stopping a study early. If one of two treatment arms appears to be superior to the other, ethical concerns might argue for early termination of the study. If the two treatments appear to be equivalent, we do not have the same ethical problem. However, we might want to devote our resources to other studies. Thus we need to consider rational criteria for early termination of a study in that situation as well.

One approach is to consider the probability, given the current data, that the study, if allowed to continue as originally planned, will produce a significant result favoring one of the treatment arms. If that probability is high, we might feel justified in stopping the study early and concluding the superiority of that arm. If that probability is low, we might feel justified in stopping the study early and concluding that there is little evidence of a difference between the arms. But such probabilities depend not only on the current data, but also on the true, but unknown, survival distributions for the two arms. The following criteria, based on the original null and alternative hypothesis, have been suggested:

- If the probability, given the current data, of a significant result if the study is continued to its planned conclusion is high (perhaps .90 or more), even under the null hypothesis, then we can terminate the study with rejection of the null hypothesis.

- If the probability, given the current data, of a significant result if the study is continued to its planned conclusion is low (perhaps .10 or less), even under the alternative hypothesis, then we can terminate the study without rejection of the null hypothesis

The only remaining problem is how to compute the probabilities described in these criteria. Those computations are rather difficult to do, but the results can be estimated through simulation. That is what is done in the macro described in the next section.

3.13.2 The CONDPOW Macro

The CONDPOW macro takes an existing data set and simulates the results of allowing the patients still being followed to continue until that planned termination of the study. It also simulates new patients entering until the end of the planned accrual period and followed for the planned follow-up period. The survival function in each group must be of the form $S(t) = \pi + (1 - \pi)\exp(-\lambda t)$. π, which may be zero, is the assumed cure rate, and λ is the constant hazard among those not cured. The macro is invoked with a statement of the form

```
%condpow(lam1=   , lam2=   , atime=   , arate=    ,follow=   , pi1=   ,
pi2=   , grp1=   , n=     ,dataset =   , stat=  );
```

where

LAM1 and LAM2	are the presumed hazards of noncured patients in groups 1 and 2.
ATIME	is the remaining accrual time.
ARATE	is the presumed accrual rate.
FOLLOW	is the amount of planned post-accrual follow-up time.
PI1 and PI2	are the presumed cure rates in groups 1 and 2. The defaults are zero for both.
GRP1	is the proportion of those to be accrued who will be in group 1. The default is .5.
N	is the number of replications of the simulation.
DATASET	is the name of the existing data set. The default is to use the last data set defined. There is a tricky point about this data set. As with survival data generally, we need a time variable and a censoring variable. However, we need to distinguish between patients who are censored because they are still alive when the analysis is done and those who are censored because they are no longer being followed. The former must have 0 as the value of the censoring variable. The latter have the value -1 for the censoring variable. Those who died have a censoring value 1.
STAT	is the test statistic to be used. The choices are Log-Rank (the default) or Wilcoxon.

In order to avoid excessive output from running PROC LIFETEST many times, we suppress the output by using the statement `ods listing off;` The results are found in the SAS log, but are not shown here.

3.13.3 Example

Consider the interim data set described in Section 3.13.1. The null hypothesis is that the median survival times in both arms is one year. This is equivalent to both hazards being .69. If the study were to continue to its planned conclusion, there would be two more years of accrual at 48/year followed by one year of additional follow-up. The Condpow macro can be invoked by the following statement:

```
%condpow(lam1=.69, lam2=.69, atime=2, arate=48, follow=1,
n=1000, dataset = x);
```

The results are as follows.

Output 3.13

```
Results for Conditional Power Simulation for Log-Rank test


Existing Dataset = x   Significance Level =  .05
After 1000 Replications, Estimated Power = 0.476
Group1 percentage = .5  Group1 lamda = .69  Group1 cure rate = 0
Group2 lamda = .69 Group2 cure rate = 0
accrual time = 2 accrual rate = 48 follow up time = 1
```

Notice that the conditional power is estimated to be 0.476. In other words, under the null hypotheses, the probability of rejecting the null hypothesis, if the study is carried to conclusion, is 0.476. Early stopping is not justified.

3.14 Listings of Macros

3.14.1 Listing of the LINRANK Macro

```
%macro linrank(dataset=_last_, time=time, cens=  ,
             censval=  ,groupvar= method=logrank,rho=1,
             stratvar= _none_, s
          stratmis=no,trend=order );

/*      Delete invalid observations and
        print list of observations deleted. */

data xx deleted;
   set &dataset;
   obsnumb = _n_;
   if &time <0  or &groupvar=''  or &cens = . then delete=1;
   if "&stratvar" ne "_none_" and "&stratmis" = "no" and &stratvar
   = '' then delete =1;
   _none_ = 1;
   if delete=1 then output deleted;
   else output xx;
proc print data=deleted;
   title 'Deleted Observations';
   var  obsnumb &time &cens &groupvar
%if "&stratvar" ne "_none_" %then &stratvar;;

/*      Determine number of groups, their names,
        and the weights to use for trend test.   */
```

```
proc sort data = xx;
   by &groupvar;
data y;
   set xx;
   by &groupvar;
   if first.&groupvar then do;
       n+1;
       call symput('ngrps',left(n));
   end;
run;
data grpnames;
   set y;
   by &groupvar;
   keep &groupvar n;
   if first.&groupvar;
data groupwts;
   set grpnames;
   keep
   %if "&trend" = "order" %then n;
   %else &groupvar;;

/* Find number of strata */

proc sort data=xx;
   by &stratvar;
data xx;
   set xx;
   by &stratvar;
   retain stratn 0 ;
   if first.&stratvar then do;
       stratn+1;
       call symput('stratcnt', left(stratn));
   end;
run;

/*      Start loop on strata        */

%do ii = 1 %to &stratcnt;

/*    Form stratum subset, find number of
      groups, number in each group, and
      group weights in stratum              */

   data x;
      set xx;
      if stratn = &ii;
      call symput('stratval', &stratvar);
   run;
   proc freq;
      table &groupvar/ noprint out= counts;
   proc sort data=x;
         by &groupvar;
   data x;
      set x;
      by &groupvar;
         retain grpn 0 ;
      if first.&groupvar then do;
                       grpn+1;
         call symput('grpcount', left(grpn));
call symput('grpname'||left(grpn), &groupvar);
         end;
   run;
   data grpnames;
      set x;
      by &groupvar;
      keep &groupvar grpn;
      if first.&groupvar;
   data grpwts;
      set grpnames;
      keep
      %if "&trend" = "order" %then grpn;
      %else &groupvar;;
```

```
/*      Create table          */

   proc sort data=x;
      by descending &time;
   data y;
      set x;
      keep r1-r&grpcount rtot;
      array r{*} r1-r&grpcount;
      retain r1-r&grpcount rtot 0;
      %let countsq = %eval(&grpcount*&grpcount);
      r{grpn}+1;
      rtot+1;
   data x;
      merge x y;
   proc sort;
      by &time;
   data x;
      set x;
      by &time;
      array d{*} d1-d&grpcount;
      retain d1-d&grpcount dtot;
      if first.&time then do i=1 to &grpcount;
         d{i}=0;
         dtot=0;
         end;
      if &cens not in (&censval) then do;
         d{grpn}+1;
         dtot+1;
         end;
      if last.&time then output;
   data x;
      set x;
      if dtot>0;
      retain km km_  1;
      all=1;
      array e{*} e1-e&grpcount;
      array diff{*} diff1-diff&grpcount;
      array r{*} r1-r&grpcount;
      array d{*} d1-d&grpcount;
         array wdiff{*} wdiff1-wdiff&grpcount;
      array s{*} sum1-sum&grpcount;
array cov{&grpcount, &grpcount} cov1-cov&countsq;
array sumcov{&grpcount,&grpcount} sumcov1-sumcov&countsq;
      if _n_ = 1 then km_ = 1;
      else km_ = km;
      km=km*(rtot-dtot)/rtot;
      do j=1 to &grpcount;
         e{j} = dtot*r{j}/rtot;
         diff{j} = d{j} - e{j};
         if "&method"="logrank" then w=1;
         if "&method"="gehan" then w=rtot;
if "&method"="tarone" then w=sqrt(rtot);
if "&method"="harrington" then w=km_**&rho;
         wdiff{j} = w*diff{j};
         s{j} + wdiff{j};
        do l=1 to &grpcount;
if dtot=1 then c=1; else c=(rtot-dtot)/(rtot-1);
if j=l then cov{j,l}=w**2*(dtot*(rtot*r{j}-r{j}**2)*c)/rtot**2;
else cov{j,l}=-w**2*(r{j}*r{l}*dtot*c)/rtot**2;
            sumcov{j,l}+cov{j,l};
            end;
       end;

/*       Sum over times and reformat for printout       */

   proc means sum noprint;
       var d1-d&grpcount e1-e&grpcount diff1-diff&grpcount
       wdiff1-wdiff&grpcount;
       output out = out sum=;
   data out;
```

```
      set out;
         array e{*} e1-e&grpcount;
         array d{*} d1-d&grpcount;
         array difff{*} diff1-diff&grpcount;
         array wdif{*} wdiff1-wdiff&grpcount;
         do j = 1 to &grpcount;
               group = j;
               events = d{j};
               expected = e{j};
               diff = difff{j};
               wdiff = wdif{j};
               output;
               end;
         label wdiff = 'Weighted Diff';
         label events = 'Events';
         label expected = 'Expected';
         label diff = 'Diff';
data xxx;
      merge out grpnames counts;
      proc print l noobs;
      var &groupvar count percent events expected diff wdiff;
      sum   count events;
      title1 'Summary of Events vs Expected';
      %if "&stratvar" ne "_none_" %then title2 "&stratvar = &stratval";;
      title3 "Method = &method";
run;

/*   Accumulate vectors and matrices for pooled stats   */

      %if "&ii" = "1" %then %do;
            data pooled;
               set xxx;
            %end;
            %else %do;
            data pooled;
            set pooled xxx;
            %end;
      data x;
            set x;
      proc sort;
            by all;
data s (keep = sum1-sum&grpcount) cov (keep = col1-col&grpcount);
            set x;
            by all;
            if last.all;
            array s{*} sum1-sum&grpcount;
            array sumcov{&grpcount, &grpcount}
                  sumcov1-sumcov&countsq;
            array col{*} col1-col&grpcount;
            output s;
            do j=1 to &grpcount;
                  do l=1 to &grpcount;
                  col{l}=sumcov{j,l};
                  end;
            output cov;
            end;
      data yy;
            merge grpnames cov;

/* Give columns of covariance matrix group names */
      %do j = 1 %to &grpcount;
            label col&j = "&&grpname&j";
            %end;
      proc print l noobs;
            var &groupvar col1-col&grpcount;
            title1 'Covariance Matrix';
```

```
%if "&stratvar" ne "_none_" %then title2 "&stratvar =
        &stratval";;
        title3 "Method = &method";
        %if "&ii" = "1" %then %do;
        data poolcov;
            set yy;
        %end ;
        %else %do;
        data poolcov;
        set poolcov yy;
        %end;

/*      Use proc iml to do matrix calculations
        for test statistic.                      */

    proc iml;
        reset noprint;
        use s;
        read all into x;
        use cov;
        read all into v;
        use grpwts;
        read all var _all_ into grpwts;

/*      Omit first row and column       */

        xx=x[1:1,2:&grpcount];
        vv=v[2:&grpcount,2:&grpcount];
        stat= xx*inv(vv)*xx`;
        df = &grpcount - 1;
        p_val = 1-probchi(stat,df);
        results = stat||df||p_val;
        cols={ChiSquare df p_value};
        title1 ' ';
%if "&stratvar" ne "_none_" %then title1 "&stratvar =
    &stratval";;
        title2 "Method = &method";
        print results[colname=cols];

/*      Test for trend.          */

        if %eval(&grpcount) > 2 then do;
            wts=grpwts[2:&grpcount, 1:1];
            xxx=xx*wts;
            vvv=wts`*vv*wts;
            stat = xxx*xxx/vvv;
            df=1;
            p_val= 1-probchi(stat,df);
            trend = stat||df||p_val;
            print trend[colname=cols];
            end;
        quit;
    %end;

 /* end of loop on strata */

/*      Pooled results if stratified analyis    */

%if "&stratvar" ne "_none_" %then %do;
   proc freq data=xx;
        table &groupvar / noprint out=counts;
   proc sort data=pooled;
        by &groupvar;
   proc means noprint sum data=pooled;
        var count events expected diff wdiff;
        by group;
        output out=pooled1 sum=;
   data;
        merge pooled1 grpnames counts;
   proc print l noobs;
        var &groupvar count percent events expected diff wdiff;
        sum   count events;
```

```
                    title1 'Summary of Events vs Expected';
                    title2 "Pooled Over All Values of &stratvar";
         proc sort data=poolcov;
                by &groupvar;
         proc means noprint sum data=poolcov;
                var col1-col&ngrps;
                by &groupvar;
                output out=pooled2 sum=;
         proc print l noobs;
                var &groupvar col1-col&ngrps;
                title1 'Covariance Matrix';
     title2 "Pooled Over All Values of &stratvar";
         data pooled2;
                set pooled2;
                keep col1-col&ngrps;
         run;
         proc iml;
                reset noprint;
                use pooled1;
                read all var {wdiff} into x;
                use pooled2;
                read all into v;
                xx=x[2:&ngrps,1:1];
                vv=v[2:&ngrps,2:&ngrps];
                stat = xx'*inv(vv)*xx;
                df = &ngrps - 1;
                p_val=1-probchi(stat,df);
                cols={ChiSquare df p_value};
                title1 'Pooled Results';
                title2 "Method = &method";
                results = stat||df|| p_val;
                print results[colname=cols];

  /*     Test for trend.          */

                if %eval(&ngrps) > 2 then do;
                use groupwts;
                read all var _all_ into weights;
                wts = weights[2:&ngrps, 1:1];
                xtrend = xx'*wts;
                vtrend = wts'*vv*wts;
                stattrnd = xtrend**2/vtrend;
                p_valtrd = 1-probchi(stattrnd,1);
                df=1;
                trend=stattrnd||df||p_valtrd;
                print trend[colname=cols];
                run;
                end;
         %end;
  %mend;
```

3.14.2 Listing of the RAND_GEN Macro

```
%macro rand_gen(
  indata= ,
  time =  ,
  cens =   ,
  group =   ,
  numreps=1000,
  seed=0);

/* This is a minor modification of a macro presented as part of a talk
by David Cassell during the SAS Users Group International (SUGI)
Conference 27 (2002) */

%let indata=&indata;  /* forces evaluation of &INDATA at the right time
*/

   /* Get size of input dataset into macro variable &NUMRECS */
```

```
   proc sql noprint;
     select count(*) into :numrecs from &INDATA;
     quit;

  /* Generate &NUMREPS random numbers for each record, so records can
be
     randomly sorted within each replicate */

  data __temp_1;
    retain seed &SEED ;  drop seed;
    set &INDATA;
    do replicate = 1 to &NUMREPS;
      call ranuni(seed,rand_dep);
      output;
      end;
    run;

    proc sort data=__temp_1;  by replicate rand_dep;  run;

/* Now append the new re-orderings to the original dataset.  Label the
original as Replicate=0, so the %TEST macro will be able to pick out
the correct p-value.  Then use the ordering of __counter within each
replicate to write the original values of &time and &cens, thus
creating a randomization of these variables in every replicate. */

  data reps ;
    array timelist{ &NUMRECS } _temporary_ ;
    array censlist{ &NUMRECS } _temporary_;
    set &INDATA(in=in_orig) __temp_1(drop=rand_dep);
    if in_orig then do;
      replicate=0;
      timelist{_n_} = &time ;
      censlist{_n_} = &cens ;
      end;
    else do ;
      &time = timelist{ 1+ mod(_n_,&NUMRECS) };
      &cens = censlist{ 1+mod(_n_, &NUMRECS) };
    end;
    run;

%mend rand_gen;
```

3.14.3 Listing of the PERM_GEN Macro

```
%macro perm_gen(indata = _last_, time = ,cens = ,  n1 = ,
                     n2 = ,group = );
%let n = %eval(&n1 + &n2);
%let ncomb = %sysfunc(comb(&n, &n1));
ods output Plan=Combinations;
   proc plan ;
      factors replicate= &ncomb ordered
            r= &n1 of &n comb;
   run;

data reps; set combinations; keep replicate  i &group ;
array r{*} r1 - r&n1;
array grp{*} group1 - group&n;
do i = 1 to &n;
grp{i} = 2;
do j = 1 to &n1;
if r{j} = i then grp{i} = 1;
end;
&group = grp{i};
output;
end;
run;
data temp; set _null_;
%do i = 1 %to &ncomb;
```

```
data temp; set temp &indata; keep &time &cens;
%end;

data reps; merge reps temp;
data temp2; set &indata;
replicate = 0;
data reps; set temp2 reps;

run;
%mend;
```

3.14.4 Listing of the TEST Macro

```
%macro test(time =   , cens =   , censval =    , test = , group = ,
                  type = );
proc lifetest data = reps outtest = out noprint;
time &time*&cens(&censval); test &group;
    by replicate;
    run;
    data out2 ; set out;
    if "&test" = 'logrank' then type = 'LOG RANK';
    if "&test" = 'gehan' then type = 'WILCOXON';
    if _TYPE_ = type and _NAME_ = "&time" then output;
data out3; set out2 end = last; retain chisq;
    if replicate = 0 then chisq = &time;
    else do;
    if &time + .00000001  ge chisq then num+1;
    end;
    if last then do;
            pvalue = num/(_n_ - 1);
            stderr = sqrt((pvalue*(1-pvalue))/(_n_ - 1));
            lowbound = max(pvalue - 1.96*stderr, 0);
            upperbound = min(pvalue + 1.96*stderr, 1);
            n = _n_ - 1;
            output;
            end;
%if &type = rand %then %do;
    label n = 'Number of Replicates';
    label pvalue = "Randomization &test Test Estimated P-Value (2-
      sided)";
    label lowbound = 'Lower 95 Pct Bound';
    label upperbound = 'Upper 95 Pct Bound';
    %end;
%else %do;
label pvalue = "Permutation &test Test P-Value (2-sided)";
%end;
%if &type = rand %then %do;
    proc print noobs l; var pvalue stderr lowbound upperbound n;
    %end;
%else %do;
proc print noobs l ; var pvalue;
%end;
run;
data; set out2; if replicate = 0;
p = 1 - probchi(&time, 1);
label p = 'Asymptotic P-Value';
proc print noobs l ; var p; run;
%mend;
```

3.14.5 Listing of the SURVPOW Macro

```
%macro survpow(s1=   , s2=      , nsub=365, actime= ,
               futime=  ,rate=        ,p=.5, loss1=0, loss2=0,
               w=1, siglevel=.05) ;

/* Find number of points in data set for group 1 and convert to vectors
*/

data _null_;
   set &s1;
   i=_n_;
   call symput('counta',left(i));
run;
data y;
   set &s1;
   retain sa1-sa&counta ta1-ta&counta ;
   array surv{*} sa1-sa&counta;
   array ttime{*} ta1-ta&counta;
   t=t*&nsub;
   all=1;
   i=_n_;
   surv{i}=s;
   ttime{i}=t;
   output;
   proc sort;
   by all;
data y;
   set y;
   by all;
   if last.all;
   keep  all ta1-ta&counta sa1-sa&counta;
/*  Find number of points in data set for group 2 and convert to vector
*/
data _null_;
   set &s2;
   i=_n_;
   call symput('countb', left(i));
run;
data yy;
   set &s2;
   retain sb1-sb&countb tb1-tb&countb;
   array surv{*} sb1-sb&countb;
   array ttime{*} tb1-tb&countb;
   t=t*&nsub;
   all=1;
   i=_n_;
   surv{i}=s; ttime{i}=t;
   output;
proc sort;
   by all;
data yy;
   set yy;
   by all;
   if last.all;
   keep  all tb1-tb&countb sb1-sb&countb;
/*  Find hazards at each partition point  */
data z;
   all=1;
   do t=0 to (&actime+&futime)*&nsub-1;
         output;
         end;
proc sort;
   by all;
data merged;
   merge z y yy;
   by all;
   if trim("&counta") = "1" then lam1=-log(sa1)/ta1;
   %do i=1 %to &counta -1 ;
       %let j = %eval(&i+1);
```

```
          if ta&i le t lt ta&j then lam1 =
          (sa&i-sa&j)/((sa&j-sa&i)*(t-ta&i)+sa&i*(ta&j-ta&i));
%end;
     if trim("&counta") = "2" and ta2 = . then do;
          lambda = -log((sa1-sa2)/(1-sa2))/ta1;
          lam1 = lambda*(1-sa2)*exp(-lambda*t)/(sa2+
          (1-sa2)*exp(-lambda*t));
          end;
     if trim("&countb") = "1" then lam2=-log(sb1)/tb1;
     %do i=1 %to &countb -1 ;
          %let j = %eval(&i+1);
               if tb&i le t lt tb&j then
               lam2 =(sb&i-sb&j)/
               ((sb&j-sb&i)*(t-tb&i)+sb&i*
               (tb&j-tb&i));
          %end;
          if trim("&countb") = "2" and tb2 = . then do;
     lambda = -log((sb1-sb2)/(1-sb2))/tb1;
     lam2 = lambda*(1-sb2)*exp(-lambda*t)/
     (sb2+(1-sb2)*exp(-lambda*t));
     end;

/*  Calculate ratio of hazards and number at risk at each partition
point and accumulate needed sums */

data;
     set merged;
     by all;
     retain n1 n2 n;
     if _n_ = 1 then do;
          n1=&rate*&p*&actime;
          n2=&rate*(1-&p)*&actime;
          n=n1+n2;
     end;
     tau=&futime*&nsub;
     psi1=&loss1/&nsub;
     psi2=&loss2/&nsub;
     phi=n1/n2;
     theta=lam1/lam2;
     d1=lam1*n1;
     d2=lam2*n2;
     d=d1+d2;
     c1=psi1*n1;
     c2=psi2*n2;
     if _n_ > tau then do;
          c1=c1+n1/(&actime*&nsub+tau-_n_+1);
          c2=c2+n2/(&actime*&nsub+tau-_n_+1);
          end;
     n1=n1-d1-c1;
     n2=n2-d2-c2;
     sum1+(d*&w*(phi*theta/(1+phi*theta) - phi/(1+phi)));
     sum2+d*&w**2*phi/(1+phi)**2;
     n=n1+n2;

/*  Calculate e and power */

     if last.all then do;
          e=sum1/sqrt(sum2);
          z=-probit(&siglevel/2);
          power = 1 - probnorm(z-e) +  probnorm(-z-e);
          ac_time=symget('actime');
          fu_time=symget('futime');
          ac_rate=symget('rate');
          n=ac_rate*ac_time;
          alpha = symget('siglevel');
          prop=symget('p');
          los_rat1=symget('loss1');
          los_rat2=symget('loss2');
          weights = symget('w');
          output;
          end;
```

```
        label ac_time='Accrual Time';
        label power='Power';
        label fu_time = 'Followup Time';
        label ac_rate = 'Accrual Rate';
        label n = 'N';
        label prop = 'Prop in Grp 1';
        label los_rat1 = 'Loss Rate 1';
        label los_rat2 = 'Loss Rate 2';
        label weights = 'Weights';

   /*  Print results */

   proc print l noobs;
        var ac_time fu_time ac_rate n alpha prop los_rat1 los_rat2 weights
        power;
   run;
   %mend;
```

3.14.6 Listing of the MANTBYAR Macro

```
   %macro mantbyar(dataset= last_ , state= , time=time ,nstates=2 ,
                   format= default.,id=id);

   /* Create Format for States */

   %let form=%str(proc format; value default 1='state1');
   %do i=2 %to &nstates;
       %let form=&form &i= %str(%')STATE&i %str(%');
       %end;
   &form;

   /* Create Table */

   proc sort data= &dataset;
       by &id &time;
   data d;
       set &dataset end=last;
       by &id;
       retain id 0;
       if first.&id then id+1;
       if last then call symput('nobs',left(id));
   proc sort;
       by &time descending &state;
   %let nstat2=%eval(&nstates*&nstates);
   %let nm1=%eval(&nstates-1);
   data dd;
       set d;
       by &time descending &state;
       retain s1-s&nobs r1-r&nstates o1-o&nstates;
       retain e1-e&nstates 0;
       retain v1-v&nstat2 0;
       retain d1-d&nstates 0;
       array s(*) s1-s&nobs;
       array r(*) r1-r&nstates;
       array e(*) e1-e&nstates;
       array o(*) o1-o&nstates;
       array ot(*) ot1-ot&nstates;
       array v(&nstates,&nstates) v1-v&nstat2;
       array d(*) d1-d&nstates;
       if &time=0 then do;
           s(id)=&state; r(&state)+1;
           nt+1;
           end;
       if &time>0 and &state<&nstates+1 then do;
           prior=s(id);
           r(prior)+(-1);
           if &state>0 then r(&state)+1; s(id)=&state;
           if &state=0 then nt+(-1);
           end;
```

```
          if &state=&nstates+1 then do;
              if first.&state then do i=1 to &nstates;
                  ott=0;
                  ot(i)=0;
                  end;
              prior=s(id);
              ot(prior)+1;
              ott+1;

/* Calculate covariance matrix */

              if last.&state then do;
                  do i=1 to &nstates;
                      do j= 1 to &nstates;
                      if i=j then v(i,i)+
                      r(i)*(nt-r(i))*ott*(nt-ott)/(nt**2*(nt-1));
                      else v(i,j)+ (-r(i)*r(j)*ott*
                      (nt-ott)/(nt**2*(nt-1)));
                      end;
                      end;
                  do i=1 to &nstates;
                  e(i)+r(i)/nt*ott;
                  r(i)+(-ot(i));
                  o(i) + ot(i);
                  d(i)+ (o(i)-e(i));
                  end;
                  nt+(-ott);
                  output;
              end;
              end;
data ddd;
    set dd end=last;
    array e(*) e1-e&nstates;
    array o(*) o1-o&nstates; if last;
    df=&nstates-1;
    do &state=1 to &nstates;
        expected=e(&state); observed=o(&state);
            ratio=observed/expected;
        diff=observed-expected;
        output;
        end;
data cov;
    set ddd;
    keep v1-v&nstat2;
    %let slist=;
    %do i=1 %to &nstates;
        data _null_ ;
            call symput('s', put(&i,&format));
        run;
        %let slist= &slist &s ;
        %end;
data exp ;
    set ddd;
    keep e1-e&nstates;
data obs;
    set ddd;
    keep o1-o&nstates;

/* Use IML to calculate test statistic and print results */

proc iml;
    use cov;
    read into covmat;
    cov=shape(covmat,&nstates);
    statlist={&slist};
    tranlist=statlist`;
    use exp;
    read into expmat;
    print 'Covariance Matrix';
    print cov[r=tranlist c=statlist format=10.4];
    v=diag(cov);
    use obs;
```

```
      read into obsmat;
      rmat=obsmat#expmat##(-1);
      r=rmat`;
      difmat=obsmat-expmat;
      d=difmat`;
      obs=obsmat`; exp=expmat`;
      z=difmat*inv(v##(.5));
      p=(1-probnorm(abs(z)))`; p=2*p;
      state =state||obs||exp||r||d||p;
      top={'Observed' 'Expected' 'O/E' 'O-E' 'P-      Value'};
      print 'Summary of Results for Each State';
      print state[r=tranlist c=top format=12.6];
      cov=cov[1:&nm1,1:&nm1];
      expmat =expmat[1,1:&nm1];
      obsmat=obsmat[1,1:&nm1];
      chisq=(expmat-obsmat)*inv(cov)*(expmat-obsmat)`;
      print 'Test of Homogeneity of States';
      p=1-probchi(chisq,&nm1);
      df=&nm1;
      print chisq [format=11.4] df [format=5.0] p  [format=9.7] ;
%mend mantbyar;
```

3.14.7 Listing of the CONDPOW Macro

```
%macro condpow(dataset=_last_,lam1=,lam2=, atime=,arate=,follow=,
                grp1=.5, pi1=, pi2=,stat=Log-Rank,
                alpha=.05, n=);
options printmsglist=0 source=0 notes=0;  /*to avoid excessive log;*/
ods listing close;   **to avoid excessive output;
/*creating 'all' dataset for record the output of lifetest;*/
data all;
probchisq= .;
run;
/*begin the loop for n replications of lifetest;*/
%do i=1 %to &n;

/*bring the existing dataset;*/
%if "&dataset" ne "none" %then %do;
data b;
set &dataset;
cure1=(&pi1/(&pi1+(1-&pi1)*exp(-&lam1*time)));
cure2=(&pi2/(&pi2+(1-&pi2)*exp(-&lam2*time)));
rand1=ranuni(0);
rand2=ranuni(0);
if cens=0 and group=1 and rand1 < cure1 then addtime=1000000;
  else if cens=0 and group=1 and rand1 >=cure1 then addtime=
ranexp(0)/&lam1;
  else if cens=0 and group=2 and rand2 < cure2 then addtime= 1000000;
  else if cens=0 and group=2 and rand2 >=cure2 then addtime=
ranexp(0)/&lam2;
  else addtime=0;
if cens=0 and addtime >= (&atime+&follow) then
do;
   survtime= time + (&atime + &follow);
   endcens=0;
end;
  else if cens=0 and addtime < (&atime +&follow) then
  do;
     survtime =time + addtime ;
     endcens=1;
  end;
  else if cens=1 then
  do;
     survtime = time;
     endcens= 1;
  end;
```

```
    else if cens=-1 then
      do;
          survtime = time;
          endcens= 0;
      end;
drop cure1 cure2 rand1 rand2;
%end;

/*allow the power estimate without existing data set;*/
data c;
do j=1 to &arate*&atime;
    accurday=ranuni(0)*&atime;
    group=(ranuni(0)>&grp1) + 1;
    piran1=ranuni(0);
    piran2=ranuni(0);
    if group=1 and piran1 <&pi1 then addtime=1000000;
    else if group=1 and piran1 >=&pi1 then addtime=ranexp(0)/&lam1;
    else if group=2 and piran2 <&pi2 then addtime=1000000;
    else if group=2 and piran2 >=&pi2 then addtime=ranexp(0)/&lam2;
    if addtime >=(accurday + &follow) then
      do;
          survtime = accurday + &follow;
          endcens=0;
      end;
    else if addtime <(accurday +&follow) then
      do;
          survtime = addtime;
          endcens=1;
      end;
output;
end;
run;

/*combine the new dataset b and c together for lifetest;*/
%if "&dataset" ne "none" %then %do;
data d (keep=survtime endcens group);
set b c;
run;
%end;
%else %if "&dataset" = "none" %then %do;
data d (keep=survtime endcens group);
set c;
%end;
run;

/*Do lifetest 1 to i times and write the output to the out&i files;*/
ods output homtests=out&i;
proc lifetest data=d notable;
time survtime*endcens(0);
strata group;
run;

data out&i;
set out&i;
if test = "&stat";
run;
data all; set all out&i; run;
%end;

/*calculating the power as the # of reject Ho vs. the # of total
lifetests;*/
data all;
set all;
if probchisq ne .;
if probchisq < &alpha then reject+1;
power=reject/(_N_ - 1);
n=_N_ -1;
```

```
if n =&n then do;
/*put results into log;*/
put;
put;
put "Results for Conditional Power Simulation for &stat test" ;
put;
put "Existing Dataset = &dataset   Significance Level =  &alpha";
put 'After ' n 'Replications, Estimated Power = ' Power;
put "Group1 percentage = &grp1  Group1 lamda = &lam1  Group1 cure rate
= &pi1";
put "Group2 lamda = &lam2 Group2 cure rate = &pi2";
put "accrual time = &atime accrual rate = &arate follow up time =
&follow" ;
end;
run;
%mend condpow;
```

Chapter 4   Proportional Hazards Regression

4.1   Some Thoughts about Model-Based Estimation and Inference.. 111
4.2   The Cox (Proportional Hazards) Regression Method 112
4.3   The Hazard Ratio and Survival 113
4.4   Multiple Covariates... 114
4.5   Defining Covariates 114
4.6   Scaling the Covariates... 115
4.7   Survival Probabilities.. 116
4.8   Maximum Likelihood Estimation of the Coefficients... 116
4.9   Using PROC PHREG 117
4.10 Model-Building Considerations 131
4.11 Time-Dependent Covariates 134
4.12 More Complex Models 136
4.13 Checking the Proportional Hazards Assumption... 136
4.14 Exercise 138
4.15 Survival Probabilities.. 138
4.16 Residuals.. 143
4.17 Power and Sample Size.. 145
4.18 Imputing Missing Values 148
4.19 Listings of Macros 150

4.1 Some Thoughts about Model-Based Estimation and Inference

Up to now we have based our methods of estimation and inference on only the data. No assumptions about the hazard function, density, or distribution function were made. With this chapter we begin a different approach: we look at methods based upon assumptions about these functions. You may wonder why. After all, we showed in Chapters 2 and 3 that survival functions could be estimated and compared without such assumptions. And what if our assumptions are wrong? I think George Box summarized the situation with his aphorism:

> All models are wrong.
> Some are useful.

All models are wrong because the real world is invariably more complex than can be captured in any mathematical formula, no matter how complicated. Consider, in particular, a person afflicted with a life-threatening disease and being treated by some therapeutic regimen. We can't hope to understand the complex interplay of forces and reactions going on in that patient's body and affecting the patient's survival. How can we possibly hope to capture all that in some mathematical formula?

And yet, we often find that some mathematical formula expresses something about the survival of such patients that seems to hold reasonably well in practice. In such cases, taking advantage of that fact can result in analyses that are more precise and more informative. That is the sense in which some models are useful. This chapter and the next illustrate these points.

Before we proceed, I would like to suggest an addendum to Dr. Box's statement.

> Models that specify less are less wrong
> and less useful.

The model that we discuss in this chapter is not as specific as the models that we will discuss in the next chapter. The model makes certain assumptions about the hazard function, but does not assume its complete form. Thus this model is less subject to the errors inherent in model mis-specification, although it will, therefore, be less informative. But, as you will see, it will enable us to say things about the survival of a cohort that could not have been said based on the methods of earlier chapters.

4.2 The Cox (Proportional Hazards) Regression Method

4.2.1 The Basic Model

In the last chapter you learned how to compare groups with respect to survival. The methods presented were valid without regard to any assumptions concerning the survival distributions of the groups. In this chapter you will see how to analyze the effect of a numeric variable on survival. Cox (1972) introduced the method, which is known as Cox regression, or proportional hazards regression. It is based on a model of the same name. This model makes the assumption that additive changes in the value of a numeric variable cause corresponding multiplicative changes in the hazard function or, equivalently, additive changes in the log of the hazard. The SAS PHREG procedure, which implements this method, is discussed in this chapter.

Consider a population in which a variable, x, is observed in addition to the survival time and censoring variables. Such a variable is called a covariate. It could be dichotomous (e.g., $x = 0$ for treatment A, $x = 1$ for treatment B) or quantitative (e.g., weight). For now, only one such covariate will be considered. The extension to more than one will follow. We might then expect the hazard to be a function of both the time and the value of x. Let $h(t, x)$ be the hazard at time t for an individual having a value of x for the covariate. Then the proportional hazards model assumes that for some parameter, β, and nonnegative function, $h_0(t)$, we have

$$h(t, x) = h_0(t)\exp(\beta x) \tag{4.1}$$

The function, $h_0(t)$ is called the underlying, or baseline, hazard function. Note that it is independent of x. In fact, it is the hazard function of a patient for whom $x = 0$. It follows that, for any values of t and x, $h(t, x + 1)/h(t, x) = \exp(\beta)$. In other words, this assumption implies that a unit increase in x multiplies the hazard by the same value for all values of t, namely $\exp(\beta)$. Of course, the key to analysis of survival with this model is to estimate β and make inferences about its value. For example, if the hypothesis that $\beta = 0$ is rejected, then it can be inferred that the variable x influences the hazard, and hence, the survival function. If $\beta > 0$ then the hazard increases (and survival worsens) as x increases. Similarly if $\beta < 0$ then the hazard decreases (and survival improves) as x increases. The estimated value of β leads to an estimate of $\exp(\beta)$ which is called the hazard ratio. Sometimes this ratio is called the risk ratio and abbreviated RR. (I prefer to use hazard ratio because "risk" has other meanings in epidemiology.)

You may be wondering about the other part of Equation 4.1, the baseline hazard, $h_0(t)$ and whether we need to estimate it as well. Here's where the genius of Cox's method is seen. His method of estimating β, that we will outline later in this chapter, is based on a partial likelihood in which the factor $h_0(t)$ is canceled out. Thus the proportional hazards assumption allows us to estimate the effect of a covariate on the hazard function without estimating the baseline hazard.

When Cox regression is used to study the effect of a dichotomous variable, such as treatment group, which is coded as 0 or 1, then $\exp(\beta)$ is the ratio of the hazard for group 1 to the hazard for group 0. That ratio is assumed to be constant for all time. In this case $\beta > 0$ means that group 0 has better survival. Thus the method of this chapter provides an alternative to the log rank test and the other linear rank tests of the previous chapter.

4.2.2 The Proportional Hazards Assumption

It should be noted, before we proceed further, that the proportional hazards assumption that underlies this model is fairly strong and may not always be reasonable. Because analyses based on this assumption are so easy to do using software such as SAS, it is tempting to do them without much thought about their appropriateness. Consider a covariate, x, which equals 1 for a surgical intervention and 0 for a nonsurgical intervention. Suppose that the surgical intervention has high early risk, but excellent long-term survival prospects once a patient has survived the surgery and its effects. On the other hand, the nonsurgical intervention does not have high early risk, but also does not have very good long-term survival. In this case, the hazard ratio would be high initially, but decreased as time increases. Thus the hazard ratio, for this situation, would not be constant. For another example, consider the covariate, age at diagnosis. It might be the case that hazard increases considerably as age increases from 60 to 70 years old, but very little or not at all as age increases from 15 to 25 years old. The proportional hazards assumption implies that $h(t, 70)/h(t, 60) = h(t, 25)/h(t, 15)$ for all values of t. In both of these examples the proportional hazards assumption would not be valid and the method of this chapter would be inappropriate. Ways to study the validity of the proportional hazards assumption are considered later in this chapter.

4.3 The Hazard Ratio and Survival

There is a common misconception that a hazard ratio is a ratio of death probabilities. For example, it is thought that a hazard ratio of 1.6 means that the probability of death for any time is 60% greater in one group than in the other. Let's take a moment, before we continue, to explore what a hazard ratio really says about survival and death probabilities. Suppose the hazard ratio of treatment 1 vs treatment 0 is r. Writing $S_1(t)$ and $S_0(t)$ for the survival functions associated with these treatments we have

$$S_1(t) = \exp[-\int_0^t h(u, 1)du] = \exp[-\int_0^t rh(u, 0)du] = \exp[-r\int_0^t h(u, 0)du]$$

$$= \{\exp[-\int_0^t h(u, 0)du]\}^r = [S_0(t)]^r$$

(4.2)

Thus we see what a hazard ratio of r says about the relationship of two survival functions. The survival probability in the group with value 1 equals the survival probability in the group with value 0 raised to the r power. To see what this says about the death probabilities, consider a hazard ratio of 2.0. Then for a value of t with $S_0(t) = .2$, we would have $S_1(t) = .2^2 = .04$. The corresponding death probabilities are, therefore, .8 and .96. The hazard ratio of 2.0 did not double the probability of death. Now consider another value of t for which $S_0(t) = .9$. Then we would have $S_1(t) = .9^2 = .81$. Now the corresponding death probabilities are .1 and .19. This time, the probability of death is approximately doubled. In fact, the idea that a hazard ratio of r multiplies a death probability by r, while not true, is approximately true for death probabilities near 0. Readers familiar with logistic regression will recognize this as similar to the behavior of the odds ratio.

4.4 Multiple Covariates

Now suppose that, for each patient, we observe p covariates, which will be labeled $x_1, x_2, \ldots, x_p$. Then, for each patient, there is a corresponding column vector $\mathbf{x} = (x_1, x_2, \ldots, x_p)'$ of covariates. Let $h(t, \mathbf{x})$ be the hazard function at time t for a patient whose covariates have values given by the components of $\mathbf{x}$. To extend the proportional hazards model to multiple covariates, we assume that, for some vector of parameters $\boldsymbol{\beta} = (\beta_1, \beta_2, \ldots, \beta_p)'$

$$h(t, \mathbf{x}) = h(t_0)\exp(\boldsymbol{\beta}' \mathbf{x}) \tag{4.3}$$

Since $\boldsymbol{\beta}' \mathbf{x} = \beta x_1 + \beta_2 x_2 + \ldots + \beta_p x_p$, this means that the proportional hazards assumption holds for each of the individual covariates with the others held constant. This model allows for the estimation of the effect of each covariate in the presence of the others. As in the univariate case, the focus of the analyses is estimation of and inference about the parameters $\beta_1, \beta_2, \ldots, \beta_p$. The hazard ratio for x_j is given by $\exp(\beta_j)$ and the hazard ratio for any set of the covariates is the product of their hazard ratios.

4.5 Defining Covariates

4.5.1 Interactions

Interactions among the covariates, that is, the tendency of the effect of one covariate on survival to vary according to the value of another covariate can be studied by defining new covariates as products of the original covariates. For example, suppose that x_1 is a covariate, which takes on the value of 0 or 1 depending upon the treatment group, and x_2 is a patient's weight in kilograms. If you wish to include the interaction of weight and treatment in the model, you can introduce a new covariate, x_3, which is defined as $x_1 x_2$. Now suppose that β_3, the coefficient of x_3 in the Cox regression model, is positive. What does that mean? To answer this question, write expression (4.3) as

$$h(t, x_1, x_2, x_3) = h_0(t)\exp(\beta_1 x_1 + \beta_2 x_2 + \beta_3 x_1 x_2) = h_0(t)\exp[\beta_1 x_1 + (\beta_2 + \beta_3 x_1)x_2]. \tag{4.4}$$

This way of looking at it suggests the following interpretation: When $x_1 = 0$ (that is, in group 0) each additional unit of x_2 (weight) multiplies the hazard at any time by $\exp(\beta_2)$. But when $x_1 = 1$ (that is, in group 1) each additional unit of weight multiplies the hazard at any time by $\exp(\beta_2 + \beta_3)$ Thus a positive value for β_3 means that the effect of weight is greater in group 1 than in group 0. By writing the exponent in (4.4) as $\beta_2 x_2 + (\beta_1 + \beta_3 x_2)x_1$ you can see another interpretation. The group effect is greater among heavier patients.

4.5.2 Exercise

Consider the example above and suppose that $\beta_1 = -.8$ and $\beta_3 = .1$. For what weights does group 0 have better survival than group 1?

4.5.3 Categorical Variables with More Than Two Values

You may sometimes have a grouping variable that takes on more than two values. For example, you might be studying a type of cancer with four main histologies. For convenience, call them A, B, C, and D. This variable can be studied by the methods above by converting histology into three covariates as follows:

x_1 which is 1 for histology A, 0 otherwise.
x_2 which is 1 for histology B, 0 otherwise.
x_3 which is 1 for histology C, 0 otherwise.

Do not define a fourth covariate, x_4, for histology D. If you do so, the values of the four covariates will sum to 1 for every patient, creating a numerical problem.

If β_1 is the coefficient of x_1 in the model of expression (4.3), then $\exp(\beta_1)$ is the ratio of the hazard for those with histology A to the hazard for those with histology D. Similar statements can be made for the coefficients of x_2 and x_3. For i and j chosen from 1, 2, and 3, $\exp(\beta_i - \beta_j)$ is the ratio of the hazard for the histology represented by x_i to the hazard of the histology represented by x_j.

PROC TPHREG, which is experimental in Version 9, allows us to specify that a variable, which may take on character string values, is a classification variable. In that case, if the variable has k values, SAS creates the $k{-}1$ dichotomous variables as described above. The last value is the reference value. The results are the same as if you used PROC PHREG with the $k{-}1$ dichotomous variables that you defined yourself. The syntax used to do this is as follows:

```
PROC TPHREG;
  CLASS catvarname;
  MODEL timevar*censvar(value(s)) = catvarname <othervars>;
```

4.6 Scaling the Covariates

It is tempting not to be concerned about the scale in which covariates are measured. After all, the question of whether a patient's weight affects survival should, with any reasonable statistical method, be answered the same whether weight is measured in kilograms, pounds, grams, or tons. In fact, that is the case for proportional hazards regression. However, the scale used can make large differences in the estimate of the hazard ratio and can lead to results that are easily misinterpreted.

To make the discussion specific, suppose a covariate is measured in millimeters and PROC PHREG produces an estimate of 0.049 for its beta coefficient and thus an estimate of $\exp(0.049) = 1.05$ for its hazard ratio. That means that a millimeter increase in the covariate is estimated to increase the hazard by 5%. An increase of 10 millimeters, or 1 centimeter, would then multiply the hazard by $1.05^{10} = 1.63$. If the analysis were done with the covariate measured in centimeters, the estimate of the beta coefficient would be $10{\times}0.049 = 0.49$ and the estimated hazard ratio would be 1.63. But both analyses are really saying the same thing. The only difference is in the units of measurement. The lesson here is that it is important to report the unit of measurement along with the hazard ratio for a continuous variable.

A more extreme situation can result from dealing with covariates based on dates, such as a patient's age at diagnosis. Suppose age is simply defined in a SAS DATA step as date of diagnosis minus date of birth. This produces, of course, the patient's age in days. If you obtained .0001 as an estimate for β and a hazard ratio of $\exp(.0001) = 1.0001$ you might be inclined to think that the effect of age is minimal. However, this would be equivalent to a hazard ratio of 1.44 ($= 1.0001^{3650}$) for a decade of age. Thus a 50-year-old would have an estimated 44% greater hazard than a 40-year-old. (If you think this example is based on the author's personal experience, you are right.)

4.7 Survival Probabilities

Until now the discussion has dealt with the hazard function. When analyzing survival data, however, you are probably more concerned with survival probabilities and how they are affected by the values of the covariates under study. If we let $S(t, \mathbf{x})$ represent the value of the survival function at time t for a patient with covariate vector $\mathbf{x}$, the proportional hazards model implies that

$$S(t, \ \mathbf{x}) = \exp[-\int_0^t h_0(u)\exp(\boldsymbol{\beta}'\mathbf{x})du] \tag{4.5}$$

But the right side can be written as $\left\{\exp[-H_0(t)]\right\}^{\exp(\boldsymbol{\beta}'\mathbf{x})}$. Here $H_0(t)$ is the integral $\int_0^t h_0(u)du$.

That integral is called the baseline cumulative hazard. Once we have estimates for the beta's, survival probabilities can be estimated for any vector of covariates if we can estimate this baseline cumulative hazard. In fact, as we discuss later in this chapter, we will be able to do this as well.

4.8 Maximum Likelihood Estimation of the Coefficients

As described in Appendix B, any attempt to use maximum likelihood estimation to estimate the beta coefficients immediately runs into two problems. First, we have the problem of how to handle the censored observations. Second, we have the problem that, even with values for the beta coefficients, we still do not have the survival function completely specified. We still have the baseline hazard to deal with. In his landmark 1972 paper introducing proportional hazards regression, Cox presented a variation of the likelihood function, called the partial likelihood function, that is independent of the unknown baseline hazard function. That is accomplished by conditioning the likelihood on the ordering of the complete and censored observations.

Let the data be represented by the triples $(t_i, d_i, \mathbf{x}_i)$ for $i = 1, 2, \ldots, n$ where t_i is the observation time, $d_i = 0$ (censored) or 1 (uncensored), and $\mathbf{x}_i$ is a column vector of covariate values for the ith patient. For now assume no tied times so that all of the t_i are distinct. That assumption will be removed later. To simplify the notation below, let the times be ordered so that $t_1 < t_2 < \ldots < t_n$. Now consider a particular time t_i for which $d_i = 1$ so that a death occurred at time t_i. By the definition (4.3) of the proportional hazards model, the probability of that death within an interval of width Δt containing t_i is approximately

$$h_0(t_i)\exp(\boldsymbol{\beta}'\mathbf{x}_i)\Delta t \tag{4.6}$$

But all of the patients who were observed for time t_i or more, that is with time t_j where $j \geq i$, had similar probabilities of dying in that interval (with $\mathbf{x}_i$ replaced by $\mathbf{x}_j$). Thus the probability that one of them died in that interval is approximately

$$\sum_{j \geq i} h_0(t_i)\exp(\boldsymbol{\beta}'\mathbf{x}_j)\Delta t \tag{4.7}$$

To form an estimate of the conditional probability of the death of the patient whose observation time was t_i given that there was a death among those observed for at least that long, divide the probability given by (4.6) by the probability given by (4.7). Then, taking the product of all such quotients over all deaths yields

$$\prod_{d_i=1} \frac{\exp(\boldsymbol{\beta}'\mathbf{x}_i)}{\sum_{j\geq i} \exp(\boldsymbol{\beta}'\mathbf{x}_j)} \qquad (4.8)$$

Notice that, for each i, the unknown baseline hazard $h_0(t_i)$ is canceled from the numerator and denominator. Of course, that's the whole idea.

Now what if ties are allowed? There are different approaches for dealing with ties. The one described below is Breslow's (1974). Let d_i represent the number of deaths at time t_i. The numerator is then derived from the product of the probabilities of each of the d_i deaths. But this can be obtained by simply adding the exponents. In other words, $\mathbf{x}_i$ can be replaced by $\mathbf{s}_i$, the sum of the covariate vectors for the patients who died at time t_i. For the denominator, the probability of d_i deaths at time t_i is approximately the denominator in (4.7) raised to the d_i power.

The final result, then, is what is known as the partial likelihood and is given by

$$\prod_{d_i \geq 1} \frac{\exp(\boldsymbol{\beta}'\mathbf{s}_i)}{\left[\sum_{j\geq i} \exp(\boldsymbol{\beta}'\mathbf{x}_j)\right]^{d_i}} \qquad (4.9)$$

The Newton-Raphson iterative procedure can be used to find the vector $\boldsymbol{\beta}$ that maximizes (4.9). Expression (4.9) is not a true likelihood. It is called, instead, a partial likelihood. Nevertheless, it has been shown that the value of $\boldsymbol{\beta}$ that maximizes (4.9) has the properties of maximum likelihood estimators described in Appendix B.

For a stratified analysis, the products of the form in (4.9) are created separately for each level of the stratification variable. This allows for different underlying hazard functions for different strata. The likelihood to be maximized is the product of the partial likelihoods over all of the strata.

4.9 Using PROC PHREG

4.9.1 The Basic Usage

In order to use PROC PHREG, you should have, for each patient, a time variable and a censoring (or event) variable to indicate survival status. In addition, you will have values for one or more covariates that you wish to analyze for possible effect on survival. To invoke the procedure, you need the PROC statement, followed by a MODEL statement giving the time and (optionally) censoring variable and the covariates to be used in the analysis. The basic syntax looks like this:

```
PROC PHREG;
    MODEL timevar*censvar(censval(s)) = covariate(s);
```

Here *timevar* is the time variable, and *censvar* is the censoring variable. If no observations are censored, then *censvar* is not needed. In the syntax, *censval (s)* represents the values of *censvar* that indicate that a time is censored, and *covariate(s)* represents the list of variables to be considered as the covariates of the regression. The MODEL statement can also include an option to specify how ties in the time variable are handled. The default is to use the Breslow (1974) method. This will generally be satisfactory.

PROC PHREG uses only those observations for which all of these variables are nonmissing. You might, therefore, be cautious about including covariates for which many patients have missing values. Section 4.18 discusses an alternative method of dealing with missing data.

4.9.2 Example: Univariate Analyses

Consider the following analysis of a cohort of melanoma patients. The variable Biopsy is the date of biopsy and is taken as the starting date. The variable Followup is the date each patient was last seen. The patient's survival status is indicated by a variable named Status which has the value 'Dead' if the patient died. Other variables thought to influence survival are included in the data set. They are tumor thickness, in millimeters, Clark level (scored as I, II, III, IV, or V) as a measure of the tumor's spread, and ulceration. We are interested in the effect of these variables on survival. The following statements were used to create the data set:

```
data; set sas.melanoma;
if clarklevel = 'I' then clark = 1;
if clarklevel = 'II' then clark = 2;
if clarklevel = 'III' then clark = 3;
if clarklevel = 'IV' then clark = 4;
if clarklevel = 'V' then clark = 5;
months = (followup - biopsy)/30.4;
if ulceration = 'Yes' then ulcer = 1;
if ulceration = 'No' then ulcer = 0;
if status = 'Dead' then d = 1;
else d = 0;
```

Note that Clark level and ulceration needed to be converted to numeric variables (although we could have chosen to treat Clark level as a categorical variable). Thickness is already a numeric variable, so nothing is done with it. Also, the time variable, Months, needed to be created from the beginning and end dates and the censoring variable needed to be created from the variable called Status. Finally, variable names of length greater than eight characters were not permitted prior to Version 7 of SAS. If you use an earlier version, change the variable names accordingly.

A word of warning: code like the following can be dangerous.

```
if status = 'Dead' then d = 1;
else d = 0;
```

A patient with status missing, or erroneously entered as 'DEAD' or 'dead' will have d = 0 and thus be considered censored. In this case, I knew that this did not happen, so the code is all right.

We can first look at the separate impact of each variable on survival with the following statements:

```
proc phreg; model months*d(0) = clark;
proc phreg; model months*d(0) = ulcer;
proc phreg; model months*d(0) = thickness;
run;
```

The output for the analysis of ulceration is given below as Output 4.1.

Output 4.1

```
                          The SAS System
                         The PHREG Procedure
                         Model Information

                      ❶  Data Set
                         WORK.DATA1
                     Dependent Variable        months
                     Censoring Variable        d
                     Censoring Value(s)         0
                     Ties Handling             BRESLOW


           Summary of the Number of Event and Censored Values
                                            Percent
         Total        Event      Censored   Censored

    ❷  1113             90         1023       91.91


                     Convergence Status

         Convergence criterion (GCONV=1E-8) satisfied.


                   ❸  Model Fit Statistics

                       Without        With
          Criterion    Covariates     Covariates

           -2 LOG L    1082.215       1028.572
           AIC         1082.215       1030.572
           SBC         1082.215       1033.072


            Testing Global Null Hypothesis: BETA=0
    ❹
     Test                Chi-Square     DF    Pr > ChiSq

     Likelihood Ratio     53.6434       1       <.0001
        Score             61.7522       1       <.0001
        Wald              50.7451       1       <.0001




            Analysis of Maximum Likelihood Estimates

     Parameter         Standard                          Hazard
     Variable  DF  Estimate  Error   Chi-Square  Pr > ChiSq  Ratio

     ulcer      1   1.58764  0.22287  50.7451      <.0001    4.892
```

The output presents the following:

❶ Information about the data set used, the time and censoring variables, and the method of handling ties.

❷ The number of observations and the number censored.

❸ Three model fit statistics.

❹ Three tests of the null hypothesis that the beta coefficient is zero. The first is $-2[\log L(0) - \log L(\hat{\beta})]$ as discussed in Appendix B. The Wald statistic is $\hat{\beta}^2 / \text{var}(\hat{\beta})$. The score statistic has not been discussed previously in this book. It is defined to be $-[d\log L(0)/d\beta]^2 / [d^2\log L(0)/d\beta^2]$. All three of these statistics have asymptotic χ^2 distributions with one degree of freedom in the univariate case. The generalizations to more than one covariate are discussed in the following section. An estimate of the beta coefficient, the standard error of that estimate, and the hazard ratio, which is just the antilog of the beta coefficient, are also given. In this case, the value of 4.892 for the hazard ratio indicates that the hazard for a patient with an ulcerated tumor is estimated to be about five times the hazard for a patient whose tumor is not ulcerated.

4.9.2.1 Exercise

Analyze the variable Clarklevel as a categorical variable using PROC TPHREG. Also run the program shown earlier to treat Clarklevel as an ordinal variable satisfying the proportion hazards assumption. Compare the estimates of the hazard ratio of Clarklevel I vs IV produced by the two approaches.

4.9.3 Multivariate Analyses

One of the major reasons that proportional hazards regression is so useful is that it allows us to look at several variables at one time, each in the presence of the others. To do this in the preceding example we can use the statements:

```
proc phreg;
model months*d(0) = ulcer clark thickness;
run;
```

The output is given as Output 4.2.

Output 4.2

```
                          The SAS System
                         The PHREG Procedure

                        Model Information

                     Data Set
                       WORK.DATA1
                 Dependent Variable        months
                 Censoring Variable        d
                 Censoring Value(s)        0
                 Ties Handling             BRESLOW


         Summary of the Number of Event and Censored Values


                                    Percent
                                    Censored
     Total       Event    Censored  Censored

     1096         89       1007      91.88


                        Convergence Status

            Convergence criterion (GCONV=1E-8) satisfied.


                      Model Fit Statistics

                          Without         With
             Criterion    Covariates      Covariates

             -2 LOG L     1066.026        993.006
             AIC          1066.026        999.006
             SBC          1066.026        1006.472


              Testing Global Null Hypothesis: BETA=0

    Test                 Chi-Square      DF      Pr > ChiSq

    Likelihood Ratio     73.0197         3        <.0001
    Score                92.3698         3        <.0001
    Wald                 74.5334         3        <.0001


               Analysis of Maximum Likelihood Estimates

                      Parameter Standard                        Hazard
    Variable    DF    Estimate  Error   Chi-Square Pr > ChiSq   Ratio

    ulcer       1     1.20581   0.23874  25.5102    <.0001      3.339
    clark       1     0.29558   0.17257   2.9337    0.0867      1.344
    thickness   1     0.12105   0.04655   6.7615    0.0093      1.129
```

Now the analyses are extended to the multivariate analysis of the three covariates. The global null hypothesis is now that the vector of coefficients for the three covariates is the zero vector and the Wald test statistic is $\hat{\beta}'\mathbf{V}\hat{\beta}$, where $\hat{\beta}$ is the vector of parameter estimates and $\mathbf{V}$ is the negative of the inverse of the matrix created by taking the second partial derivatives of the log likelihood with respect to the parameters. The score statistic, in the multivariate case, becomes

$$-[\partial \log L(\mathbf{0})/\partial \beta]'[\partial^2 \log L(\mathbf{0})/\partial \beta^2]^{-1}[\partial \log L(\mathbf{0})/\partial \beta]$$

where $\partial \log L(\mathbf{0})/\partial \beta$ is the vector of partial derivatives of the log likelihood with respect to the β_i evaluated at the zero vector and $\partial^2 \log L(\mathbf{0})/\partial \beta^2$ is the matrix of second partial derivatives of the log likelihood evaluated at the zero vector. The p-value for each of the covariates is based on the square of the estimated beta coefficient divided by its estimated variance. It's important to recognize that in this multivariate analysis, each of the covariates is analyzed in the presence of the others. For example, if you just look at ulceration in the univariate analysis, you would estimate that the hazard for a patient with an ulcerated tumor is about five times as great as for a patient whose tumor is not ulcerated. However, the multivariate analysis shows us that a patient with an ulcerated tumor would have about three times the hazard of a patient with the same Clark level and tumor thickness and a nonulcerated tumor.

As mentioned earlier, hazard ratios need to be interpreted in terms of the units of the associated covariates. Since ulcer = 1 for an ulcerated tumor and 0 for one that is not ulcerated, the hazard ratio is the ratio of the hazard for an ulcerated tumor over the hazard for one that is not ulcerated. Since thickness is measured in millimeters, the hazard ratio is the ratio of the hazard of a patient with a particular tumor thickness to the hazard for a patient whose tumor thickness is one millimeter less. If the tumor had been measured in centimeters the hazard ratio would have been $1.129^{10} = 3.365$, but the effect of thickness would not be any different.

4.9.4 Interactions

In order to consider the interaction of ulceration and thickness, we form a new covariate, the product of thickness and ulceration. The following program can perform a proportional hazards analysis of ulceration, thickness, and their interaction:

```
data; set sas.melanoma;
months = (followup - biopsy)/30.4;
if ulceration = 'Yes' then ulcer = 1;
if ulceration = 'No' then ulcer = 0;
if status = 'Dead' then d = 1;
else d = 0;
thicknessxulcer = thickness*ulcer;
proc phreg; model months*d(0) =  ulcer thickness thicknessxulcer;
run;
```

The last part of the output is as follows:

Output 4.3

		Analysis of Maximum Likelihood Estimates				
Variable	DF	Parameter Estimate	Standard Error	Chi-Square	Pr > ChiSq	Hazard Ratio
ulcer	1	1.85845	0.31287	35.2829	<.0001	6.414
thickness	1	0.28774	0.04208	46.7659	<.0001	1.333
thicknessxulcer	1	-0.19318	0.06448	8.9750	0.0027	0.824

The interaction term is statistically significant and its estimated coefficient is –0.19318. But what does this mean? To answer this question, rewrite

$$\exp(1.85845*ulcer + .28774*thickness -.19318*thicknessxulcer)$$

as

$$\exp[1.85845*ulcer + thickness*(.28774 - .19318*ulcer)].$$

This helps us to see what the interaction means. The effect of thickness on the hazard is to multiply it by $\exp(.28774) = 1.333$ for each millimeter of thickness when ulcer = 0 (i.e., for nonulcerated tumors). However, when ulcer = 1 (i.e., for ulcerated tumors), the effect of tumor thickness is to multiply the hazard by $\exp(.28774 - .19318) = \exp(.09456) = 1.099$ for each millimeter of thickness. In other words, the meaning of the interaction of thickness and ulceration is that the presence or absence of ulceration modifies the effect of thickness on the hazard and thus on survival. With a little thought, we can see that this result becomes intuitively logical. (Of course, some people have more highly developed intuitions than others.) Ulceration is apparently a pretty serious thing for a melanoma tumor. If the tumor is ulcerated, that's such bad news that tumor thickness does not add as much to the negative prognosis.

You should rewrite

$$\exp(1.85845*ulcer + .28774*thickness -.19318*thicknessxulcer)$$

as

$$\exp[.28774*thickness + ulcer*(1.85845 - .19318*thickness)]$$

to figure out for yourself what this says about the way that thickness modifies the effect of ulceration.

This might be a good time to pause and reflect upon how much more informative the analyses that we have done thus far in this chapter are when compared to the nonparametric analyses of the previous chapter. But being able to say more is not much of an accomplishment if what we are saying is wrong because it is based on false assumptions. We will return to this issue later.

4.9.5 Exercise

Using the melanoma example, explain, in your own words, what the interaction model implies about the way that thickness modifies the effect of ulceration. According to the model, how thick would a tumor need to be for ulceration not to matter at all?

4.9.6 Stratification

Suppose we have a vector of covariates, **x**, that we feel may affect survival and suppose we also have a dichotomous variable q that takes on the values 1 and 2. We are not interested in estimating the effect of q, but we do want to take that effect into consideration when analyzing the effect of **x**. In this case we don't need to assume that q satisfies the proportional hazards assumption. The variable q can be thought of as a stratification variable. The partial likelihood can be taken to be the product of the two partial likelihoods formed as previously shown for each value of q. Specifically, we can write that partial likelihood as

$$\prod_{\substack{d_i \geq 1 \\ q_i = 1}} \frac{\exp(\boldsymbol{\beta}' \mathbf{s}_i)}{\left[\sum_{j \geq i} \exp(\boldsymbol{\beta}' \mathbf{x}_j)\right]^{d_i}} \prod_{\substack{d_i \geq 1 \\ q_i = 2}} \frac{\exp(\boldsymbol{\beta}' \mathbf{s}_i)}{\left[\sum_{j \ni i} \exp(b' \mathbf{x}_j)\right]^{d_i}} \qquad (4.10)$$

This formulation is more general than simply treating q as another variable in the proportional hazards regression because it allows for different baseline hazards for different values of q. The following statements show how to form a stratified analysis to assess the effect of thickness while stratifying for ulceration.

```
proc phreg;
model months*d(0) = thickness;
strata ulcer;
run;
```

These statements would cause any observation that has a missing value for the variable Ulcer to be omitted. If we had used the statement `strata ulcer/missing`, observations with a missing value for Ulcer would have formed a third stratum. The results are given as Output 4.4.

Output 4.4

```
                        The SAS System
                      The PHREG Procedure

                    Model Information
                      Data Set                    WORK.DATA1
              Dependent Variable        months
              Censoring Variable        d
              Censoring Value(s)        0
              Ties Handling             BRESLOW

          Summary of the Number of Event and Censored Values

                                           Percent
     Stratum   ulcer   Total  Event  Censored  Censored
        1        0       756    32      724      95.77
        2        1       357    58      299      83.75
     ------------------------------------------------------
     Total               1113   90     1023      91.91
```

Output 4.4 (continued)

```
                    Convergence Status

         Convergence criterion (GCONV=1E-8) satisfied.


               Model Fit Statistics

                  Without         With
     Criterion    Covariates    Covariates

     -2 LOG L      913.895        897.843
     AIC           913.895        899.843
     SBC           913.895        902.342



        Testing Global Null Hypothesis: BETA=0

     Test                Chi-Square      DF     Pr > ChiSq
     Likelihood Ratio     16.0526        1        <.0001
     Score                21.9149        1        <.0001
     Wald                 21.2792        1        <.0001


                     The SAS System
                    The PHREG Procedure

          Analysis of Maximum Likelihood Estimates

                  Parameter   Standard                         Hazard
     Variable DF  Estimate     Error   Chi-Square Pr > ChiSq   Ratio

     thickness 1   0.16499    0.03577   21.2792      <.0001     1.179
```

In this case, the results are quite similar to those obtained if we treat ulceration as another variable satisfying the proportional hazards assumption.

4.9.7 Other PROC PHREG Features

PROC PHREG has a rich collection of additional features. Only those that are most useful are discussed here. As with many other SAS procedures, a statement of the form

    BY varname;

causes separate analyses to be done for each value of *varname*. The data set must by sorted by *varname*. A statement of the form

    WHERE expression;

causes the analyses to be restricted to those patients for whom *expression* is true. There are also statements that can be used to produce estimates of survival functions over time for specified values of the covariates. These are discussed later in this chapter.

Specifying the option SIMPLE in the PROC statement causes simple descriptive statistics for each variable in the right side of the MODEL statement to be printed. Several important options can be specified in the MODEL statement. They must follow a slash (/) that follows the list of independent variables. RISKLIMITS (or RL) causes the output to include $(100 - \alpha)100\%$ confidence intervals for the risk ratios. The default value for α is 0.05. This can be altered by using the option ALPHA = *value*.

There are several options, called model-building options, that control which of a set of covariates that you supply actually gets used in the model. These options are used when you are looking for a set of covariates that can distinguish patients with respect to their anticipated survival prospects. Their use is tricky and somewhat controversial among statisticians. Some will argue that such methods should not be used at all. Some issues you should think about when using these methods are discussed in Section 4.10.

By using the option SELECTION = FORWARD, you cause the covariates to be included in the model to be chosen one at a time. The procedure starts by performing univariate proportional hazards regressions with each independent variable in the MODEL statement. The variable with the largest score χ^2 is entered into the model first. The procedure then performs the two variable proportional hazards regressions by using each of the remaining covariates with the one already chosen. The covariate with the largest score χ^2 in the model that contains the first one entered is then added to the model. The process continues in this fashion until none of the remaining covariates has score χ^2 values large enough to be included. The default is for the process to stop when none of the remaining covariates is significant at the 0.05 level. Other values can be chosen by including the option SLENTRY (or SLE) = VALUE. If you wish to limit the model to *n* covariates, you can use the option STOP = *n*. If you wish to force *m* particular covariates to be included in the model you can list them first in the MODEL statement and use the option START = M.

There are other model-building options that can be used to build models in different ways. Using SELECTION = STEPWISE will cause the procedure to go through a process similar to the one previously described for SELECTION = FORWARD. The difference is that SELECTION = STEPWISE will allow covariates previously entered to be removed from the model if they are no longer significant using the Wald χ^2 statistic. The default threshold for significance is 0.05. This can be altered by using the option SLSTAY = *value* where *value* is the desired significance threshold. Again the process stops when all of the covariates not in the model have score χ^2 p-values exceeding the SLE value. The process also stops if a covariate is entered into the model and then removed in the same step. If the process didn't stop under this condition, you could have that covariate both entered and removed indefinitely.

The option SELECTION = BACKWARD causes the procedure to begin by estimating the coefficients for all of the covariates in the MODEL statement. The covariate having the smallest value for the one degree of freedom Wald χ^2 statistic is then removed from the model if the p-value for that covariate is larger than the SLSTAY value specified. The default is 0.05. The process stops when all of the covariates still in the model have Wald χ^2 p-values smaller than the SLSTAY value.

Another way to specify the models created is to use the options SELECTION = SCORE and BEST = n. These will cause the best n models of each size to be found and printed. Best in this case means having the highest score statistic. That statistic is one of the three described earlier that provide a measure of the collective significance of the covariates in the model. For example, if ten covariates are specified in the MODEL statement and the options SELECTION = SCORE and BEST = 5 are used, then the procedure prints the five best one-covariate models, the five best two-covariate models, and so on, until it gets to the five best nine-covariate models. Of course, there is only one ten-covariate model. It will be printed as well. If the BEST = n option is omitted and there are ten or fewer covariates in the MODEL statement, then the procedure prints all models with each number of covariates. If you think that can be a lot of models, you are right. With ten covariates, this will result in $2^{10} - 1 = 1023$ models being printed. If there are more than ten covariates in the MODEL statement, then the number of models of each size printed will not exceed the number of covariates.

4.9.8 A Model-Building Example

For an example of the use of PROC PHREG for creating a proportional hazards model for survival based on a set of survival data and covariate values, consider another melanoma data set. The data are based on 1396 patients who had their melanomas surgically removed. Disease-free survival (DFS) time is defined as the time, in months, until either death or tumor relapse. Several covariates are recorded and analyzed for association with DFS. Location is coded as 1 (extremity), 2 (trunk), 3 (face/neck), or 4 (mucous membrane). Sex was coded as 0 for females and 1 for males. Thickness and Clark level are recorded as described above, as is the presence or absence of ulceration. Three dichotomous location covariates need to be defined as described earlier. Loc1 equals 1 if the location is 1, 0 otherwise. Loc2 and Loc3 are defined similarly.

A forward selection method is used with the default significance threshold of 0.05. The option RL requests 95% confidence intervals. The DETAILS option causes the details of the selection process to be printed. Here are the SAS statements to perform the analysis on a SAS data set previously defined.

```
proc phreg;
    model dfstime*dfscens(0) = loc1-loc3 sex clark
        thickness ulcer/ selection = forward rl
        details;
  title1 'Proportional Hazards Regression Analysis';
  title2 'Of Melanoma Data';
  run;
```

The results are given in Output 4.5.

Output 4.5

```
                  Proportional Hazards Regression Analysis
                            Of Melanoma Data
                           The PHREG Procedure

                            Model Information

                  Data Set                     WORK.DATA8
                  Dependent Variable           DFSTIME
                  Censoring Variable           DFSCENS
                  Censoring Value(s)           0
                  Ties Handling                BRESLOW


            Summary of the Number of Event and Censored Values

                                          Percent
           Total      Event    Censored   Censored

           968        201        767       79.24


                ❶ Analysis of Variables Not in the Model

                           Score
          Variable      Chi-Square     Pr > ChiSq

          loc1            1.0273         0.3108
          loc2            0.0283         0.8663
          loc3            3.0090         0.0828
          sex             1.8951         0.1686
          CLARK          37.1010         <.0001
          thickness      73.9724         <.0001
          ulcer          24.9179         <.0001


                     ❷ Residual Chi-Square Test

             Chi-Square        DF       Pr > ChiSq

              80.7527           7          <.0001

        ❸
     Step  1. Variable thickness is entered.  The model contains the following
     explanatory
               variables:

               thickness

                          Convergence Status

       Convergence criterion (GCONV=1E-8) satisfied.
```

Output 4.5 (continued)

```
              Proportional Hazards Regression Analysis
                        Of Melanoma Data

                       The PHREG Procedure
                      Model Fit Statistics

                         Without            With
           Criterion    Covariates        Covariates
           -2 LOG L      2274.798          2219.676
           AIC           2274.798          2221.676
           SBC           2274.798          2224.979


           ❹   Testing Global Null Hypothesis: BETA=0

Test                    Chi-Square        DF       Pr > ChiSq
Likelihood Ratio          55.1218          1          <.0001
Score                     73.9724          1          <.0001
Wald                      72.9631          1          <.0001


           ❺   Analysis of Maximum Likelihood Estimates

              Parameter  Standard                         Hazard    95% Hazard Ratio
Variable   DF  Estimate    Error   Chi-Square  Pr > ChiSq  Ratio   Confidence Limits

thickness  1   0.33820   0.03959   72.9631      <.0001    1.402     1.298      1.516


           ❻   Analysis of Variables Not in the Model

                        Score
Variable             Chi-Square    Pr > ChiSq

loc1                   2.3063        0.1289
loc2                   0.2266        0.6341
loc3                   2.0602        0.1512
sex                    0.3358        0.5623
CLARK                  9.5331        0.0020
ulcer                  2.5655        0.1092


                 ❼   Residual Chi-Square Test

              Chi-Square        DF       Pr > ChiSq

               14.6913           6         0.0228

❽
Step  2. Variable CLARK is entered.  The model contains the following
explanatory variables:
```

Output 4.5 (continued)

```
                         CLARK  thickness

                       Convergence Status

          Convergence criterion (GCONV=1E-8) satisfied.

                      Model Fit Statistics

                    Without            With
   Criterion       Covariates       Covariates
   -2 LOG L         2274.798         2209.735
   AIC              2274.798         2213.735
   SBC              2274.798         2220.341


        ❽   Testing Global Null Hypothesis: BETA=0

   Test                  Chi-Square        DF      Pr > ChiSq

   Likelihood Ratio       65.0634          2         <.0001
   Score                  75.8003          2         <.0001
   Wald                   69.7922          2         <.0001


           ❾ Analysis of Maximum Likelihood Estimates

                Parameter  Standard                        Hazard  95% Hazard Ratio
   Variable DF   Estimate    Error   Chi-Square  Pr > ChiSq  Ratio Confidence Limits

   CLARK      1   0.36925   0.12024    9.4316      0.0021     1.447  1.143     1.831
   thickness  1   0.26488   0.04847   29.8596      <.0001     1.303  1.185     1.433


            ❿ Analysis of Variables Not in the Model

                                 Score
                  Variable     Chi-Square      Pr > ChiSq

                    loc1         1.1965          0.2740
                    loc2         0.0763          0.7824
                    loc3         1.6817          0.1947
                    sex          0.0580          0.8097
                    ulcer        2.0892          0.1483

             Proportional Hazards Regresion Analysis
                        Of Melanoma Data

                       The PHREG Procedure

           ⓫ Residual Chi-Square Test

          Chi-Square         DF        Pr > ChiSq

            5.3010           5           0.3803

NOTE: No (additional) variables met the 0.05 level for entry into the model.

           ⓬ Summary of Forward Selection

           Variable    Number      Score
   Step    Entered       In      Chi-Square    Pr > ChiSq
   1       thickness      1       73.9724        <.0001
   2       CLARK          2        9.5331        0.0085
```

Note the following features of the output:

❶ The seven univariate proportional hazards regression models are calculated.

❷ The highly significant residual χ^2 indicates that the model containing the seven covariates is superior to the model with none of them.

❸ Thickness, the most highly significant of the seven covariates, is entered into the model

❹ Three tests of the significance of the model containing thickness are reported. All are highly significant.

❺ The estimated beta coefficient for thickness in the one-covariate model, its standard error, and its significance level are given. An estimate of the hazard ratio associated with a thickness increase of one millimeter is given as well as a 95% confidence interval for that hazard ratio.

❻ Score χ^2 statistics along with their p-values for the six two-covariate proportional hazards models using thickness and each of the remaining covariates are computed. The highest χ^2 value is for the model in which Clark is added.

❼ The residual χ^2 is significant, indicating that at least one of the remaining variables is relevant in determining survival probabilities.

❽ Clark is added to the model. The three statistics for the two-covariate model are calculated. All are significant.

❾ Beta coefficient estimates, their standard errors, and p-values for each of the two covariates now in the model are reported. Estimates of the risk ratios and 95% confidence intervals for each of the covariates are also given.

❿ The five three-covariate proportional hazards regressions using thickness, Clark, and each of the remaining five covariates are calculated. None meet the significance threshold of 0.05.

⓫ The residual χ^2 is not significant, indicating no evidence that the remaining covariates influence survival.

⓬ The model-building process ends. A summary of the covariate selection process is given.

4.10 Model-Building Considerations

4.10.1 Correlated Covariates

Other SAS regression procedures, LOGISTIC and REG, have model-building options similar to those described earlier. The remarks that follow apply to them as well. First, you need to be aware that the different methods can, and often do, produce different final models. Each has some logical basis, and it would be difficult to say that one is better than the others. Also you need to realize that a covariate that is omitted from the model may, on its own, be highly significant. That can happen if that covariate is highly correlated with a covariate (or a linear combination of covariates) currently in the model. Suppose, for example, that x_1 and x_2 have values for score χ^2 in univariate proportional hazard regressions of 5.62 and 5.64, respectively. Then, in a stepwise or forward selection, x_2 will be entered into the model. Now if x_1 and x_2 are highly correlated, then x_1 may not be significant in the model containing x_2. Thus x_1 will not appear in the model. If another sample were similarly analyzed, x_1 might, simply by chance, have a larger χ^2 than x_2. Thus it would be entered into the model, and x_2 might be left out.

4.10.2 The "Multiple Testing" Problem

Another thing to realize is that when you use a subset of the original covariates in the final model, the p-values reported for those covariates are seriously biased. With a large number of covariates in the model, the probability that at least one will be considered "significant" and entered into the model is much higher than the stated or default value of Slentry. For example, if a MODEL statement lists 25 independent covariates that are not related to survival at all and SLENTRY = 0.05, then there is a probability of 0.72 $(1 - .95^{25})$ that at least one will be "significant" and entered into the model with a p-value less than 0.05 and a probability of 0.36 that at least two will. For this reason, you should avoid thoughtlessly putting a large number of covariates into a MODEL statement. Use only covariates that make sense clinically or biologically. Even so, models created in one of the ways described earlier need to be confirmed in additional data sets. If you have a sample that is large enough, you might want to divide it into two parts. Use one part to build a model and the other to test it.

4.10.3 Prescreening Covariates

As noted previously, a patient will be excluded from the analysis if any of the covariates in the MODEL statement have missing values. Unfortunately, missing values are very common when dealing with medical data. Tests that are supposed to generate values of the covariates are sometimes not done. Sometimes clinical problems prevent their being done. Sometimes tests are done, but the results are technically inadequate or equivocal. With a large number of covariates, even if each is nonmissing for 90%-95% of the patients, you might have data on all of the covariates for fewer than half of the patients in the sample. This is even more serious if "missingness" is not at random but is in some way related to patient or disease characteristics that are, in turn, related to prognosis. This can happen, for example, if certain tests on tumor tissue can be done only when there is enough tissue, which may be the case only for larger tumors. One way to lessen this problem is to prescreen the covariates with univariate proportional hazard regressions. You would then perform a second proportional hazards regression using only those covariates passing through the first screen with p-values less than some threshold value, say 0.05 or 0.10. In this way, missing values for covariates that are apparently not associated with survival and are unlikely to wind up in the final model will not cause a patient to be excluded.

Two SAS procedures, PROC MI and PROC MIANALYZE, introduced on an experimental basis in Version 8 and production in Version 9, allow us to impute missing covariate values and perform analyses using the imputed values. This is discussed in Section 4.18.

4.10.4 Grouping Covariates

Sometimes there are great differences in the cost of acquiring values for covariates. The term "cost" is used here in a broad sense to include such factors as risk to the patient, morbidity, inconvenience, and so forth. It's only reasonable to consider these factors in seeking a model for hazard. A covariate might be highly associated with prognosis and thus provide a useful guide to therapy. However, its determination might cause considerable morbidity or be very expensive. We would prefer to avoid obtaining this covariate if another covariate, or set of covariates, can provide the same information. One way to accomplish this is as follows:

1. Group the covariates according to the costs associated with their determination.

2. Perform a series of proportional hazards regressions using those of less cost in the earlier steps.

3. In each step, add the covariates in the next group to those added to the model in the previous steps.

Suppose, for purposes of illustration, we come up with three such groups of covariates, which we label A, B, and C, with group A being the least and C being the most costly to acquire. For example, the group A covariates might be obtained from the patient history, the second group from expensive lab tests, and the third group from exploratory surgery. Here are the steps:

1. Run PROC PHREG with some model-building options on the covariates in group A only. Presumably n of them will be in the final model.

2. Re-run PROC PHREG with these n covariates listed first in the MODEL statement followed by those in group B using the option START $= N$. This will cause the n covariates from the first step to be included as well as the m group B covariates that are significant in the model containing these covariates.

3. Run PROC PHREG once again listing the $m + n$ covariates from this second model first, followed by the covariates in group C. Use the option START = R where R = N+M. This procedure ensures that a covariate is in the final model only if it has an influence on the hazard, hence survival, which is not accounted for by covariates that are less costly to acquire.

4.10.5 *Using Cutpoints on a Continuous Covariate*

When dealing with a continuous covariate, you have two approaches that you can use. One is to use the actual value that is observed in a Cox regression as described earlier. The other is to convert it to a dichotomous, or perhaps ordinal covariate by using cutpoints. For example, instead of using the age of a woman with breast cancer, you can create a dichotomous covariate to use. This covariate might take on the value 0 if the woman is 60 years old or less and 1 if the woman is over 60 years old. This covariate could be used in a proportional hazards regression or as the grouping variable in one of the linear rank tests as we did in the Chapter 3. Arguments can be made for and against both approaches. Here are two arguments against the use of cutpoints:

- By converting from a continuous variable to a dichotomous variable, you are throwing out potentially useful information. After all, ages of 47, 62, or 85 are more informative than "less than 60" or "greater than 60". It doesn't make sense to consider a 59-year-old and a 61-year-old to be different, but a 62-year-old and an 85-year-old to be the same.

- The choice of a cutpoint or cutpoints is arbitrary. If dichotomizing age, for example, where do you draw the line? Using a cutpoint of 50 might lead to a statistically significant beta coefficient, while a cutpoint of 60 might not. You might simply use the median value of the covariate. Many analysts will try a variety of cutpoints and use the one with the largest χ^2 statistic. If you do that you need to understand that the resultant p-value is subject to the multiple testing effect discussed in Section 4.10.2. A recent report (Altman et al., 1994) and a letter commenting on it (Cantor and Shuster, 1994) discuss this issue in greater detail.

Here are two arguments for the use of cutpoints:

- Although it might be reasonable to assume that the effect of a covariate's value on the hazard function is monotonic, it might not be reasonable to assume that it satisfies the proportional hazards assumption. The hazard ratio for an 80-year- old vs a 70-year-old might differ from the corresponding ratio for a 50-year-old vs a 40-year-old. Dichotomizing age avoids this problem.

- The results for a dichotomous variable are easier to interpret to other people, particularly those not statistically sophisticated. It's easier for such a person to understand (or at least think he or she understands) that older patients have a 40% greater hazard (i.e., a hazard ratio of 1.40) than that each year increases the hazard by 3% (i.e., a hazard ratio of 1.03 per year). In fact, if a continuous covariate is dichotomized, then the log rank test or one of the other linear rank tests can be used. Then the results can be interpreted in terms of the observed vs expected number of deaths in each group. This is a convenient way to visualize the magnitude of the effect of a dichotomous variable.

There is no single simple answer to the question of whether it is better to use the actual value of a continuous covariate or to dichotomize it with a cutpoint. To a certain extent, I think it's a "culture clash" issue. Most statisticians come from mathematical backgrounds. It is natural for them to think in terms of continuous measurements. To such a person, a systolic blood pressure of 146 mm Hg is not just "greater than 140," and he or she might think it strange to consider someone with a systolic blood pressure of 139 to be at normal risk while someone with a systolic blood pressure of 141 is at high risk. For a physician, however, a decision needs to be made. Does he or she treat this patient for systolic hypertension or not? The physician naturally wants someone to provide a cutpoint and say that above this value hazard is elevated and should be treated. You need to consider the way that you expect the covariate to affect survival as well as the anticipated audience for your analyses and decide accordingly.

Whatever your thoughts on this matter, or the planned analyses, I generally advise researchers I work with to enter the actual values of continuous variables. It is then easy for me to convert them to dichotomous or ordinal variables in a DATA step if that is desired. Of course, reconstructing continuous values from dichotomous or ordinal ones is not as easy.

4.11 Time-Dependent Covariates

The method of proportional hazards regression and PROC PHREG can be used in a manner that has not yet been discussed. You may want to consider the effect on survival of a covariate that is not constant over time. Such a covariate is called a time-dependent covariate. Some examples might be a patient's weight, diastolic blood pressure, or levels of certain serum markers. A dichotomous variable might also vary with time. Consider patients who are candidates for an organ transplant. They are followed from the time that determination is made, but it might be some time before the transplant can be accomplished. Some will die before that is done. Others may die post-transplant. To study the effect of transplantation on survival you can consider "transplantation state" as a covariate. If the patient is transplanted at time t_0, then that covariate can be assigned a value of 0 for $t < t_0$ and 1 for $t \geq t_0$. In Chapter 3 you saw how the Mantel-Byar method could be used to analyze such data. The technique described here offers an alternative.

Notation of the form x(t) will be used for a covariate that may vary over time. The column vector $(x_1(t), x_2(t), \ldots, x_p(t))'$ will be denoted $\mathbf{x}(t)$. The proportional hazards regression model with time-dependent covariates can then be written

$$h(t, \mathbf{x}(t)) = h(t_0)\exp(\boldsymbol{\beta}'\mathbf{x}(t)) \qquad (4.11)$$

where $\boldsymbol{\beta}$ is, as before, a column vector of regression coefficients.

If x(t) is a time-dependent covariate that you wish to consider in a proportional hazards regression, you need to provide information on the value of x for all values of t. This is done through programming statements that follow the MODEL statement. These statements can use many of the statements, and all of the functions, that can be used in the DATA step. As an example, suppose you are following patients who are candidates for an organ transplant. That data might contain the variables Time, for the patients' time on study and Censor, to indicate whether the patient was alive (0) or dead (1). In addition you might have a variable, Trantime, which represents the time at which the patient was transplanted. If the patient never received a transplant, this variable would have a missing value. The following SAS statements could be used to do proportional hazards regression analysis with "transplant state" which is denoted by Trans as a time-dependent covariate:

```
proc phreg:
   model time*censor(0) = trans;
   trans = 0;
   if time ge trantime and trantime ne . then trans= 1;
run;
```

A positive (negative) value for the coefficient of Trans would indicate that transplantation increased (decreased) the hazard and thus diminished (improved) survival.

Continuous time-dependent covariates cause greater trouble. Generally you could not monitor a patient continuously for values of such a covariate. Even if you could, how would you translate the values for that function into programming statements? Instead, what is usually done is to record values of the covariate at certain times, say $t_1, t_2, \ldots, t_k$ where $t_1 = 0$. Suppose those corresponding values are $a_1, a_2, \ldots, a_k$. Then the programming statements to assign, for any time, the most recently recorded value might look like this (for $k=10$):

```
array t{10} t1 - t10;
array a{10} a1 - a10;
x = a1;
do i = 1 to 10;
    if t{i} ne . and time ge t{i} then x = a{i};
    end;
run;
```

Remember, although this looks like DATA step programming, these statements do not appear in the DATA step. They are placed after the MODEL statement that goes with the PROC PHREG statement. This code assigns the most recent value to a covariate. Of course, more complicated time-dependent variables can be defined as well. Here are some examples:

- $x(t)$ equals the average of the a_i for $t_i \leq t$.
- $x(t)$ equals the maximum (or minimum) of the a_i for $t_i \leq t$.
- $x(t)$ equals the slope of the least squares line determined by the a_i.
- $x(t)$ equals the range of the a_i.
- $x(t)$ equals the (approximation of the) cumulative values of the $a(t_i)$ over time. I.e. $\Sigma a_i(t_{i+1}-t_i)$.
- $x(t)$ is interpolated from a_i and a_{i+1} where $t_i < t < t_{i+1}$.

Leslie Kalish (2000) has written a macro that can be used to calculate the first four of these time-dependent covariates in this setting as well as the most recent value. He has graciously allowed me to include it with the other macros in this book. The macros and other code and data can be found on the companion Web site for this book.

4.11.1 Exercise

Modify the code in the previous section to define the value of the time-dependent variable, x, by interpolation between the preceding and succeeding values. For example, for a time midway between t_i and t_{i+1}, $x(t)$ should equal $(a_i + a_{i+1})/2$.

4.12 More Complex Models

By using time-dependent covariates, you can also create more complex models in situations where the proportional hazards property does not hold. To reprise an example mentioned earlier in this chapter, let $x_1 = 1$ if a patient was treated surgically and 0 if otherwise. Suppose you believe that the hazard ratio is different after $t = 90$ days from the hazard ratio prior to that time. You might use the following statements to analyze the survival data:

```
proc phreg;
    model t*cens(0)= x1 x2;
    if t < 90 then x2 = 0;
    else x2 = x1;
```

Note that x_1 is time *independent*, but x_2 is time *dependent*. Now let's assume proportional hazards and suppose β_1 and β_2 are the regression coefficients for x_1 and $x_2(t)$ respectively. Then the hazard function can be written $h(t, x_1, x_2(t)) = h_0(t)\exp[\beta_1*x_1 + \beta_2*x_2(t)]$. This means that the x_1 (surgery) effect is β_1 prior to $t = 90$, and $\beta_1 + \beta_2$ thereafter. If surgery is associated with increased hazard during the first 90 days and diminished hazard thereafter, you might then have $\beta_1 > 0$ and $\beta_1 + \beta_2 < 0$.

4.13 Checking the Proportional Hazards Assumption

As pointed out in Section 4.1, the appropriateness of the proportional hazards regression method and the validity of the results depend on the correctness of the proportional hazards assumption given by Equation (4.3). This section discusses some graphical and analytic methods of checking on that assumption. In each case, the check will be for one dichotomous covariate. Of course, the proportional hazards assumption can be checked separately for each covariate.

Let $S_1(t)$ and $S_2(t)$ be the survival functions for the two values of this covariate. As shown in Section 4.3, these functions, under the proportional hazards assumption, will be related by $S_1(t) = [S_0(t)]^r$ for some positive number, r. In fact, $r = \exp(\beta)$. Taking natural logarithms of both sides produces

$$\log S_1(t) = r\log S_0(t) \tag{4.12}$$

Taking the natural logarithms of the negatives of both sides (note that both sides of (4.12) are negative) yields

$$\log[-\log S_1(t)] = \log(r) + \log[-\log S_0(t)] \tag{4.13}$$

According to (4.13), the proportional hazards assumption implies that graphs of $\log[-\log S_0(t)]$ and $\log[-\log S_1(t)]$ are parallel. In fact, the constant vertical distance between them should be the coefficient β. You may recall from Chapter 3 that one of the options in PROC LIFETEST is to print graphs of certain functions of the estimated survival function and that the graph of $\log[-\log(\hat{S}(t))]$ vs $\log(t)$ was one of them. Thus, one way to check on the proportional hazards assumption in this case is to invoke PROC LIFETEST with the dichotomous covariate as a stratification variable and use the option PLOTS = (LLS) or PLOTS = (LOGLOGS). You can then inspect the plots visually to see if the curves seem to be vertically separated by a near constant amount. The same approach can be used for a categorical variable with more than two values. The following code shows how this is done for the melanoma data described at the beginning of this chapter and the covariate ulcer. The NOPRINT option is used because we want only the graph in this case.

```
symbol1 c=black l=1 w=3;
symbol2 c=black l=3 w=3;
proc lifetest noprint plots = (lls) nocensplot;
    time months*d(0);
    strata ulcer;
run;
```

Figure 4.1 shows the graphs of $\log[-\log \hat{S}_1(t)]$ and $\log[-\log \hat{S}_0(t)]$ vs $\log(t)$ where $\hat{S}_1(t)$ and $\hat{S}_0(t)$ are the Kaplan-Meier estimates of the survival curves for the patients with and without ulcers and t is survival time. The graphs are roughly parallel and the proportional hazards property appears to hold.

Figure 4.1

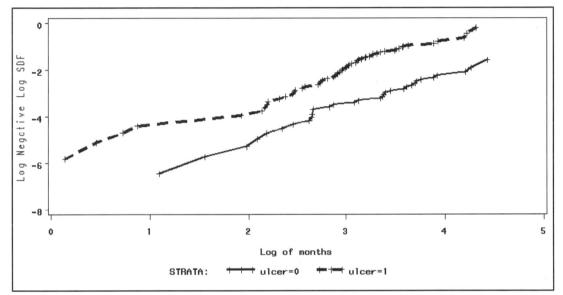

Another way to check on proportional hazards using PROC LIFETEST for each group is to specify the lifetable, or actuarial, method of producing survival function estimates, with the same intervals, for each. Then the printed output will include estimates of the hazard at the midpoints of each interval for each group. If the proportional hazards assumption holds, their ratio should be relatively constant. A problem with this approach is that unless the samples are fairly large, the hazard estimates will not be very good and this method may not work too well.

PROC PHREG itself provides a way to test for certain deviations from proportional hazards. This method is described in the SAS PROC PHREG documentation. Suppose you have a dichotomous (0 or 1) covariate group, for which you want to check the proportional hazards assumption. Define a time-dependent covariate by $x(t) = \text{group}*t$ where t is the time variable. The SAS documentation suggests $\log(t)$ instead of t. This avoids numeric problems if the time variable takes on large values– for example, if time is measured in days over several months. Then $x(t)$ is 0 for group 0 and t for group 1. The proportional hazards model based on these two covariates is then

$$h(t, \ x(t)) = h_0(t) \exp(\beta_1 * \text{group} + \beta_2 * \text{group} * t) \tag{4.14}$$

The hazard ratio for group 1 relative to group 0 is $\exp(\beta_1 + \beta_2 t)$. If the estimate of β_2 differs significantly from 0 then that indicates that the hazard ratio for group increases ($\beta_2 > 0$) or decreases (if $\beta_2 < 0$) over time. In either case, the hazard ratio is not constant.

This test is not a general test of the proportional hazards assumption. Its alternative to the null hypothesis of a constant hazard ratio is one that changes monotonically over time. If the hazard ratio increases for a while and then decreases, you might not get a statistically significant result for the test.

As an example, the SAS statements to test the proportional hazards assumption for the variable Ulcer in the first melanoma data set would be

```
proc phreg;
model months*d(0) = ulcer x;
if ulcer = 1 then x = months;
if ulcer = 0 then x = 0;
run;
```

The parameter estimates and their significance are given in Output 4.6:

Output 4.6

```
              Analysis of Maximum Likelihood Estimates


             Parameter   Standard                              Hazard
Variable  DF  Estimate     Error   Chi-Square  Pr > ChiSq      Ratio
ulcer      1   1.67009    0.39965   17.4629       <.0001        5.313
x          1  -0.00325    0.01303    0.0622        0.8031       0.997
```

The p-value for the coefficient of x, 0.8031, offers no evidence that the hazard ratio for Ulcer is either increasing or decreasing over time.

4.14 Exercise

Note that in Figure 4.1 the graphs of log[–log(S(t))] vs log(t) appear to be approximately linear for both groups. What kind of survival function does this suggest? What does the slope of the line tell you?

Hint: Write log[–log(S(t)] = a + blog(t) and exponentiate both sides twice.

4.15 Survival Probabilities

4.15.1 The BASELINE Statement

As mentioned earlier in this chapter, you and researchers you are working with are probably more interested in survival probabilities than in hazards. Suppose you use PROC PHREG to establish that higher values of certain covariates and lower values of others are associated with better survival (their beta coefficients are negative and positive, respectively). You would next want to know more about the survival probabilities over time for patients with certain specified values of those covariates. PROC PHREG provides such estimated survival probabilities for models in which none of the covariates are time dependent. The technical details underlying the derivation of these estimated survival probabilities are beyond the scope of this book and, for those who are interested, can be found in the PROC PHREG documentation. But it is not necessary to understand those details to obtain the estimates. The syntax for a typical statement to obtain survival function estimates for specified values of the covariates would look like this:

BASELINE OUT=*datasetname1* COVARIATES=*datasetname2*
    SURVIVAL=*varname* STDERR=*varname* LOWER=*varname*
    UPPER = *varname*;

In the syntax, *datasetname1* is the name of the output SAS data set that will contain the estimates produced. This data set will contain the estimates produced for each value of the time variable in the data set used by PROC PHREG. If it is omitted, SAS uses the DATAn convention to assign a name. *Datasetname2* is the name of a SAS data set that you have previously defined. It contains the values of the covariates for which you want survival function estimates. Estimates at the means of the covariates are produced by default. This may not make sense for a dichotomous variable. If COVARIATES = *datasetname2* is omitted, only the estimates at the means of the covariates are output to *datasetname1*. The statement produces estimates for the survival function, its standard error, and upper and lower bounds for 95% confidence intervals. They will have the variable names specified in the variable names that follow the equal signs. Several other statistics can be calculated in addition to (or instead of) these. Several options can be used after a slash (/). Among them are ALPHA = *value,* which allows you to specify an alpha value other than 0.05 for the (1 – alpha) 100% confidence intervals and NOMEAN to keep from calculating estimates for the means of the covariates.

4.15.2 Example

For an example, consider once again the melanoma data used previously. We saw that survival is worse for patients with thick and ulcerated tumors and best for those whose tumors are thin and nonulcerated. PROC PHREG will be used with a BASELINE statement to produce survival estimates and their standard errors for three hypothetical patients: one with good anticipated survival (thin, nonulcerated), one with poor anticipated survival (thick, ulcerated), and one with intermediate prognosis (thick, nonulcerated). The SAS statements are as follows:

```
data cov_vals;
    input thickness ulcer;
    datalines;
4.0  1
 .3  0
4.0  0
;
proc phreg data=melanoma noprint;
   model months*d(0)= thickness ulcer;
baseline  covariates=cov_vals  survival=survival
stderr=se lower=lo_bound  upper=up_bound  out=estsurv / nomean;
proc print;
run;
```

The results are printed in Output 4.7. For each pair of covariate values in the data set Cov_vals, only the first and last 20 lines of the output are reproduced. The NOMEAN option causes the output associated with the mean values of Thickness and Ulcer to be suppressed. It doesn't make much sense to talk about patients with Ulcer = .32 when Ulcer only has values of 0 and 1.

Output 4.7

				The SAS System			
Obs	thickness	ulcer	months	survival	se	lo_bound	up_bound
1	4	1	0.0000	1.00000	.	.	.
2	4	1	1.1513	0.99785	0.002146	0.99366	1.00000
3	4	1	1.5789	0.99562	0.003101	0.98956	1.00000
4	4	1	2.0724	0.99335	0.003850	0.98583	1.00000
5	4	1	2.4013	0.99106	0.004488	0.98230	0.99989
6	4	1	2.9934	0.98874	0.005063	0.97886	0.99871
7	4	1	4.7368	0.98630	0.005633	0.97532	0.99740
8	4	1	6.8421	0.98110	0.006749	0.96796	0.99442
9	4	1	7.2697	0.97846	0.007262	0.96433	0.99280
10	4	1	8.0921	0.97577	0.007762	0.96067	0.99110
11	4	1	8.4868	0.97306	0.008237	0.95705	0.98934
12	4	1	8.7500	0.97031	0.008699	0.95341	0.98752
13	4	1	8.9145	0.96753	0.009152	0.94976	0.98564
14	4	1	8.9803	0.96476	0.009583	0.94616	0.98372
15	4	1	9.0132	0.96198	0.009997	0.94259	0.98178
16	4	1	10.0987	0.95906	0.010435	0.93883	0.97974
17	4	1	10.3947	0.95608	0.010871	0.93501	0.97763
18	4	1	10.7895	0.95308	0.011297	0.93119	0.97548
19	4	1	11.6118	0.94995	0.011740	0.92722	0.97324
20	4	1	11.6776	0.94683	0.012169	0.92327	0.97098
68	4.0	1	34.5395	0.71789	0.03526	0.65200	0.79044
69	4.0	1	35.6250	0.71084	0.03592	0.64382	0.78483
70	4.0	1	36.0197	0.70371	0.03657	0.63557	0.77916
71	4.0	1	36.2171	0.69649	0.03722	0.62722	0.77341
72	4.0	1	37.1711	0.68827	0.03806	0.61756	0.76706
73	4.0	1	37.7961	0.67992	0.03889	0.60782	0.76058
74	4.0	1	39.0789	0.67134	0.03973	0.59781	0.75391
75	4.0	1	40.6250	0.66209	0.04068	0.58697	0.74683
76	4.0	1	41.2171	0.65281	0.04160	0.57616	0.73966
77	4.0	1	42.9934	0.64317	0.04256	0.56493	0.73223
78	4.0	1	48.8487	0.63029	0.04428	0.54920	0.72334
79	4.0	1	48.9474	0.61726	0.04589	0.53357	0.71408
80	4.0	1	50.6908	0.60302	0.04779	0.51627	0.70436
81	4.0	1	50.8224	0.58898	0.04947	0.49958	0.69437
82	4.0	1	66.2500	0.55847	0.05672	0.45766	0.68147
83	4.0	1	67.0066	0.52732	0.06304	0.41717	0.66656
84	4.0	1	68.0921	0.49508	0.06823	0.37789	0.64860
85	4.0	1	71.1513	0.46033	0.07346	0.33670	0.62936
86	4.0	1	74.7368	0.41433	0.08060	0.28298	0.60664
87	4.0	1	83.5526	0.32314	0.10547	0.17044	0.61264
88	0.3	0	0.0000	1.00000	.	.	.
89	0.3	0	1.1513	0.99968	0.00032	0.99905	1.00000
90	0.3	0	1.5789	0.99935	0.00047	0.99842	1.00000
91	0.3	0	2.0724	0.99901	0.00060	0.99784	1.00000
92	0.3	0	2.4013	0.99867	0.00071	0.99728	1.00000
93	0.3	0	2.9934	0.99832	0.00081	0.99674	0.99990
94	0.3	0	4.7368	0.99795	0.00091	0.99617	0.99973
95	0.3	0	6.8421	0.99717	0.00112	0.99498	0.99936
96	0.3	0	7.2697	0.99677	0.00122	0.99439	0.99916
97	0.3	0	8.0921	0.99636	0.00132	0.99378	0.99894
98	0.3	0	8.4868	0.99595	0.00141	0.99318	0.99872
99	0.3	0	8.7500	0.99553	0.00151	0.99258	0.99849
100	0.3	0	8.9145	0.99511	0.00161	0.99196	0.99826
101	0.3	0	8.9803	0.99468	.001699833	0.99135	0.99802
102	0.3	0	9.0132	0.99425	.001792219	0.99075	0.99777
103	0.3	0	10.0987	0.99381	.001890598	0.99011	0.99752
104	0.3	0	10.3947	0.99335	.001989749	0.98945	0.99725
105	0.3	0	10.7895	0.99288	.002088989	0.98880	0.99698
106	0.3	0	11.6118	0.99240	.002192475	0.98811	0.99670
107	0.3	0	11.6776	0.99191	.002294851	0.98742	0.99642
108	0.3	0	11.7763	0.99142	.002396253	0.98674	0.99613
156	0.3	0	35.6250	0.95053	0.009979	0.93117	0.97029
157	0.3	0	36.0197	0.94910	0.010233	0.92926	0.96937
158	0.3	0	36.2171	0.94765	0.010494	0.92730	0.96844
159	0.3	0	37.1711	0.94598	0.010776	0.92509	0.96734
160	0.3	0	37.7961	0.94426	0.011064	0.92283	0.96620
161	0.3	0	39.0789	0.94248	0.011367	0.92046	0.96503
162	0.3	0	40.6250	0.94054	0.011704	0.91788	0.96376
163	0.3	0	41.2171	0.93857	0.012043	0.91526	0.96247
164	0.3	0	42.9934	0.93649	0.012401	0.91250	0.96112
165	0.3	0	48.8487	0.93368	0.012942	0.90866	0.95940

Output 4.7 (continued)

166	0.3	0	48.9474	0.93079	0.013479	0.90474	0.95759
167	0.3	0	50.6908	0.92757	0.014090	0.90036	0.95560
168	0.3	0	50.8224	0.92432	0.014682	0.89599	0.95355
169	0.3	0	66.2500	0.91704	0.016761	0.88477	0.95049
170	0.3	0	67.0066	0.90925	0.018857	0.87303	0.94697
171	0.3	0	68.0921	0.90076	0.020962	0.86060	0.94280
172	0.3	0	71.1513	0.89107	0.023384	0.84640	0.93810
173	0.3	0	74.7368	0.87723	0.027171	0.82556	0.93214
174	0.3	0	83.5526	0.84541	0.040897	0.76893	0.92949
175	4.0	0	0.0000	1.00000	.	.	.
176	4.0	0	1.1513	0.99940	0.000609	0.99821	1.00000
177	4.0	0	1.5789	0.99877	0.000891	0.99703	1.00000
178	4.0	0	2.0724	0.99813	0.001120	0.99594	1.00000
179	4.0	0	2.4013	0.99749	0.001322	0.99490	1.00000
180	4.0	0	2.9934	0.99683	0.001509	0.99388	0.99980
181	4.0	0	4.7368	0.99615	0.001699	0.99282	0.99948
182	4.0	0	6.8421	0.99467	0.002083	0.99060	0.99876
183	4.0	0	7.2697	0.99392	0.002266	0.98949	0.99838
184	4.0	0	8.0921	0.99316	0.002448	0.98837	0.99797
185	4.0	0	8.4868	0.99239	0.002625	0.98725	0.99754
186	4.0	0	8.7500	0.99160	0.002801	0.98613	0.99711
187	4.0	0	8.9145	0.99080	0.002976	0.98499	0.99665
188	4.0	0	8.9803	0.99001	0.003146	0.98386	0.99619
189	4.0	0	9.0132	0.98921	0.003313	0.98274	0.99573
190	4.0	0	10.0987	0.98837	0.003491	0.98155	0.99523
191	4.0	0	10.3947	0.98751	0.003669	0.98034	0.99473
192	4.0	0	10.7895	0.98664	0.003850	0.97912	0.99421
193	4.0	0	11.6118	0.98573	0.004041	0.97784	0.99368
194	4.0	0	11.6776	0.98482	0.004229	0.97657	0.99315
242	4	0	34.5395	0.91140	0.017399	0.87793	0.94615
243	4	0	35.6250	0.90889	0.017827	0.87461	0.94451
244	4	0	36.0197	0.90633	0.018258	0.87124	0.94283
245	4	0	36.2171	0.90371	0.018697	0.86780	0.94111
246	4	0	37.1711	0.90072	0.019240	0.86378	0.93923
247	4	0	37.7961	0.89765	0.019793	0.85968	0.93729
248	4	0	39.0789	0.89446	0.020371	0.85541	0.93529
249	4	0	40.6250	0.89100	0.021010	0.85075	0.93314
250	4	0	41.2171	0.88748	0.021650	0.84605	0.93094
251	4.00000	0.00000	42.9934	0.88379	0.022322	0.84111	0.92864
252	4.00000	0.00000	48.8487	0.87880	0.023316	0.83427	0.92571
253	4.00000	0.00000	48.9474	0.87368	0.024297	0.82733	0.92262
254	4.00000	0.00000	50.6908	0.86799	0.025403	0.81960	0.91924
255	4.00000	0.00000	50.8224	0.86228	0.026469	0.81194	0.91576
256	4.00000	0.00000	66.2500	0.84954	0.030216	0.79234	0.91088
257	4.00000	0.00000	67.0066	0.83600	0.033912	0.77211	0.90518
258	4.00000	0.00000	68.0921	0.82137	0.037548	0.75098	0.89836
259	4.00000	0.00000	71.1513	0.80481	0.041638	0.72720	0.89070
260	4.00000	0.00000	74.7368	0.78144	0.047933	0.69292	0.88126
261	4.00000	0.00000	83.5526	0.72892	0.068704	0.60596	0.87681

4.15.3 Graphs of the Estimated Survival Functions - The Macro PHPLOT

While output such as this provides information about the estimated survival functions for patients with particular covariate values, you would probably like to see this displayed graphically as well. The macro PHPLOT, which is patterned after KMPLOT in Chapter 2, provides graphs of the model-based estimated survival functions. Before using this macro, you should have run PROC PHREG with a BASELINE statement to produce the survival function estimates as described in Section 4.15.1. You must also must add a numeric variable taking on the value 1, 2, 3, . . . etc., to represent the distinct covariate vectors used in the Covariates data set. You might also want to provide a label for this variable and a format for its values. This is illustrated in the following example:

```
proc format;
    value c 1 = 'Low' 2 = 'Intermediate' 3 = 'High';
    proc sort data = estsurv;
    by thickness ulcer;
```

```
data estsurv;
    set estsurv;
    by thickness ulcer months;
    retain c 0;
    if first.ulcer then c+1;
    format c c. ;
label c = 'Risk';
```

Now the macro PHPLOT can be invoked. The following template can be used.

```
%phplot(data=      /*Name of data set to be used.  Default is
                     last */
,ci=               /*Put confidence intervals on the graphs
                     (yes/no).
                     Default is no */
,yvar=             /*Variable name associated with keyword
                     survival of statement */
,ylabel=           /*Label for vertical axis.  Default is Pct
                     Survival */
,byvar=            /*Variable used to distinguish covariate
                     vectors */
,xvar=             /*The time variable used in the proc statement.
                     The default is time */
,xlabel=           /*The label for the horizontal axis.  The
                     default is Time */
,combine=          /*yes to combine curves on one graph, no (the
                     default) to produce separate graphs for each
                     curve.  If curves are combined on one graph,
                     confidence intervals cannot be plotted. */
,title=            /*Title to be printed. Default is  Proportional
                     Hazards Survival Curve */
,lcl=              /*Variable name associated with lower keyword
                     in baseline statement. Default is lcl */
,ucl=              /*Variable name associated with upper  keyword
                     n baseline statement.  Default is ucl */
)
```

The following example of an invocation of the macro PHPLOT produced Figure 4.2:

```
%phplot(
       yvar=survival        /*Variable name associated with
                              keyword survival of baseline statement */
       ,ylabel=Pct Survival /*Label for vertical axis.  Default
                              is Pct Survival */
       ,byvar=c             /*Variable used to distinguish covariate
                              vectors */
       ,xvar=months         /*The time variable used in the proc
                              statement. The default is time */
       ,xlabel=Months       /*The label for the horizontal axis.  The
                              default is Time */
```

```
,combine = yes          /*yes to combine curves on one graph, no
                          (the default) to produce separate
                          graphs for each curve.  If curves
                          are combined on one graph, confidence
                          intervals can not be plotted. */
,title = Figure 4.2     /*Title to be printed. Default is
                          Proportional Hazards Survival Curve */
,lcl = lo_bound         /*Variable name associated with lower
                          keyword in baseline statement.  Default
                          is lcl */
,ucl = up_bound         /*Variable name associated with upper
                          keyword in baseline statement. Default
                          is ucl */
)
```

Figure 4.2

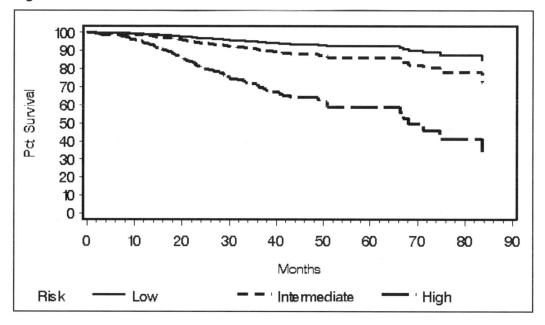

4.16 Residuals

Readers who are familiar with linear regression are probably also familiar with the use of residuals in that setting. For each observed value, y_i, of the dependent random variable, Y, the residual is the difference between y_i and its predicted value $\hat{y}_i$. By looking at these residuals, the adequacy of the model can be assessed and aberrant observations can be detected.

Defining residuals in Cox regression is not as straightforward. For one thing, we are not modeling the survival time, but instead are modeling the logarithm of the hazard. In addition, there is the problem of the censored observations. In spite of this (or perhaps because of this) there are several approaches to defining residuals in the context of Cox regression. PROC PHREG can produce martingale residuals, deviance residuals, Schoenfeld residuals, and score residuals. We will discuss only the first two of these.

Consider an observation of the form $(t_i, d_i, \mathbf{x}_i)$ where t_i is the time of observation, $d_i = 0$ for a censored observation and 1 for an uncensored observation, and $\mathbf{x}_i$ is a vector of covariates. Although residuals can be defined for time-dependent variables, we will deal only with covariates that are constant over time. The martingale residual is defined as $M_i = d_i - \hat{\Lambda}_0(t_i)\exp(\hat{\boldsymbol{\beta}}'\mathbf{x}_i)$ where $\hat{\Lambda}_0(t_i)$ is the estimated baseline cumulative hazard function. Thus the martingale residual is the difference between the actual number of deaths for this patient (of course, 0 or 1) and the cumulative hazard associated with that patient's covariate values. It can be shown that martingale residuals, asymptotically, are uncorrelated and have a mean of zero. This mimics desirable properties of residuals in linear regression. These residuals must be less than 1; however, they have no lower bound. Thus they are not symmetric about zero. In addition, a patient with high hazard could have negative residual with large absolute value, even if he dies on the study.

The deviance residual is defined as $D_i = \text{sign}(M_i)\sqrt{2[-M_i - d_i\log(d_i - M_i)]}$ where M_i is the martingale residual defined earlier and $\text{sign}(M_i)$ is 1 if M_i is positive and -1 if it is negative. It's probably not obvious, but this formula will increase the values of positive martingale residuals and bring negative ones closer to zero. The result will be to produce residuals that are reasonably symmetric if the proportional hazards property holds.

4.16.1 Producing Residuals with PROC PHREG

By using the OUTPUT statement you can use PROC PHREG to produce residuals, and many other useful statistics. This statement takes the following form:

    OUTPUT OUT = datasetname keyword1 = varname keyword2 = varname . . . ;

The OUT = *datasetname* is optional. If you leave it out, the DATAn convention is applied. The keywords are the statistics that you want to include in this data set, and the variable names that you want to use for them are on the right sides of the equal signs. Among the keywords you can use are RESMART for martingale residuals, RESDEV for deviance residuals, RESSCH for Schoenfeld residuals, RESSCO for score residuals, and XBETA for the value of the linear combination, $\hat{\boldsymbol{\beta}}'\mathbf{x}$. The time variable, censoring variable, covariates, and any stratification, FREQ, and BY variables are automatically included. It is useful to view the relationship of the residuals to values of the covariates and $\hat{\boldsymbol{\beta}}'\mathbf{x}$ using PROC GPLOT.

4.16.2 Example

Consider Example 52.7 in the *SAS/STAT User's Guide Version 9*. Martingale and deviance residuals are calculated along with the statistics of the model for survival based on Logbun (the logarithm of blood urea nitrogen) and Hgb (serum hemoglobin). The graph of the deviance residuals vs $\hat{\boldsymbol{\beta}}'\mathbf{x}$ does not indicate any problem with the model. It would also be useful to plot the graph of these residuals vs Logbun and Hgb.

4.16.3 Exercises

Copy the example code from Example 52.7 in the *SAS/STAT User's Guide, Version 9* into your Program Editor. Then do the following:

a) Produce the graphs of the deviance residuals for this model vs Logbun and Hgb.

b) Write a SAS program to calculate the estimated cumulative hazard for each patient in this data set. Hint: Start with the output data set produced in this example and use the formula for martingale residuals in Section 4.16.

c) What if Bun (= exp(logbun)) were used in the model instead of Logbun? Re-do this example with Bun and Hgb.

d) Make up two artificial patients to add to this data set. One should be a high-risk patient who survives a long time. The other should be a low-risk patient who dies very quickly. See how these patients show up in the graphs of the deviance residuals.

4.17 Power and Sample Size

4.17.1 The Nature of the Problem

Turning to the issues of power and sample size, there are two related questions that can be asked.

1. How large a sample do I need to ensure a specified power for a test of a null hypothesis that one of the beta coefficients is zero?

2. Given a sample of a particular size, what is the power for the test of a null hypothesis that one of the beta coefficients is zero?

The first type of question should be answered when you are planning a study. The second is relevant when you are given an existing set of data to analyze. In particular, if you find that a beta coefficient estimate is not significantly different from zero, you might want to know if there was much probability of getting a significant result, even for meaningful values of the beta coefficient, with the available sample. The macro PHPOW described in the following section addresses both types of questions.

In thinking about the nature of the proportional hazards model, it is clear that a general approach to these problems is not practical. There are just too many sources of complexity. In order to say anything about power or sample size for the general model, you would need to specify the beta coefficients of all of the covariates. In addition, the joint distribution of the covariates in the population from which the sample is drawn would have to be specified. Finally, the underlying hazard function, $h_0(t)$ would affect the calculations as well.

4.17.2 The Method of Hsieh and Lavori

Hsieh and Lavori (2000), describe a sample size method for Cox regression with one nonbinary covariate, X. Without any assumptions on the distributions of the covariate X and survival time T, the total number of deaths required is shown to be

$$D = (z_{1-\alpha} + z_{1-\beta})^2 [\sigma^2 (\log\Delta)^2]^{-1} \tag{4.15}$$

where σ^2 is the variance of X and Δ is the hazard ratio for that covariate. $z_{1-\alpha}$ and $z_{1-\beta}$ are standard normal deviates at the desired significance level α and power $1-\beta$, respectively. The required sample size is then calculated by dividing the number of deaths by the overall proportion expected to die.

Now suppose we are performing a proportional hazards regression with k covariates $X_1, X_2, \ldots, X_k$. Generally, our main interest will be on the significance of each of these covariates in the model containing the others. Unless these covariates are independent, the sample size needed to achieve a specified power for one of them is altered by the inclusion of the others in the model. In fact, it is increased. Hsieh and Lavori suggest that the number of deaths, and hence the sample size, needed can be found by considering the result without taking the other covariates into consideration and then multiplying by the factor $1/(1 - R^2)$ where R is the multiple correlation coefficient of the variable of interest with the other variables in the model. For example, if we are estimating the sample size needed to have adequate power for a test of the covariate X_1, and we assume that the multiple correlation coefficient of X_1 with the other variables in the model is 0.5, we would multiply the sample size found as described in the following section by $1/(1 - .25) = 1.33$.

4.17.3 The PHPOW Macro

Now suppose a study is designed to accrue patients at rate r for time T and then to follow them for additional time τ. Suppose the baseline survival function (the survival function when X equals its mean value) is $S_0(t)$ and that the study's planner is willing to assume proportional hazards with a hazard ratio of $\Delta \neq 1$ for X as the alternative to the null hypothesis that $\Delta = 1$. The probability of death on the study for a patient with X = x and who enters the study at time t in [0, T] is $1 - [S_0(T + \tau - t)]^{\Delta^x}$. Here we assume, without loss of generality, that the mean of X is zero. If we assume that accrual is uniform in [0,T] and that X has density function f(x), the probability of death for a patient on the trial is given by

$$\frac{1}{T}\int_{t=0}^{T}\int_{x=-\infty}^{\infty} f(x)\{1-[S_0(T+\tau-t)]^{\Delta^x}\}dxdt \quad \text{which can be written as}$$

$$\frac{1}{T}\int_{t=\tau}^{T+\tau}\int_{x=-\infty}^{\infty} f(x)\{1-[S_0(t)]^{\Delta^x}\}dxdt. \quad \text{The expected number of deaths is then}$$

$$\frac{N}{T}\int_{t=\tau}^{T+\tau}\int_{x=-\infty}^{\infty} f(x)\{1-[S_0(t)]^{\Delta^x}\}dxdt \quad \text{where N = rT, the sample size. Replacing the left side of the Lavori/Hsieh equation by this final result, we get}$$

$$\frac{N}{T}\int_{t=\tau}^{T+\tau}\int_{x=-\infty}^{\infty} f(x)\{1-[S_0(t)]^{\Delta^x}\}dxdt = (z_{1-\alpha} + z_{1-\beta})^2[\sigma^2(\log\Delta)^2]^{-1}.$$

Taking $f(x)$ to be the normal density with variance σ^2 and mean zero, we can, at least in theory, solve for any of the parameters given the others and an assumed baseline survival function. In particular, we can find the sample size, N, needed to achieve a given power or the power for a given sample size given values of the other parameters. The macro PHPOW uses the module Quad in PROC IML to perform the indicated double integral and thus accomplish these calculations. You need to license SAS/IML software to use it.

Use the following syntax to invoke the macro PHPOW:

%PHPOW (T = *value*, TAU = *value*, ALPHA = *value*, N = *value*,
    POWER = *value*, VAR = *value*, DELTA = *value*, S0 = *value*);

where

T	specifies the accrual time,
TAU	specifies the follow-up time,
ALPHA	specifies the significance level, the default is .05,
N	specifies the sample size,
POWER	specifies the power,
VAR	specifies the variance of the covariate,
DELTA	specifies the hazard ratio,
S0	specifies the baseline survival function. It should be a function of the variable, time.

Either *n* or *power* must be omitted from the macro call or given the missing value ".". The macro will calculate the value of the missing parameter.

An example shows how the macro works. Suppose that we are planning a study of the effect of a variable, X, which has variance one, on survival. We feel that it is reasonable to assume that, for any particular value of X, survival will be exponential and that an average patient (i.e., with a mean value of X) will have median survival of about 1.75 years. This implies a constant hazard of about 0.4. We will be testing the hazard ratio for X at a two-sided significance level of 0.05, and we plan to accrue 100 patients over three years and to follow them for an additional year. We would like to estimate the power of this study if the hazard ratio is 1.5. The statement

```
%phpow (T = 3, tau = 1, n = 100, var = 1, delta = 1.5,
        s0 = exp(-.4*time))
```

can be invoked to calculate power. The SAS output will look like this:

Output 4.8

```
                Power and Sample Size Results

Alpha    =       0.05

Hazard Ratio  =        1.5

Accrual Time  =        3

Followup Time  =        1

Covariate Variance  =        1

Sample Size  =       100

Power(Calculated)  =       0.88
```

If we specify the power, say 90%, the following statement can be used to calculate the required sample size:

```
%phpow ( t = 3, tau = 1, power = .9, var = 1, delta = 1.5,
         s0 = exp(-.4*time));
```

The output follows:

Output 4.9

```
                 Power and Sample Size Results

Alpha    =      0.05

Hazard Ratio   =        1.5

Accrual Time   =        3

Followup Time  =        1

Covariate Variance   =        1

Power  =      0.9

Sample Size (Calculated)   =        105
```

Note that nothing about this method or the macro requires that the baseline survival distribution be exponential. For example, we might feel that the "average" patient has a 30% chance of being cured and that the noncured patients have exponential survival with a median survival of 1.75 years. In that case the baseline survival function would be given by `s0 = .3 + .7*exp(-.4*time)`.

4.17.4 Exercise
Re-do the previous example to calculate the sample size needed if 20% of the patients are cured, the others have exponential survival, and the median survival of all patients is 1.75 years. What does this suggest about the effect of a nonzero cure rate on the sample size needed for a proportional hazards analysis? Hint: First you will need to solve $.5 = .2 + .8\exp(-1.75\lambda)$ for λ. Use the resulting expression as the value of `s0`.

4.18 Imputing Missing Values

We spoke earlier of the problem posed by missing data. PROC PHREG excludes any cases for which any of the covariates is missing. Now you might feel that this approach wastes a lot of useful information. It's tempting to think about somehow replacing a missing value with some nonmissing value so that the observation is not lost completely. A lot of work has been done to show that, if done carefully with consideration of the effect such imputations on the uncertainty of the result, such efforts can be useful.

4.18.1 PROC MI and PROC MIANALYZE
SAS PROC MI, (which stands for multiple imputation) and PROC MIANALYZE can be used together to implement one method of dealing with missing data. PROC MI starts with a data set that has some values of specified variables missing. It then creates a data set consisting of several (the default number is five) replicates of the original data set with the missing values replaced by imputed

values. These imputed values are chosen randomly to be consistent with the structure seen in the nonmissing data. Each replicate is distinguished by a distinct value of the variable _IMPUTATION_, which is added to the data set. You can then perform PROC PHREG by _IMPUTATION_, using the OUTEST statement with the COVOUT option to create an output data set containing the parameter estimates and their estimated covariance matrices for each value of _IMPUTATION_. PROC MIANALYZE can then be used to generate estimates of the parameters and their standard errors.

Here's an example of how these two procedures can be used with PROC PHREG. Consider a data set with two covariates, x1 and x2, a time variable, Time, and an event variable, Cens, which takes on the values 0 and 1 for censored and complete observations respectively.

```
proc mi data = dataset out = imputations noprint;
var x1 x2;
run;
```

This code starts with the data set named Dataset that presumably has some values of x1 and x2 missing. It creates a data set consisting of five replicates of the original data set. The NOPRINT option is used because we do not need to have the details printed. A variable, _REPLICATE_, is added to this data set. We follow this by

```
proc phreg outest = out covout noprint;
model time*cens(0) = x1 x2;
by _imputation_;
```

This code performs PROC PHREG on each of the five replicates of the original data set with the missing values replaced by imputed values. The use of OUTEST = OUT COVOUT creates a data set which is used by PROC MIANALYZE. We then use these statements.

```
proc mianalyze data = out;
var x1 x2;
run;
```

Here's an example of part of the output.

Output 4.10

```
          Multiple Imputation Parameter Estimates

Parameter      Estimate      Std Error    95% Confidence Limits      DF

x1             0.219244      0.134968     -0.07327   0.511759 12.604
x2             0.319188      0.097486      0.12328   0.515098 48.961

          Multiple Imputation Parameter Estimates

          Parameter        Minimum        Maximum

          x1              0.072097       0.313587
          x2              0.283353       0.389769

          Multiple Imputation Parameter Estimates

                                        t for H0:
          Parameter      Theta0    Parameter=Theta0   Pr > |t|

          x1               0             1.62          0.1290
          x2               0             3.27          0.0019
```

Using the five data sets with imputed values, we obtain estimates of .219244 and .319188 for the Cox regression parameters of x1 and x2. The standard errors are computed using the within-imputation and between-imputation variances and are used to compute 95% confidence intervals and for the significance tests. Both are based on the fact that these estimates can be shown to have approximate *t* distributions, with the degrees of freedom given in the output.

4.18.2 Exercise

Apply PROC MI and PROC MIANALYZE to the data set associated with this exercise containing data and macros in this book by imputing values for the missing values of x1 and x2. (The example code and data sets can be found on the companion Web site for this book.) Print out the data set as well as the derived data set containing the imputed values. Print the data set produced by the OUTEST option. Find the mean of the parameters found for the five replicates of the original data set and compare that to the results of PROC MIANALYZE.

4.19 Listings of Macros

4.19.1 The PHPLOT Macro

```
%macro phplot(data =      , ci=no, yvar=survival,
              ylabel=Pct Survival, byvar= none,
              xvar=time,xlabel=Time,combine=no,
              title=Proportional Hazards Survival Curve,
              lcl=lcl, ucl = ucl );

/* Symbol statements for up to 4 curves on one graph */

%if &combine=yes %then %do;
    %let ci=no;
        symbol1 l=1  v=none  i=stepjl w=5;
        symbol2 l=3 v=none i=stepjl w=5;
        symbol3 l=5 v=none i=stepjl w=5;
        symbol4 l=33 v=none i=stepjl w=5;
        %end;

/* Symbol Statements for separate graphs */

%if &combine=no %then %do;
        symbol1 l=1  v= none i=stepjl w=5;
        symbol2 l=3 v=none i=stepjl w=5;
        symbol3 l=3 v=none i=stepjl w=5;
        %end;

%if &byvar=none %then goptions cby=white;
data;
    set &data;
    survival=&yvar*100;
    lcl=100*&lcl;
    ucl=100*&ucl;
    y=survival;
    curve=1;
    output;
    y=ucl;
    curve=2;
    %if &ci=yes %then output;
    y=lcl;
    curve=3;
    %if &ci=yes %then output;
proc sort;
    by &byvar curve &xvar;
run;
```

```
proc format;
value curve 1='PH curve'
               2='UCL'
               3='LCL';
axis1 width=5 minor=none label=(h=2 f=swiss a=90 j=center
"&ylabel")value=(h=1.5 f=swiss) order=(0 to 100 by 10);
axis2 width=5 label=(h=2 f=swiss  "&xlabel") value=(h=1.5
f=swiss);
%if &combine=no %then legend1 label=(f=swiss h=1.5  'Curve')
                                value=(f=swiss h=1.5 j=l
                                'PH Curve' "UCL" "LCL");
legend2 label=(f=swiss h=1.5) value=(f=swiss h=1.5 j=l);

/* PROC GPLOT for separate graphs */
%if &combine=no %then %do;
        proc gplot;
        plot y*&xvar= curve /
        legend=legend1
        vaxis=axis1 haxis=axis2
        %if &ci=no %then nolegend;;
        ;
        by &byvar;
        format curve curve.;
        %end;

/* PROC GPLOT for combined graphs */

%if &combine=yes %then %do;
    proc gplot;
        plot y*&xvar=&byvar/ legend=legend2
        vaxis=axis1 haxis=axis2;
        %end;
title &title;
run;
%mend phplot;
```

4.19.2 *The PHPOW Macro*

```
%macro phpow(t = , tau = , alpha = .05, n = ., power = ., var = ,
delta = , s0 = );

/*This is a SAS macro for calculating power and sample size. It is
based on Hsieh and Lavori (2000), Controlled Clinical Trials, 21: 552-
560*/

proc iml;
file print;
title 'Power and Sample Size Results';

 /*The inner integrand is calculated*/

    start integrand(time) global(yv,delta,var);
        pi = 4*atan(1);
        part1 = 1/sqrt(2*pi*var)*exp(-yv**2/(2*var));
      part2 = 1 - (&s0)**(delta**yv);
        p = part1*part2;
      return(p);
    finish;

 /*The inner integral is calculated*/

    start marginal(v) global(yv,t, tau );
    tt = t;
    ttau = tau;
    upper = tt + ttau;
        interval = ttau||upper;
     yv = v;
     call quad(pm,"integrand",interval);
```

```
      return(pm);
      finish;

   /*The outer integral and probability of death are calculated*/

   start outer(tt,ttau,  svar, ddelta) global( t, tau, var, delta );
      t = tt;
      tau = ttau;
      var = svar;
      delta = ddelta;
      interval= .M ||.P;
      call quad(per,"MARGINAL",interval);
      prob_d = per/t;
      return(prob_d);
      finish;
      prob_d =  outer(&t, &tau,  &var, &delta);

   /* Power is calculated if it is missing */

      %if &power = . %then %do;
      deaths = prob_d*&n;
      zpower = sqrt(&var)*abs(log(&delta))*sqrt(deaths)-
      probit(1 - &alpha/2);
      power_calculated = round(probnorm(zpower), .1);
      sample_size = &n;
      %end;

   /* Sample size is calculated if it is missing */

      %else %do;
      zpower = probit(&power);
      deaths =
      (zpower+probit(1-&alpha/2))**2/(abs(log(&delta)))**2/&var;
      sample_size_calculated = round(deaths/prob_d, 1);
      power = &power;
      %end;

   /*Output results*/

      Alpha = &alpha;
      hazard_ratio = &delta;
      accrual_time = &t;
      followup_time = &tau;
      covariate_variance = &var;
      baseline_survival = "&s0";
      put 'Alpha    ='alpha;
      put;
      put 'Hazard Ratio   ='hazard_ratio;
      put;
      put 'Accrual Time   ='accrual_time;
      put;
      put 'Followup Time   ='followup_time;
      put;
      put 'Covariate Variance   ='covariate_variance;
      put;
      put 'Baseline Survival = 'baseline_survival;
      put;
      %if &power=. %then %do;
      put 'Sample Size   =' sample_size;
      put;
      put 'Power(Calculated)   ='power_calculated;
      put;
      %end;
      %else %do;
      put 'Power   ='power;
      put;
      put 'Sample Size (Calculated)   =' sample_size_calculated;
      %end;
      run;
   %mend;
```

Chapter 5   Parametric Methods

5.1	Introduction	153
5.2	The Accelerated Failure Time Model	155
5.3	PROC LIFEREG	156
5.4	Example Using PROC LIFEREG	156
5.5	Comparison of Models	159
5.6	Estimates of Quantiles and Survival Probabilities	160
5.7	The PROC LIFEREG Parameters and the "Standard" Parameters	163
5.8	The Macro PARAMEST	163
5.9	Example Using the Macro PARAMEST	166
5.10	An Example with a Positive Cure Rate	169
5.11	Comparison of Groups	173
5.12	One-Sample Tests of Parameters	176
5.13	The Effects of Covariates on Parameters	176
5.14	Complex Expressions for the Survival and Hazard Functions	179
5.15	Graphical Checks for Certain Survival Distributions	179
5.16	A Macro for Fitting Parametric Models to Survival Data	180
5.17	Other Estimates of Interest	183
5.18	Listings of Macros	183

5.1 Introduction

This chapter brings to a logical conclusion a process that was begun in Chapter 2. That chapter and Chapter 3 introduced you to methods of survival analysis that made no assumptions about the underlying survival distribution(s). Such methods are said to be non-parametric. Chapter 4 made certain assumptions about the nature of the hazard function for the proportional hazards regression method. Since the underlying hazard is left unspecified, this method is called semiparametric. This chapter takes the next step. It will be assumed that the survival function is of a certain form, such as exponential, Weibull, and so on, with one or more parameters whose values are unknown. The idea, of course, is to estimate those values from a set of survival data. These estimates, then, complete the specification of the survival function.

The chapter presents two approaches to this problem. The first uses PROC LIFEREG. This procedure is based on a model known as the accelerated failure time model. It allows for the specification of a vector of covariates and provides information about the effect of these covariates on survival times. In this sense it resembles PROC PHREG, which was discussed in Chapter 4. You will see, however, that the effect of a covariate in this model is quite different from that of the proportional hazards model. PROC LIFEREG requires the assumption of one of five types of survival functions. The second approach uses a macro, PARAMEST, which will be described later in this chapter. This macro allows you to specify any survival function with any number of parameters. Estimates of the values of the parameters are produced. Explanatory covariates are permitted by this macro as well. Using PARAMEST is a bit more difficult than using PROC LIFEREG. It is necessary to specify both the survival distribution and the hazard function as functions of the covariates and time, with parameters whose values are not known. In addition, using this macro requires more computer time. However, it does permit greater flexibility in specifying the underlying distribution and the effects of the covariates.

Both of these parametric approaches have an important feature not found in the methods presented previously. They both allow for right-censored, left-censored, or interval-censored data. A survival time is left censored if what is known about it is that it is no more than a value, t. A survival time is interval censored if what is known about it is that it is at least some value, say t_1, and less than some greater value, t_2.

Interval censoring is fairly common. If patients are followed periodically for recurrence of disease, one might be disease free when checked at time t_1 but have the disease when checked at a later time t_2. If you don't know when the disease recurred, but only that it was between t_1 and t_2, then the recurrence time is interval censored by the interval (t_1, t_2). When using methods that do not allow for interval censoring, analysts generally define the event time to be the time at which the event was first observed, that is t_2. A consequence of this is that one investigator checking for the event annually, will, all other factors being equal, tend to report longer times than another investigator checking for the event every six months. The ability to deal with interval censoring is an important feature of the methods of this chapter.

Left censoring is less common. In the situation we just discussed, a patient found to have recurred at the time of his or her first follow-up visit would be left censored. Of course, left censoring can be thought as interval censoring with the left endpoint of the censoring interval being zero. In order for PROC LIFEREG *or* the macro PARAMEST to deal with these forms of censoring, the data set must convey the necessary information. This is accomplished by having two time variables in the data set, say t_1 and t_2. The roles of t_1 and t_2 are described as follows:

If . . .	Then . . .
t_2 is a missing value	t_1 is considered a right-censored time
t_1 is a missing value	t_2 is considered a left-censored time
neither t_1 nor t_2 is a missing value and if $t_1 < t_2$	time is considered censored in the interval (t_1, t_2)
$t_1 = t_2$ and if t_1 is not a missing value	time is complete with the common value

Consider, for example, the following data:

PatId	t1	t2
1	.	7.8
2	2.3	5.9
3	4.6	.
4	7.3	7.3

Patient #1 had the event occur sometime prior to time 7.8. Patient #2 had the event occur between times 2.3 and 5.9. Patient #3 was last observed and event-free at time 4.6. Patient #4 had the event occur at time 7.3. The fact that the form of the survival function is specified allows us to accommodate these forms of censoring.

5.2 The Accelerated Failure Time Model

You are probably already familiar with the linear regression model presented in most elementary statistics texts. The basic assumption is that a dependent variable, y, is related to a set of independent variables, $x_1, x_2, \ldots, x_k$ by a relationship of the form

$y = \beta_0 + \beta_1 x_1 + \ldots + \beta_k x_k + \sigma\varepsilon$ where $\beta_0, \beta_1, \ldots, \beta_k$ are unknown regression coefficients, ε is random variable having a standard normal distribution, and σ is a positive number. You might wonder whether this approach would work with y replaced by survival time. That could be done. But since survival time cannot be negative, it is more common to use the natural logarithm of the survival time as the dependent variable. Also, in addition to the standard normal distribution, the random variable ε can be assumed to have other distributions as well. Of course the distribution chosen for ε determines the distribution of survival time. In the following discussion, T represents the random survival time, and Y its natural logarithm. Assume that, for each patient, k covariates, x_1, $x_2, \ldots, x_k$, are observed. Then the accelerated failure time model implies that for some set of coefficients $\beta_0, \beta_1, \ldots, \beta_k$, random variable, ε, and positive number, σ, we have

$$Y = \beta_0 + \beta_1 x_1 \cdots \beta_k x_k + \sigma\varepsilon$$

or equivalently   (5.1)

$$T = \exp(\beta_0 + \beta_1 x_1 + \ldots \beta_k x_k + \sigma\varepsilon)$$

The parameters β_0 and σ are called the intercept and scale parameters. The parameters $\beta_1, \ldots, \beta_k$ describe the way that survival time is affected by the values of the covariates. A value of zero for one of these coefficients implies that its associated covariate has no effect. A positive value means that an increase in the value of the associated covariate leads to an increase in survival time, i.e., that larger values of the covariate are better. A negative coefficient means that an increase in the value of the associated covariate leads to lesser times, i.e., that larger values of the covariate are worse. Note that this is the opposite of the situation for the regression coefficients in the proportional hazards model. But the difference between these models goes beyond this. Remember that in the proportional hazards model we are modeling the effect of a covariate on the hazard function. In the accelerated failure time model we are modeling the effect of a covariate on the survival times themselves.

Consider a covariate x which has the value 0 for the standard treatment and 1 for the experimental treatment. Suppose that in the model given by (5.1) its coefficient is 0.5. By (5.1) that means that the logarithm of the survival time is increased by 0.5 for the experimental treatment. Equivalently, the survival times for that treatment are $\exp(0.5)$, or about 1.65, times the survival times for the standard treatment. If the median survival time for the standard treatment is three years, then the median survival time for the experimental treatment is 3 times 1.65 or 4.95 years. Similar statements can be made for other percentiles.

5.2.1 Exercise

Suppose that ε is a random variable whose distribution is exponential with hazard = 1. Let β_0 and σ be constants with $\sigma > 0$. Show that $\exp[\beta_0 + \sigma\log(\varepsilon)]$ has a Weibull distribution. We usually write the Weibull survival function as $S(t) = \exp(-\lambda t^\gamma)$. Express λ and γ in terms of β and σ. For what restriction on these parameters do we get an exponential distribution? (Hint: if $T = \exp[\beta_0 + \sigma\log(\varepsilon)]$, then $\Pr[T > t] = \Pr[\beta_0 + \sigma\log(\varepsilon) > \log(t)] = \Pr[\varepsilon > \ \ ???] = ???$ Now use the survival function of ε to write the survival function of T.)

5.3 PROC LIFEREG

PROC LIFEREG uses syntax very much like that of PROC PHREG. After the PROC statement

```
proc lifereg;
```

you need a MODEL statement. This statement can take one of three forms. The first, which can be used if there is no left or interval censoring, is the same as that of PROC PHREG except for the optional specification of a distribution function.

```
MODEL TIMEVAR*CENSVAR(CENSVALS) = covariates / D = distribution;
```

Here Timevar is the time variable, Censvar is the variable that tells whether the time is right censored or not, Censvals is a list of values of Censvar that indicate that the time is right censored, and Covariates is the list of covariates to be considered in the model. You specify the type of distribution for the time variable after the slash. The permissible choices are exponential, Weibull, gamma, lognormal, and loglogistic. Weibull is the default. Section 5.15 discusses some considerations that may help to make that choice. If you want to allow for left and interval censoring, then change the MODEL statement as follows:

```
MODEL (TIMELO, TIMEHI) = covariates / D = distribution;
```

Here Timelo and Timehi are time variables as described in Section 5.1. If Timelo is missing, then Timehi is considered a left-censored time. If Timehi is missing, then Timelo is considered a right-censored time. If neither is missing and Timelo < Timehi, then the time is interval censored in the interval (Timelo, Timehi). If both are equal and not missing, then the time is uncensored at their common value.

There is a third form of the MODEL statement that is not generally used in survival analyses and will not be discussed here. In both of the statements shown here, the covariates can be omitted. In that case only the intercept, scale parameter, and, if gamma is chosen as the distribution for ε, a shape parameter, will be estimated.

PROC LIFEREG has no provision for specifying a method of entering or dropping covariates. You can, however, try several different models in the same SAS session by using several different MODEL statements. These models may differ in the distribution as well as the covariates used. This permits you to perform various significance tests "by hand," as shown in the next example.

5.4 Example Using PROC LIFEREG

Let's reconsider the melanoma example discussed in the previous chapter. Patients with melanoma had their tumors removed surgically and were followed for relapse. Among the tumor characteristics that were studied for their effect on relapse time were the Clark and Breslow scores of the tumor. The following statements can be used to study the effect of these scores in models based on exponential, Weibull, and gamma distribution for the time to recurrence.

```
proc lifereg;
    model dfstime*dfscens(0) = clark breslow / d = exponential;
    model dfstime*dfscens(0) = clark breslow;
    model dfstime*dfscens(0) = clark breslow / d = gamma;
    run;
```

The output is printed below.

Output 5.1

```
                        The SAS System

                      Lifereg  Procedure

Data Set          =WORK.MELANOMA
Dependent Variable=Log(DFSTIME)
Censoring Variable=DFSCENS
Censoring Value(s)=     0
Noncensored Values=  275  Right Censored Values=   1010
Left Censored Values=   0  Interval Censored Values=   0
Observations with Missing Values=  98
Observations with Zero or Negative Response=  13


❼ Log Likelihood for EXPONENT -742.4698271
                        The SAS System

                      Lifereg  Procedure
                                ❸            ❹
Variable  DF   Estimate  Std Err  ChiSquare  Pr>Chi Label/Value

 INTERCPT  1  6.49733516 0.326373  396.3168  0.0001 Intercept
 CLARK  ❷  1 -0.3926619 0.098908  15.76055  0.0001       ❶
 BRESLOW   1 -0.2067146 0.038011  29.57444  0.0001
❺ SCALE    0      1        0                        Extreme value

Lagrange Multiplier ChiSquare for Scale 32.45002 Pr>Chi is 0.0001.



                        The SAS System

                      Lifereg  Procedure

Data Set          =WORK.MELANOMA
Dependent Variable=Log(DFSTIME)
Censoring Variable=DFSCENS
Censoring Value(s)=     0
Noncensored Values=  275  Right Censored Values=   1010
Left Censored Values=   0  Interval Censored Values=   0
Observations with Missing Values=  98
Observations with Zero or Negative Response=  13


❼ Log Likelihood for WEIBULL  -731.757061

                        The SAS System




                      Lifereg  Procedure
                                ❸            ❹
Variable  DF   Estimate  Std Err  ChiSquare  Pr>Chi Label/Value

 INTERCPT  1  6.0917069 0.274405  492.8254  0.0001 Intercept
 CLARK  ❷  1 -0.3415831 0.080442  18.03111  0.0001       ❶
 BRESLOW   1 -0.1815029 0.030888  34.52837  0.0001
❻ SCALE    1  0.81100079 0.034685                   Extreme value
```

Output 5.1 (continued)

```
                      The SAS System

                  Lifereg  Procedure

Data Set          =WORK.MELANOMA
Dependent Variable=Log(DFSTIME)
Censoring Variable=DFSCENS
Censoring Value(s)=     0
Noncensored Values=  275  Right Censored Values=   1010
Left Censored Values=   0  Interval Censored Values=   0
Observations with Missing Values=  98
Observations with Zero or Negative Response=  13


❼ Log Likelihood for GAMMA -731.2938041

                      The SAS System

                  Lifereg  Procedure
                                   ❸        ❹
 Variable  DF   Estimate  Std Err ChiSquare  Pr>Chi Label/Value

 INTERCPT   1 6.07093664 0.277994  476.9152  0.0001 Intercept
 CLARK   ❷  1 -0.3429084 0.082103  17.44387  0.0001
 BRESLOW    1 -0.1884148 0.033395  31.83285  0.0001    ❶
 SCALE      1 0.88242566 0.082996                   Gamma scale p
❻ SHAPE      1 0.83733927 0.160552                   Gamma shape p
```

Note the following features of the output:

❶ In all of the models the effects of both Breslow and Clark score are highly significant.

❷ The fact the coefficients of both are negative is consistent with what was seen in the proportional hazards model of Chapter 4. Higher values of these covariates are associated with shorter recurrence times. Specifically, a coefficient of -0.34 for Clark score implies that for each unit increase in this score, recurrence times are reduced by being multiplied by exp(-0.34) = 0.71.

❸ Each chi square statistic is the square of the ratio of the estimate to its standard error.

❹ The *p*-value (Pr > Chi) is from a χ^2 distribution with one degree of freedom and is for a test that the associated parameter is zero. Both Clark and Breslow scores are significantly nonzero in all three models. These test statistics are not given for scale and shape parameters.

❺ The scale parameter is forced to equal one in the exponential model.

❻ The scale parameter is estimated for the Weibull and gamma models, and the shape parameter is estimated for the gamma model. In these cases, zero is on the boundary of the parameter's possible interval. The chi square test statistic described earlier does not provide a valid test in such cases.

❼ The loglikelihood given for each model is the logarithm of the likelihood evaluated at the maximum likelihood estimators of the parameters. The larger it is, the more "likely" the sample is under that model. Hence, the larger the loglikelihood, the stronger the case for that model is. Note that since loglikelihoods will be negative (being the logarithms of numbers between zero and one), larger loglikelihoods have smaller absolute values.

5.4.1 Exercise

Re-do the previous example without any covariates. That is, estimate the parameters for the exponential, Weibull, and gamma models without covariates.

5.5 Comparison of Models

The next question to be considered is how to tell which of two or more models is to be preferred. While larger maximum loglikelihoods indicate a better model for the observed data, models with more parameters will, in general, have larger loglikelihoods. In fact, suppose that model A is a restriction of model B, perhaps by fixing one or more parameters at some value like zero or one. This is precisely the situation that is discussed in Appendix B. Here's a paraphrase of what is said there:

> Consider a model with m parameters and a null hypothesis that states that k of them have certain fixed values. Let L_m be the loglikelihood maximized over all m parameters. Let L_{m-k} be the log likelihood maximized over the $m - k$ parameters not fixed by the null hypothesis with the other k parameters having the values specified in the null hypothesis. Then, under the null hypothesis, $2(L_m - L_{m-k})$ has, asymptotically, a χ^2 distribution with k degrees of freedom.

This principle works equally well if the restriction of the null hypothesis states that certain regression coefficients have specified values, usually zero, or that one or more of the parameters of the baseline distribution have a specified value, usually zero or one.

Consider the three models for the melanoma data discussed previously. The Weibull distribution is a special case of the gamma distribution with the shape parameter equal to one. Using the previously discussed notation, $L_m = L_5 = -731.2938041$ and $L_{m-k} = L_4 = -731.757061$ are the maximum loglikelihoods for the gamma and Weibull models, respectively. Let's start with the assumption of a gamma model and test the restriction in which the shape parameter is one, i.e., that the data fit a Weibull distribution. Under the null hypothesis that the shape parameter is one, $2(L_5 - L_4)$ has a χ^2 distribution with one degree of freedom. In this case, $2(L_5 - L_4) = 0.92652$, which is not significant. In fact, the p-value is 0.34. We conclude that the data do not provide evidence that the shape parameter is not one. Hence we would not prefer the gamma model to the Weibull. Since the exponential distribution is a special case of the Weibull with the scale parameter equal to one, this approach can be repeated to compare these distributions. Since L_3, the maximum loglikelihood for the exponential model is -742.4698271, we have $2(L_4 - L_3) = 21.42562$, and the data provide strong evidence ($p < .0001$) that the scale parameter is not one, i.e., that the data are not modeled by an exponential distribution. Note that this discussion does not establish that tumor relapse time in this population follows a Weibull distribution. All that can be said is that in the hierarchy of exponential, Weibull, and gamma distributions, the Weibull is to be preferred. Section 5.15 discusses graphical methods of assessing the reasonableness of certain models.

5.5.1 Exercise

Re-do the discussion of Section 5.5 without any covariates in the model. Without consideration of covariates, which of the models: exponential, Weibull, or gamma is preferred?

5.6 Estimates of Quantiles and Survival Probabilities

PROC LIFEREG offers a rich set of additional options and features. Not all are discussed here. One useful feature is the ability to provide information about the estimated survival distribution defined by the model for specific covariate values. By using an OUTPUT statement you can produce a data set that can provide survival function estimates in two ways. First of all, the OUTPUT statement can give the value of the cumulative distribution determined by the model for each patient, based on that patient's observed time and covariate values. Recall that the survival function is one minus the cumulative distribution function. Another way that PROC LIFEREG can provide information about the survival function for a patient with a specified set of covariate values is to give the times associated with a set of quantiles of the cumulative distribution. The second approach is discussed here.

The OUTPUT statement goes after a MODEL statement and affects only the model that the preceding MODEL statement defines. You may use OUTPUT statements with whichever MODEL statements you like. The syntax to accomplish what is described in the previous paragraph is as follows:

```
OUTPUT OUT = datasetname CONTROL = controlvar PREDICTED = timevar
QUANTILES = list;
```

Here *datasetname* is the name of the output data set to be produced. It may be omitted. In that case, SAS names it using its DATA*n* convention. This is not recommended, however, since it can be difficult to keep track of data sets named in this way. *list* is a list of probabilities for which you want the inverse of the cumulative distribution estimated. That is, if *p* is an entry of *list* then, for each patient, the time, *t*, for which $1 - \hat{S}(t) = p$ will be reported where $\hat{S}(t)$ is the estimated survival function determined by the model and the patient's covariate values. *list* can be of the form $p_1 \, p_2 \ldots p_k$ or p_1 to p_2 by increment. All values of *p* must be between 0 and 1. *timevar* is the name of the variable that will contain the time values for each quantile. CONTROL = *controlvar* is optional. The CONTROL=keyword enables you to specify a variable, *controlvar*, in the data set used by PROC LIFEREG that controls the patients for whom these time values are estimated. If it is used, then the time values for each probability will be given only for those patients for whom *controlvar* = 1. If you want to determine the quantiles for a specific set of covariate values, you can add to the DATA= dataset an "artificial patient" with missing time value, desired covariate values, and a control variable that takes the value of one. Since the time is missing, this "patient" will not affect the parameter estimates. However the survival time for each probability in the quantile list will be produced. The output data set can, of course, be used with SAS/GRAPH to produce a graph of the estimated survival function. This is illustrated in the following example, which uses the melanoma data discussed previously.

```
/* Create artificial patient with time missing */
data add;
   c = 1;
   clark = 2 ;
   breslow = .4;
   run;
/* Add artificial patient to data set */
data mel2;
   set melanoma add;
proc lifereg data = mel2;
   model dfstime*dfscens(0) = clark breslow;
   output out = weibull cdf = cdf predicted = months
   quantiles = 0.02 to 0.98 by .02
   control = c;
data dfs;
   set weibull;
   dfs_est = 1 - _prob_;
proc print;
   var  months dfs_est ;
   title 'Weibull Model with Clark = 2.0, Breslow = 0.4';
data;
   set dfs;
   if _n_ = 1 then do;
      dfs_est = 100 ;
      months = 0;
      output;
      end;
   dsf_est=dfs_est*100;
   output;
title1 h=1.5 f=swissb 'Figure 5.1';
title2 h=1.5 f=swissb 'Weibull Model for Melanoma DFS';
title3 h=1.5 f=swissb 'Clark = 2.0, Breslow = 0.4';
axis1 width=2 minor=none label=(h=1.5 f=swissb a=90 j=center
      'Pct DFS') value = (h = 1.2 f = swissb);
axis2 width=2 label=(h=1.5 f=swissb 'Months') value=(h=1.2 f=swissb);
symbol1 v=none l=1 i=spline w = 2 c = black;
proc gplot;
   plot dfs_est*months / haxis = axis2 vaxis = axis1;
run;
```

Note that an artificial patient with the time variable missing, the control variable, C, defined to be one, and covariate values of 2.0 and 0.4 for Clark and Breslow scores, respectively, is added to the data set used by PROC LIFEREG. The variable, C, has a missing value for all other observations. The OUTPUT statement calls for calculating the times for which the cumulative distribution function (one minus the survival function) is 0.02, 0.04, . . . , 0.96, 0.98. The output generated by PROC LIFEREG has already been given. The output produced by running PROC PRINT to print the resultant data set (after subtracting the value of the probabilities from one to get dfs probabilities) is given in Output 5.2. The graph produced by SAS/GRAPH is Figure 5.1.

Note that I=SPLINE was used to produce a smooth curve instead of the steps used in the Kaplan-Meier and proportional hazards estimates survival curve estimates. That is because, in this case, we are plotting the graph of a continuous function. In the other cases we were plotting the graphs of functions whose values, by definition, were changed only at event times. Also notice that the graph is drawn well beyond the data that was used to estimate the parameters. No patients were observed for 500 months. Again, this is reasonable. Once we have estimates of the parameters, we can produce estimates of survival function values for all time values. Of course, survival function estimates for time values beyond those in the data set should be viewed skeptically.

Output 5.2

```
                        The SAS System
        Weibull Model with Clark = 2.0, Breslow = 0.4

              OBS      MONTHS      DFS_EST

                1       8.771        0.98
                2      15.517        0.96
                3      21.741        0.94
                4      27.692        0.92
                5      33.478        0.90
                6      39.161        0.88
                7      44.782        0.86
                8      50.370        0.84
                9      55.946        0.82
               10      61.528        0.80
               11      67.131        0.78
               12      72.769        0.76
               13      78.453        0.74
               14      84.194        0.72
               15      90.004        0.70
               16      95.892        0.68
               17     101.869        0.66
               18     107.946        0.64
               19     114.133        0.62
               20     120.442        0.60
               21     126.885        0.58
               22     133.475        0.56
               23     140.225        0.54
               24     147.151        0.52
               25     154.269        0.50
               26     161.597        0.48
               27     169.156        0.46
               28     176.967        0.44
               29     185.057        0.42
               30     193.454        0.40
               31     202.191        0.38
               32     211.307        0.36
               33     220.845        0.34
               34     230.858        0.32
               35     241.407        0.30
               36     252.566        0.28
               37     264.427        0.26
               38     277.100        0.24
               39     290.724        0.22
               40     305.479        0.20
               41     321.600        0.18
               42     339.401        0.16
               43     359.324        0.14
               44     382.007        0.12
               45     408.438        0.10
               46     440.256        0.08
               47     480.505        0.06
               48     535.942        0.04
               49     627.779        0.02
```

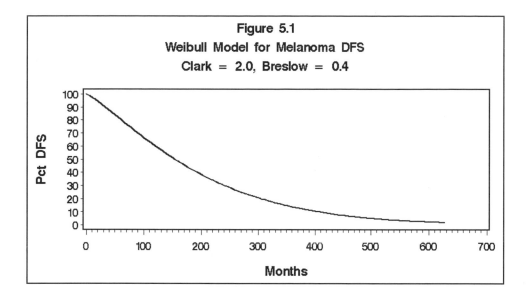

Figure 5.1
Weibull Model for Melanoma DFS
Clark = 2.0, Breslow = 0.4

5.6.1 Exercise

Compute and plot, without considering any covariates, the survival curve for the melanoma data set considered in the previous section. Do this for the exponential, Weibull, and gamma models.

5.7 The PROC LIFEREG Parameters and the "Standard" Parameters

A little care is needed when relating the parameters of the accelerated failure time model of PROC LIFEREG to the usual parameterizations of the distributions used. The parameters estimated by the procedure are not the usual ones, but the relationships between the accelerated failure time model parameters and the model's usual parameters can be readily described. For example, suppose an exponential distribution is assumed and PROC LIFEREG is used to obtain estimates of β_0 and β, the intercept and the vector of regression coefficients for the covariate vector, x. Then the hazard is now a function of x, which will be written $\lambda(x)$. The survival function for a patient with covariate values given by x is $S(t, x) = \exp[-\lambda(x)t]$. It can then be shown that $\lambda(x) = \exp[-(\beta_0 + \beta'x)]$. Thus $S(t, x) = \exp\{-\exp[-(\beta_0 + \beta'x)]t\}$. Similarly, suppose you have assumed a Weibull model and used PROC LIFEREG to estimate β_0, and β as previously shown as well as σ, the scale parameter. The survival function for a patient with covariate vector x can be written as $S(t, x) = \exp(-\lambda(x)t^\gamma)$. Then $\lambda(x) = \exp[-(\beta_0 + \beta'x)/\sigma]$ and $\gamma = 1/\sigma$.

5.7.1 Exercise

Use the delta method (see Appendix B) to derive the standard error of the hazard in an exponential distribution from the standard error of the intercept.

5.8 The Macro PARAMEST

Although PROC LIFEREG can estimate the parameters of several of the more common survival distributions, it does not permit you to specify any others. In particular, it does not permit consideration of models for which a nonzero proportion of patients are long-term survivors, or "cures." Such models, discussed in Chapter 1, have been the subject of a great deal of attention and interest by several authors (Goldman, 1984; Gamel et al. 1994; Cantor and Shuster, 1992).

The macro PARAMEST uses PROC IML. Thus you must have this product installed to use it. This macro allows you to specify any survival function and its associated hazard function. These must be functions of a time variable named t and any number of parameters which must be named THETA[1], THETA[2], . . . , THETA[k] where k is the number of parameters to be estimated. Initial values must be provided, but the macro will usually converge even if the initial values are not very good. If a parameter is bounded, the bounds can be specified, and it is a good idea to do so. This will keep the iteration from considering nonfeasible parameter values that may create large loglikelihoods. A module that calculates the loglikelihood is used by the nonlinear optimization subroutine.

The subroutine NLPTR uses finite difference methods to estimate first and second derivatives of the loglikelihood, if they are not provided as arguments. In order to make the macro PARAMEST as easy as possible to use, those arguments are not included. This adds considerably to the time needed to run the macro, but relieves you of the need to provide first and second derivatives of the survival and hazard functions. If you often need to find MLEs for a particular model, you might want to modify the macro to include first, and perhaps second, derivatives as arguments to the subroutine.

Another PROC IML function, NLLPFDD, is used to estimate the matrix of second derivatives. This matrix is then inverted to obtain estimates of the covariance matrix of the parameter estimates. As an alternative, you may provide a data set that contains time and covariate values. In that case, estimates of the survival probabilities for hypothetical patients with those times and covariate values are printed out as well. The macro PARAMEST uses the following arguments:

DATASET =   This is the name of the data set containing the survival (and, optionally, covariate) data.

METHOD =   This must be 1 or 2. It tells the macro which of two methods, as in PROC LIFEREG, are used to describe the survival data.

If METHOD = 1, then the survival data are described by two time variables. If they are both nonmissing and the second is greater than the first, the time is taken to be interval censored in the interval they define. If the second is missing, the time is right censored at the first. If the first is missing, then the time is taken to be left censored at the second. Finally, if they are both nonmissing and are equal, then the time is complete at that common value. If METHOD = 2, then only right censoring is permitted. Again, two variables are needed to describe the survival data. The first is the observation time and the second indicates whether that time is complete or right censored. The default value is METHOD = 2.

Following are the names of the time variables to be used. They describe survival time according to the method above. The defaults are t1 and t2.

```
T1=
T2=
```

Following are the names of the covariates. They should be listed with at least one space between them and no commas. The default is to have no covariates.

```
COVS=
```

Following is a row vector of the values, separated only by at least one space, that indicate a right censored observation. This is used only with method 2. The time (first time variable) will be considered (right) censored if the value of the second time variable is one of those in this vector. The default is {0}.

```
censval =
```

Following is a formula for the hazard function. The parameters to be estimated must be named THETA[1], THETA[2], . . . and so on. If you wish to consider covariates, they must be named X[1], X[2], . . . , and so on.

```
hazard =
```

Here is a formula for the survival function. As was the case for the hazard function, the parameters must be named THETA[1], THETA[2], and so on, and the covariates, if any, must be named X[1], X[2], and so on.

```
survival =
```

Here is a vector of initial values for the parameters, THETA[1], THETA[2]. The macro will usually work well even if these are rather poor estimates.

```
init =
```

The following are vectors of upper and lower bounds, respectively, for the parameter, THETA[1], THETA[2], and so on.

```
upper =
lower =
```

If there is no (upper or lower) bound for a parameter, that position in the vector should have a missing value. This can be used, for example, to indicate that a parameter can take on only positive values. In that case, the corresponding element of LOWER= should be a small positive value such 10^{-6}. The default is for all parameters to be unbounded. For example, if the first parameter, THETA[1], must be positive and the second, THETA[2], must be between 0 and 1, you can specify LOWER= {1.0e–6 1.0e–6} and UPPER = {. .99999}.

The macro PARAMEST will produce (1–alpha)*100% confidence intervals for each of the parameters. The default value of alpha is 0.05.

```
alpha =
```

This is an optional data set that contains values of time and (if they are used) covariates at which survival probabilities and their standard errors are to be estimated.

```
,pred =
```

There should be no other variables in this data set. The first variable should be the time and the others should be the same as those covariates in the COVS argument. The default is to have no such values. A word of caution is required here. In any SAS data set, the variables are ordered according to the order in which the compiler encountered them. If the dataset Pred does not include any covariates, there will be no problem. If there are covariates as well as the time variable, then you must make sure that in creating this data set the compiler encounters the time variable first. For example, if there is a time variable, T, and two covariates, X1 and X2, and the data set is created with an INPUT statement, the input statement must name the variable T first. That is, you can use

```
data pred;
   input t x1 x2;
   datalines;
```

but not

```
data pred;
   input x1 x2 t;
   datalines;
```

The macro can be called by using the following template.

```
%paramest(
         dataset =       /* The data set to be used.
                            Default is _last_*/
         ,t1 =           /* Names of time variables.  Defaults are
         ,t2 =              t1 and t2.  */
         ,covs =         /* Names of the covariates */
         ,method =       /* Method of specifying time. Default is
                            2. */
         ,hazard =       /* Formula for the hazard function */
         ,survival =     /* Formula for the survival function */
         ,init =         /* Initial values for the parameters */
         ,alpha =        /* Used for confidence intervals for the
                            parameters.  Default value is 0.05.*/
         ,lower =        /* Lower bounds for parameters.  Default
                            is no lower bounds. */
         ,upper =        /* Upper bounds for parameters.  Default
                            is no upper bounds. */
         ,pred =         /* Data set containing time and,
                            optionally, covariate values for which
                            survival probabilities are to be
                            produced.  Default is none. */
         ,censval =      /* Value(s) that indicate censoring.
                            Default is {0} */
```

5.9 Example Using the Macro PARAMEST

Consider once again the data on disease-free survival of melanoma patients that was discussed earlier and that we analyzed with PROC LIFEREG. Again, we will use the covariates Clark and Breslow. This time, however, the macro PARAMEST will be used to perform the same analyses. Although it would be possible for the parameter used by the macro to be the same intercept and scale parameters as in the previous example, it will be more instructive to use the usual parameterization of the Weibull distribution, $S(t) = \exp(\lambda t^{\gamma})$. In using the macro, λ will be identified with THETA[1] and γ with THETA[2]. The macro PARAMEST allows you to model the effects of the covariates in a variety of ways. But for comparison with the results of PROC LIFEREG, let's assume an accelerated failure time model. From the discussion of Section 5.7, it can be seen that that if X[1] and X[2] represent Clark and Breslow, respectively, then the survival function incorporating these covariates can be written $\exp(-\text{theta}[1]\text{theta}[3]^{\text{clark}}\text{theta}[4]^{\text{breslow}}t^{\text{theta}[2]})$. Letting β_0 be the intercept, β_1 and β_2 the coefficients of Clark and Breslow, and σ the scale parameter, the relationships between the parameters of this model and those of PROC LIFEREG are given by

$\text{theta}[1] = \exp(-\beta_0/\sigma)$

$\text{theta}[2] = 1/\beta_0$

$\text{theta}[3] = \exp(-\beta_1/\sigma)$

$\text{theta}[4] = \exp(-\beta_2/\sigma)$

The macro call to estimate these parameters is

```
%paramest(t1=dfstime
          ,t2=dfscens
/* Names of time variables. Defaults are t1 and t2. */
          ,covs=clark breslow
/* Names of the covariates */
          ,method=2
/* Method of specifying time.  Default is 2. */
          ,hazard=
theta[1]*theta[2]*theta[3]**x[1]*theta[4]**x[2]*t**(theta[2] - 1)
/* Formula for the hazard function */
          ,survival=
exp(-theta[1]*theta[3]**x[1]*theta[4]**x[2]*t**theta[2])
/* Formula for the survival function */
          ,init={1 1 1 1}
/* Initial values for the parameters */
          ,lower = {.0001 .0001 .0001 .0001}
/* Lower bounds for parameters.  Default is no lower bounds. */
          ,upper = {10 10 10 10}
/* Upper bounds for parameters. Default is no upper bounds. */
)
```

The results of this invocation of the PARAMEST macro are given in Output 5.3.

Output 5.3

```
                        Successful Convergence

                      MAXLL
                   -1601.163   Is Maximum Loglikelihood.

                        Parameter Estimates

            OBS      THETA      STDERR      LOWER       UPPER

             1      0.00066    0.00026    0.00015     0.00116
             2      1.18985    0.05120    1.08950     1.29021
             3      1.52837    0.15049    1.23341     1.82333
             4      1.24141    0.04713    1.14905     1.33378

                     Estimated Covariance Matrix

       Cov         theta1         theta2        theta3        theta4

     theta1     0.000000067    -.0000076     -0.000032     0.0000011
     theta2     -.000007560    0.0026218     0.000490      0.0002365
     theta3     -.000032041    0.0004895     0.022648      -.0028727
     theta4     0.000001133    0.0002365     -0.002873     0.0022209
```

Note that these estimates for THETA[1] – THETA[4] match those for the parameter estimates produced by PROC LIFEREG when the equations of Section 5.9 are applied. The columns named LOWER and UPPER contain the bounds for 95% confidence intervals, since the default alpha value of 0.05 was used.

The following example shows how to produce estimates of survival probabilities based on this model for a patient with a specified value for Clark and Breslow. Note that in creating the data set, Pred, the time variable, t, is the first to be encountered.

```
data pred;
    do t = 10 to 500 by 10;
        clark = 2.0;
        breslow = 0.4;
        output;
        end;
%paramest(
            dataset = melanoma
            ,t1 = dfstime , t2= dfscens
/* Name of time variables. Defaults are is t1 and t2.  */
            ,covs = clark breslow
/* Names of covariates */
            ,hazard =
theta[1]*theta[2]*theta[3]**x[1]*theta[4]**x[2]*t**(theta[2] - 1)
/* Formula for the hazard function */
            ,survival =
exp(-theta[1]*theta[3]**x[1]*theta[4]**x[2]*t**theta[2])
/* Formula for the survival function */
            ,init = {1 1 1 1}
/* Initial values for the parameters */
            ,lower = {.0001 .0001 .0001 .0001}
/* Lower bounds for parameters.  Default is no lower bounds. */
            ,upper = {10 10 10 10}
/* Upper bounds for parameters. Default is no upper bounds. */
            ,pred = pred
);
run;
```

This time a data set, Pred, is specified. That data set has values of 2 and 0.4 for Clark and Breslow, respectively. The values for t are 10, 20, ..., 500. The additional results are in Output 5.4 .You might want to compare it to Output 5.2.

Output 5.4

T	CLARK	BRESLOW	SURVIVAL	STDERR
10	2	0.4	0.97447	0.004417
20	2	0.4	0.94271	0.008857
30	2	0.4	0.90884	0.013287
40	2	0.4	0.87407	0.017655
50	2	0.4	0.83902	0.021915
60	2	0.4	0.80409	0.026023
70	2	0.4	0.76955	0.029945
80	2	0.4	0.73561	0.033655
90	2	0.4	0.70240	0.037134
100	2	0.4	0.67003	0.040365
110	2	0.4	0.63858	0.043341
120	2	0.4	0.60809	0.046056
130	2	0.4	0.57860	0.048507
140	2	0.4	0.55014	0.050698
150	2	0.4	0.52272	0.052630
160	2	0.4	0.49635	0.054311
170	2	0.4	0.47101	0.055747
180	2	0.4	0.44670	0.056947
190	2	0.4	0.42341	0.057921
200	2	0.4	0.40112	0.058679
210	2	0.4	0.37981	0.059233
220	2	0.4	0.35945	0.059594
230	2	0.4	0.34002	0.059775

Output 5.4 (continued)

240	2	0.4	0.32149	0.059786
250	2	0.4	0.30383	0.059640
260	2	0.4	0.28702	0.059348
270	2	0.4	0.27103	0.058922
280	2	0.4	0.25583	0.058374
290	2	0.4	0.24138	0.057713
300	2	0.4	0.22766	0.056952
310	2	0.4	0.21465	0.056099
320	2	0.4	0.20230	0.055165
330	2	0.4	0.19060	0.054160
340	2	0.4	0.17951	0.053091
350	2	0.4	0.16901	0.051967
360	2	0.4	0.15907	0.050796
370	2	0.4	0.14967	0.049586
380	2	0.4	0.14078	0.048344
390	2	0.4	0.13238	0.047075
400	2	0.4	0.12444	0.045787
410	2	0.4	0.11694	0.044484
420	2	0.4	0.10986	0.043172
430	2	0.4	0.10319	0.041856
440	2	0.4	0.09689	0.040539
450	2	0.4	0.09095	0.039227
460	2	0.4	0.08535	0.037922
470	2	0.4	0.08008	0.036628
480	2	0.4	0.07511	0.035348
490	2	0.4	0.07043	0.034084
500	2	0.4	0.06602	0.032839

5.9.1 Exercise

Re-do the previous example to estimate the disease-free survival function without regard to any covariates, assuming an exponential distribution.

5.10 An Example with a Positive Cure Rate

In the previous example, the macro PARAMEST was used to estimate the parameters of a Weibull survival distribution for a set of survival data that was previously analyzed using PROC LIFEREG. Although it was interesting to compare the two approaches, there would normally be little advantage of using this macro in this way. Indeed, the macro approach required a much greater amount of computer time. The real reason for presenting the macro PARAMEST is to enable you to perform analyses based on models not covered by PROC LIFEREG.

Consider the data set describing the survival of children with leukemia. This data set was introduced in Section 2.8. Part of Output 2.1, a graph of the Kaplan-Meier survival curve, suggests that there is a nonzero proportion of "cures." In other words, the survival curve approaches a nonzero number as time increases. None of the functions allowed by PROC LIFEREG can have this property. Two ways of forming survival functions having positive cure rates are described as follows.

- Let $S(t) = \pi + (1 - \pi)S*(t)$ where $0 < \pi < 1$ and $S*(t)$ is any survival function that goes to zero as t increases. Then π is the "cure rate" and $S*(t)$ is the survival function for those not "cured." The most widely considered function of this type is formed by letting $S*(t)$ be exponential. Thus $S(t) = \pi + (1 - \pi)\exp(-\lambda t)$. The hazard function is given by $h(t) = \lambda (1 - \pi)\exp(-\lambda t)/ S(t)$.

- Let the function h(t) be nonnegative, defined for all nonnegative values of t, and have the property that $\int_0^t h(u)du$ approaches some number c as t increases without bound. It is seen in elementary calculus courses that this last property holds if and only if the series

$$\sum_{i=0}^{\infty} h(i) \text{ converges.}$$

Then the survival function S(t) defined by

$$S(t) = \exp[-\int_0^t h(u)du]$$

approaches $\exp(-c)$, which is the cure rate, as t increases without bound. The most widely considered function of this type is formed by letting $h(t) = \alpha \exp(\beta t)$ where $\alpha > 0$. This hazard is initially (at $t = 0$) α and changes exponentially at rate β. This function is known as the Gompertz function. If $\beta < 0$, then

$$S(t) = \exp[-\int_0^t h(u)du],$$

which is $\exp\{(-\alpha/\beta)[\exp(\beta t) - 1]\}$, approaches $\exp(\alpha/\beta)$ as t increases without bound. Thus the "cure rate" is given by $\exp(\alpha/\beta)$.

The following SAS statements use two macro calls to estimate the parameters of the two survival functions described earlier and to calculate estimated survival probabilities for $t = 1, 2, \ldots 10$ years. In both cases, initial values for the parameters were found by noting from the graph that the cure rate seems to be about 0.60 and that the two-year survival rate is about 0.70. These two values allow for an initial estimate of the parameters. For the first model, the initial estimate of λ is the solution of $.6 + .4\exp(-2\lambda) = .7$. For the second model, we need to solve the equations $\exp(\alpha/\beta) = .6$ and $\exp\{(-\alpha/\beta)[\exp(\beta t) - 1]\} = .7$.

```
data pred;
   do t = 0 to 12;
   output;
   end;
title2 'Exponential with Cure Model';

%paramest(dataset =leuk
,hazard = (1 - theta[1])*theta[2]*exp(-theta[2]*t)/
          (theta[1] + (1 - theta[1])*exp(-theta[2]*t))
,t1 = time
,t2 = d
,method = 2
,survival = theta[1] + (1 - theta[1])*exp(-theta[2]*t)
,init={.6 .7}
,pred = pred
,lower = {.0001 .0001}
,upper = {.9999 .}
)
```

```
%paramest(
dataset =leuk
,hazard = theta[1]*exp(theta[2]*t)
,t1 = time
,t2 = d
,method = 2
,survival=exp(-(theta[1]/theta[2])*(exp(theta[2]*t)-1))
,init={.3 -.6}
,pred = pred
,lower = {.0001 .}
,upper = {. .}
)
```

The output is given in Output 5.5. The first part is for the exponential model. It estimates the "cure rate" to be about 0.61 and the constant hazard for the non-cures to be about 0.30/yr. These are the two values in the THETA column for that model. The second is for the Gompertz model. It estimates the initial hazard to be about 0.13/yr. and its exponential rate of change to be about –0.25/yr/yr. These are the two values in the THETA Gompertz model. The resultant estimated cure rate is about $\exp(-0.13/0.25) = 0.60$. Note that the two models predict almost indistinguishable survival probabilities and that these values are similar to those calculated by the Kaplan-Meier method in Chapter 2. In an article by Laska (1992) it is shown that the final Kaplan-Meier estimate is a reasonable non-parametric estimate for a cure rate. It is not surprising that different cure rate estimation methods yield similar results when applied to data sets that have lengthy follow-up periods.

Output 5.5

```
                    Exponential with Cure Model

                     Successful Convergence

            MAXLL
          -85.77513   Is Maximum Loglikelihood.

                    Parameter Estimates
     OBS      THETA      STDERR        LOWER        UPPER

       1    0.60707    0.068234      0.47333      0.74081
       2    0.30533    0.089005      0.13088      0.47977



              Estimated Covariance Matrix

             Cov         theta1        theta2

           theta1      .0046559      .001791
           theta2      .0017915      .0079220

          Estimated Survival Probabilities

            T       SURVIVAL       STDERR
            0       1.00000       0.00000
            1       0.89661       0.026712
            2       0.82043       0.041427
            3       0.76429       0.049234
            4       0.72292       0.053344
            5       0.69244       0.055667
            6       0.66998       0.057247
            7       0.65343       0.058573
            8       0.64123       0.059826
            9       0.63224       0.061036
```

Output 5.5 (continued)

```
                   10     0.62562    0.062177
                   11     0.62074    0.063220
                   12     0.61714    0.064141

                     (Gompertz Model)

                  Successful Convergence

                         MAXLL
            -85.82645  Is Maximum Loglikelihood.
                  Parameter Estimates

    OBS     THETA      STDERR       LOWER        UPPER

     1     0.12690    0.039649     0.04919      0.20462
     2    -0.24865    0.086704    -0.41859     -0.07872

            Estimated Covariance Matrix

        Cov          theta1          theta2

      theta1       0.0015721      -.0025601
      theta2      -.0025601       0.0075176

          Estimated Survival Probabilities

          T      SURVIVAL       STDERR
          0      1.00000       0.000000
          1      0.89373       0.028403
          2      0.81875       0.042358
          3      0.76467       0.049221
          4      0.72499       0.052728
          5      0.69548       0.054781
          6      0.67330       0.056309
          7      0.65650       0.057722
          8      0.64368       0.059154
          9      0.63387       0.060619
         10      0.62631       0.062078
         11      0.62049       0.063487
         12      0.61598       0.064807
```

5.10.1 Exercises

5.10.1.1 Let T be a random variable with hazard function $h(t) = \alpha\exp(\beta t)$ where $\alpha > 0$. Show that the survival function for T is $S(t) = \exp\{(-\alpha/\beta)[\exp(\beta t) - 1]\}$. Show that the limit of $S(t)$ as $t \to \infty$ is 0 if $\beta > 0$ and $\exp(\alpha/\beta)$ if $\beta < 0$.

5.10.1.2 Complete the work needed to show that the initial estimates for each of the models of the preceding section are reasonable. How would these initial estimates change if the Kaplan-Meier curve suggested a cure rate of about 0.35?

5.11 Comparison of Groups

In addition to providing a way of estimating parameters, the method of maximum likelihood also enables us to compare two or more groups. In Chapters 3 and 4, such comparisons focused only on whether one group was better than another with respect to survival. If you are willing to assume that two groups have the same type of survival function (for example, Weibull) with possibly different parameters, then it is easy to use the results of PROC LIFEREG or the macro PARAMEST to construct a test of the equivalence of the survival functions, i.e., equality of the parameter vectors. Tests can also be constructed to compare specific parameters or subsets of parameters.

5.11.1 An Omnibus Test

Consider two groups, 1 and 2, which will be assumed to have the same type of survival distribution but with possibly different parameter vectors θ_1 and θ_2. The null hypothesis of equivalent survival distributions in these groups can be expressed as $\theta_1 = \theta_2$. The alternative is that $\theta_1 \neq \theta_2$. To construct a test statistic for this null hypothesis you can run either PROC LIFEREG or the macro PARAMEST three times. In each case, note the value for the maximum loglikelihood. The first time use only those observations in group 1. The second time use only those observations in group 2. Call these maximum loglikelihoods LL_1 and LL_2 respectively. The third time use all of the observations. Call the resultant maximum loglikelihood LL_0. Now the maximum loglikelihood for the combined sample under the alternative is $LL_1 + LL_2$. This follows from the fact that the likelihood for the combined sample is the product of the separate likelihoods, hence the maximum loglikelihood for the combined sample is the sum of the respective loglikelihoods. LL_0 is the maximum loglikelihood under the null hypothesis. Using the principle for likelihood ratio tests stated in Appendix B, under the null hypothesis, the statistic $2(LL_1 + LL_2 - LL_0)$ has a χ^2 distribution with degrees of freedom equal to the number of parameters in the model. The null hypothesis is, therefore, rejected if that statistic exceeds the critical value associated with the chosen significance level for that χ^2 distribution.

As an example, let's turn once again to the melanoma data that was previously analyzed. This time, let's define two groups according to a Clark score which takes on the values of 1, 2, 3, and 4. Group 1 will consist of those with a Clark score of 4. Group 2 will be all others. The statements below will enable us to test the null hypothesis that, in a Weibull model, the intercept and scale parameters in these two groups are the same against the alternative that at least one of them differs for these two groups.

```
data melanoma;
   set melanoma;
/* Define group = 1 if clark = 4, 2 otherwise */
   group = 2 -(clark = 4);
proc sort;
   by group;
proc lifereg;
   model dfstime*dfscens(0) = ;
   by group;
   title 'Individual Groups';
run;
proc lifereg;
   model dfstime*dfscens(0) =;
   title 'Combined Sample';
run;
```

The output is in Output 5.6 below.

Output 5.6

```
                              Individual Groups

---------------------------- GROUP=1--------------------

                            Lifereg   Procedure

Data Set              =WORK.MELANOMA
Dependent Variable=Log(DFSTIME)
Censoring Variable=DFSCENS
Censoring Value(s)=      0
Noncensored Values=  172  Right Censored Values=    432
Left Censored Values=   0  Interval Censored Values=   0

Log Likelihood for WEIBULL -453.4687154

                            Individual Groups

---------------------------- GROUP=1 -----------------

                            Lifereg   Procedure

Variable  DF   Estimate  Std Err ChiSquare  Pr>Chi Label/Value

INTERCPT  1 4.34595117 0.079369  2998.234  0.0001 Intercept
SCALE     1 0.91660179 0.051987                   Extreme value scale

                            Individual Groups

---------------------------- GROUP=2 -----------------

                            Lifereg   Procedure

Data Set              =WORK.MELANOMA
Dependent Variable=Log(DFSTIME)
Censoring Variable=DFSCENS
Censoring Value(s)=      0
Noncensored Values=  113  Right Censored Values=    577
Left Censored Values=   0  Interval Censored Values=   0


Log Likelihood for WEIBULL -321.0223407

                            Individual Groups

---------------------------- GROUP=2 --------------------

                            Lifereg   Procedure

Variable  DF    Estimate  Std Err ChiSquare  Pr>Chi Label/Value

INTERCPT  1 4.89447835 0.092569  2795.663  0.0001 Intercept
SCALE     1 0.77839429 0.051887                   Extreme value scale

                            Combined Sample

                            Lifereg   Procedure

Data Set               =WORK.MELANOMA
Dependent Variable=Log(DFSTIME)
Censoring Variable=DFSCENS
Censoring Value(s)=      0
Noncensored Values=  285  Right Censored Values=   1009
Left Censored Values=   0  Interval Censored Values=    0
```

Output 5.6 (continued)

```
Log Likelihood for WEIBULL -797.9950515

                    Combined Sample

                  Lifereg   Procedure

Variable  DF   Estimate  Std Err  ChiSquare  Pr>Chi Label/Value

INTERCPT  1 4.66573806 0.063277  5436.941   0.0001 Intercept
SCALE     1 0.88509116 0.038424                    Extreme value scale
```

For these results, you can calculate that $2(LL_1 + LL_2 - LL_0)$ is about 47.01, which is highly significant. The critical value for the χ^2 distribution with two degrees of freedom for significance level 0.001 is 13.8. Thus, if we assume that disease-free survival in both groups is described by Weibull distributions, these results offer strong evidence that the values of the parameters for those with a Clark score of 4.0 differ from the values for those with a Clark score less than 4.0.

This procedure can easily be automated. If you use the OUTEST = *dataset* option with the PROC LIFEREG statement, you will create a SAS data set containing, among other items, the loglikelihood for the model specified. You can then use those loglikelihoods to have the SAS program calculate $2(LL_1 + LL_2 - LL_0)$.

5.11.2 Individual Parameters

Results such as those seen in the previous sections can also provide insight into whether two groups differ in the values of individual parameters. In general, the estimates are approximately normally distributed with the standard deviations equal to the standard errors in the output. Furthermore, under the null hypotheses that the parameters they estimate are equal, they have the same expected value, namely that common parameter value. Thus, their difference under the null hypothesis has a normal distribution with mean zero and variance equal to the sum of the variances of the estimates. If the parameter estimates in the two groups are denoted $\hat{\theta}_1$ and $\hat{\theta}_2$ and their standard errors are s_1 and s_2, then, under the null hypothesis, the statistic $(\hat{\theta}_1 - \hat{\theta}_2)/\sqrt{s_1^2 + s_2^2}$ has a standard normal distribution. The null hypothesis is rejected for values that exceed, in absolute value, the critical value of the standard normal distribution for the desired significance level. For the groups in the previous example, that statistic has a value of –4.50 for the intercept and 1.88 for the scale parameter. Thus the evidence is quite strong that the two groups determined by the Clark score differ in their intercept (p < 0.001). For the scale parameter, the evidence is marginal (p = 0.06).

5.11.3 Exercises

5.11.3.1 For the previous example, test for a difference in the intercept between the two groups.

5.11.3.2 Use the OUTEST = *dataset* option to automate the process in Section 5.11.1.

5.12 One-Sample Tests of Parameters

The theory for maximum likelihood provides two ways to test null hypotheses of the form $H_0: \theta = \theta_0$ where θ is one of the parameters that characterize a survival distribution and where θ_0 is a particular value. First of all, letting s be the standard error of the parameter estimate, $\hat{\theta}$, you can compare $(\hat{\theta} - \theta_0)/s$ to a critical value of a standard normal distribution. You reject the null hypothesis if the absolute value of $(\hat{\theta} - \theta_0)/s$ exceeds that critical value. Another approach is to use PROC LIFEREG or the macro PARAMEST twice. The first time, you calculate the MLEs of all of the distribution's parameters and the maximum loglikelihood at those MLEs. The second time fix the value of θ, the parameter of interest, at its hypothesized value and calculate the remaining MLEs and the resultant maximum loglikelihood. Note that the SCALE= and SHAPE= options in PROC LIFEREG enable you to restrict these values. The first of these maximum loglikelihoods is the maximum loglikelihood with θ unrestricted. Call it LL_A. The second is the maximum loglikelihood with θ equal to θ_0. Call it LL_0. Then $2(LL_A - LL_0)$ has approximately a χ^2 distribution with one degree of freedom, under the null hypothesis. Reject the null hypothesis if that statistic exceeds the critical value for this distribution.

For an example, consider the leukemia data set discussed previously in this chapter. Suppose that you would expect, based on previous experience, to have a 50% cure rate for these patients if they had been given standard therapy. Do these data offer evidence that the therapy used in this study has a cure rate that differs from 50%? If we use the survival function $S(t) = \pi + (1 - \pi)\exp(-\lambda t)$, we see that the results in Section 5.10 show an estimated "cure rate" of 0.607 with a standard error of 0.068. The first test statistic discussed in the previous paragraph is then $(0.607 - 0.500)/0.068 = 1.569$, which is not statistically significant ($p = 0.117$). Of course, this also follows from the fact that 0.500 is in the 95% confidence interval for this parameter. For a second approach you can re-do the invocation of the macro PARAMEST with the cure rate fixed at 0.5 and compare the maximum loglikelihood to that obtained without that restriction. That is, take $S(t) = 0.5 + 0.5\exp(-\lambda t)$ and $h(t) = 0.5\lambda\exp(-\lambda)/[0.5 + 0.5\exp(-\lambda t)]$. The macro can be called by

```
%paramest(
        dataset =leuk
        ,hazard =
        .5*theta[1]*exp(-theta[1]*t)/(.5 +.5*exp(-theta[1]*t))
        ,t1 = time
        ,t2 = d
        ,method = 2
        ,survival = .5 +.5*exp(-theta[1]*t)
        ,init={.7}
        ,pred = pred
        ,lower = {.0001}
        ,upper = {.}
    )
```

The maximum loglikelihood for this model is –86.81925. In Section 5.10 we saw that the maximum loglikelihood for the unrestricted model was –85.77513. The second test statistic of the previous paragraph has the value $2[-85.77513 - (-86.81925)] = 2.08824$. When we use a χ^2 distribution with one degree of freedom, the p-value is 0.148. This is similar to the result we obtained by using the first method.

5.13 The Effects of Covariates on Parameters

In Section 5.9 you saw how you could use the PARAMEST macro to evaluate the effect of covariates on the two parameters of the Weibull survival distribution. Let's look at this issue a bit more closely. Suppose there are k covariates, $x_1, x_2, \ldots, x_k$, being studied for their association with survival. Then each of the parameters of a survival function could conceivably be affected by some or all of them. You might express a parameter, θ, as a linear function of these covariates, say $\beta_0 + \beta_1 x_1 + \ldots + \beta_k x_k$. Note that β_0 is then the baseline value of the parameter, that is, the value of the parameter when $x_1 = x_2 = \ldots = x_k = 0$. But this linear function can take on all real values, so this would not be a good way to express a parameter that had a more limited set of permissible values. If a parameter can take on only positive values, a better approach to expressing it as function of the covariates might be to write it as $\exp(\beta_0 + \beta_1 x_1 + \ldots + \beta_k x_k)$. In this case, the baseline value is $\exp(\beta_0)$. If the parameter can take on only values between 0 and 1, as with a cure rate, then you might express it as $[1 + \exp(\beta_0 + \beta_1 x_1 + \ldots + \beta_k x_k)]^{-1}$. Then the baseline value becomes $[1 + \exp(\beta_0)]^{-1}$. Of course, different parameters being expressed as functions of the covariates will require distinct coefficients. A fairly large number of parameters may be needed to express a survival function in this way. If there are k covariates and p original parameters in the model, then a total of $p(k+1)$ parameters will be needed. We are fortunate to have powerful computers and software to perform matrix operations on matrices of this size.

A particularly interesting situation arises with a model for survival of the form $S(t) = \pi + (1 - \pi)S^*(t)$ where $S^*(t)$ is a survival function that gives survival probabilities for those not cured, and π is the cure rate. Suppose that $S^*(t)$ is determined by some parameter, θ. For simplicity only one such parameter will be considered, although the extension to more than one will be obvious. Then presumably both π and θ could be affected by the values of a covariate, x. Again, only one covariate will be considered. You might be interested in how x affects both the cure rate and the survival of the non-cures.

As an example, consider once again the leukemia data discussed in Chapters 2 and 3. We saw in Chapter 3 that two treatment groups did not differ significantly by the log rank test. Since both groups seem to have nonzero cure rates, you might want to assess the effect of treatment on the cure rate and the survival of those who are not cured. If survival is modeled by the exponential model with cure, then the survival and hazard functions become

$$S(t, x) = \frac{1}{1 + \exp(\theta_1 + \theta_2 x)} + \frac{\exp(\theta_1 + \theta_2 x)}{1 + \exp(\theta_1 + \theta_2 x)} \exp[-\exp(\theta_3 + \theta_4 x)t]$$

and

$$h(t, x) = -\frac{S'(t, x)}{S(t, x)} \tag{5.2}$$

where x is 0 or 1, depending on the treatment group and

$$S'(t, x) = \frac{\exp(\theta_3 + \theta_4 x)\exp(\theta_1 + \theta_2 x)\exp[-\exp(\theta_3 + \theta_4 x)t]}{1 + \exp(\theta_1 + \theta_2 x)}$$

The following SAS statements estimate these four parameters.

```
%paramest(dataset=leuk
          ,hazard=
exp(theta[3]+theta[4]*x[1])*(1-(1+exp(theta[1]+theta[2]*x[1]))**
(-1))*exp(-exp(theta[3]+theta[4]*x[1])*t)/
((1+exp(theta[1]+theta[2]*x[1]))**(-1)
+(1-(1+exp(theta[1]+theta[2]*x[1]))**(-1))*
exp(-exp(theta[3]+theta[4]*x[1])*t))
          ,t1=years
          ,t2=cens
          ,covs=group
```

```
           ,method=2
           ,survival=
  (1+exp(theta[1]+theta[2]*x[1]))**(-1)
   +(1-(1+exp(theta[1]+theta[2]*x[1]))**(-1))*
  exp(-exp(theta[3]+theta[4]*x[1])*t)
           ,init={0 0 .3 0}
  )
```

The results are printed as Output 5.7. See the full macro in Section 5.18.1.

Output 5.7

```
                     Successful Convergence

                 MAXLL
               -182.0274   Is Maximum Loglikelihood.

                    Parameter Estimates

       OBS      THETA      STDERR      LOWER       UPPER

        1     -0.43501    0.28592    -0.99540     0.12538
        2      0.36080    0.41161    -0.44593     1.16754
        3     -1.18638    0.29140    -1.75751    -0.61524
        4     -0.11637    0.40314    -0.90651     0.67376



            Estimated Covariance Matrix

      Cov        theta1      theta2      theta3      theta4

     theta1     0.081749   -0.08169   -0.024545    0.02450
     theta2    -0.081694    0.16942    0.024497   -0.05396
     theta3    -0.024545    0.02450    0.084915   -0.08486
     theta4     0.024501   -0.05396   -0.084864    0.16252
```

The second and fourth thetas measure the effect of treatment on the cure rate and the hazard among the non-cures, respectively. Note that neither is significant at the 0.05 significance level. This is clear from the fact that both 95% confidence intervals contain zero. Alternatively, you could refer the ratio theta/stderr to the standard normal distribution. The estimated cure rates are $1/[1 + \exp(-.43501)] = 0.607$ for group 0 and $1/[1 + \exp(-.43501 + 0.36080)] = 0.519$ for group 1. The corresponding hazard estimates for the non-cures are $\exp(-1.18638) = 0.305$ and $\exp(-1.18638 + -0.11637) = 0.272$.

Let's take a moment to compare the kind of information we learned from the previous example to what the log rank test can tell us. The log rank test provides insight only about the superiority of one group over the other. That insight comes from considering the relationship of the numbers of deaths in each group to the numbers that would have been expected if the groups had equivalent survivorship. The current approach is far more informative. It enables us to compare groups with respect to the proportion cured as well as the survival times of those not cured. Although it didn't happen in the previous example, it is quite possible for groups not to differ significantly by the log rank test, but for one to have a significantly higher cure rate. Of course there is a price to pay for this more informative analysis, and that price is the parametric assumption. If the groups' true survival distributions are not, at least approximately, given by a function of the assumed form the results will not be valid. Section 5.15 addresses this problem.

5.14 Complex Expressions for the Survival and Hazard Functions

One problem with the PARAMEST macro is that the expressions used with survival= and hazard= can get quite complicated, as we saw in the previous example. When that happens it may be difficult to type them correctly. Here's a suggestion that you may find helpful. When a parameter is a function of covariates, first type the survival and hazard functions without considering the covariates. Then use search and replace to replace the parameters with the appropriate function of the covariates. In the previous example, you might first type

```
survival=pi+(1-pi)*exp(-lamba*t)
```

Then use search and replace to replace pi by

```
1/(1+exp(theta[1]+theta[2]*x))
```

and to replace lambda by

```
exp(theta[3]+theta[4]*x)
```

5.15 Graphical Checks for Certain Survival Distributions

Of course all of this is contingent upon the fact that the sample being analyzed comes from a population having a survival distribution of the type chosen. While such analyses can, as has been seen, be more informative than that done by the nonparametric or semiparametric methods of Chapters 2, 3, and 4, they are invalid if the population survival distribution is not, at least approximately, of the type chosen. There are, unfortunately, no methods of deciding whether or not a given type of distribution fits a set of survival data. About the best we can do is to note that for a certain type of survival functions a simple relationship, such as linear, exists between some function of the survival function and some function of time. By plotting the graph of that relationship, using Kaplan-Meier estimates of the survival function and noting whether it appears to be linear, you can determine whether a certain model is reasonable. Furthermore, the slope and intercept of the line can provide information about the parameters that can help determine initial values. The details of this approach for several common models are discussed in the next section.

5.15.1 The Exponential and Weibull Distributions

Consider a Weibull survival function such as $S(t) = \exp(\lambda t^\gamma)$. Then it's not hard to see that $\log[-\log S(t)] = \log(\lambda) + \gamma \log(t)$. Thus, if you obtain the Kaplan-Meier estimates, $\hat{S}(t)$ of S(t) and plot a graph of $\log[-\log \hat{S}(t)]$ vs log(t), that graph should be roughly linear if the data come from a Weibull distribution. The slope would then be γ. If that slope is about one then this indicates that $\gamma = 1$ and an exponential model is reasonable. Since $\log(\lambda)$ is the intercept, applying the exponential function to the intercept provides an initial estimate of λ. If you want a graphical check of exponentiality, you can use the fact that, if $S(t) = e^{-\lambda t}$, then $\log[S(t)] = -\lambda t$. Thus you can consider the graph of $\log[\hat{S}(t)]$ vs t. For exponential survival functions, this should be a line that goes through the origin. The negative of the slope provides an initial estimate of λ. PROC LIFETEST provides the capability of producing these graphs. Just include the statement `plots = (lls)`, `plots = (ls)`, or `plots = (ls, lls)` in the PROC statement for the graph of $\log\{-\log[\hat{S}(t)]\}$ vs log(t), $\log[\hat{S}(t)]$ vs t, or both.

5.15.2 The Lognormal Distribution

This distribution is given by $S(t) = \Phi\{[\log(t) - \mu]/\sigma\}$, where $\Phi(x)$ is the standard normal cumulative distribution function. It follows that $[\log(t) - \mu]/\sigma = \Phi^{-1}[S(t)]$. Again, letting $\hat{S}(t)$ be the Kaplan-Meier estimates of $S(t)$, you might consider the graph of $\log(t)$ vs $\Phi^{-1}[\hat{S}(t)]$. This can be done easily in SAS since SAS provides the inverse of the standard normal cumulative distribution as the PROBIT function. A lognormal distribution is indicated if that graph is approximately linear. Furthermore the reciprocal of the slope will approximate σ. That value for σ multiplied by the negative of the intercept will approximate μ.

5.15.3 The Exponential Model with "Cure"

This survival distribution is given by $S(t) = \pi + (1 - \pi)\exp(-\lambda t)$. It follows that $\log[\hat{S}(t) - \pi] = \log(1 - \pi) - \lambda t$. You can plot the graphs of $\log[\hat{S}(t) - \pi]$ vs t for several values of π, where $\hat{S}(t)$ is the Kaplan-Meier estimate of $S(t)$. If one of them looks like a straight line, that indicates a model of this type. The value of π for this graph is an initial estimate of π and the negative of the slope is an initial estimate of λ.

5.15.4 The Gompertz Model

The Gompertz survival curve has a survival function $S(t) = \exp\{(-\alpha/\beta)[\exp(\beta t) - 1]\}$. It will be convenient to rewrite it as $\pi^{1 - \exp(\beta t)}$ where $\pi = \exp(\alpha/\beta)$. Recall that π is the cure rate if $\beta < 0$. It follows that $\log\{1 - \log[S(t)]/\log(\pi)\} = \beta t$. Letting $\hat{S}(t)$ be the Kaplan-Meier estimate of $S(t)$, you can plot the graphs of $\log\{1 - \log[\hat{S}(t)]/\log(\pi)\}$ vs t for several values of π. If one of them appears to be a straight line through the origin, that indicates that a Gompertz model is reasonable. The value of π for that graph is an initial estimate of the cure rate or $\exp(\alpha/\beta)$. The slope of that line is an initial estimate of β.

5.16 A Macro for Fitting Parametric Models to Survival Data

The macro CHEKDIST allows you to perform the graphical checks described in the previous section on a data set. To use it, you must provide information about the data set containing the survival data and the model, chosen from those described earlier, that you wish to fit. For the Gompertz model or the exponential model with cure, you also need to provide the value (or values) of π that you would like to check. Those values are specified in list format. Some examples are

```
pi = 0.5
pi = 0.2 to 0.8 by 0.2.
```

Because the macro processor will interpret a comma as an indication that the parameter specification has ended, you cannot use an expression like

```
pi = 0.2, 0.3, 0.4.
```

To invoke this macro, you can use the following template:

```
%chekdist(
         data =              /* The name of the data set to be used.
                                Default is _last_ */
         ,time =             /* The name of the time variable  */
         ,cens =             /* The name of the censoring variable */
         ,censvals =         /* Values of the censoring variable that
                                indicate a censored observation.
                                Default is 0 */
         ,model =            /* Model to be fit.  Choices are exp,
                                weibull, lognorm, expcure, and gomp */
         ,pi =               /* Value(s) for the cure rate */
)
```

As examples, consider the following two invocations of the macro CHEKDIST. The first checks on the fit of a Weibull model to a data set of survival data. The second checks on the fit of an exponential model with cure to another data set. Cure rates of 0.2, 0.3, 0.4, 0.5, and 0.6 are considered. In both data sets the time variable is T and the censoring variable is Cens. The only censoring value is 0, which is the default. Both data sets were artificially created to have the distribution for which they are being checked. The data set Data1 is simulated from a Weibull model with $\lambda = 0.33$ and $\gamma = 0.64$. The data set Data2 is simulated from an exponential with cure model with $\lambda = 0.23$ and $\pi = 0.4$. The results are seen in Figures 5.2 and 5.3. Note that the graph in Figure 5.2 is nearly linear. This would support the contention that the underlying data were sampled from a Weibull distribution. Furthermore, the vertical coordinate associated with $\log(t) = 0$ is about $- 1.0$. This would suggest a value for λ of about $\exp(- 1.0) = 0.37$. The slope of the line appears to be about 0.6, suggesting that value for γ. Both values are close to those of the population sampled. In Figure 5.3 the graph for $\pi = 0.4$ is nearly linear. This indicates that a model with about 40% surviving and exponential survival for the non-cures is reasonable. The slope for the graph with $\pi = 0.4$ appears to be about $- 0.2$, suggesting a value for λ of about 0.2.

```
%chekdist(
         data=data1    /* The name of the data set to be used.
                          Default is _last_ */
         ,time=t       /* The name of the time variable  */
         ,cens=cens    /* The name of the censoring variable */
         ,model=weibull/* Model to be fit.  Choices are exp,
                          weibull, lognorm, expcure, and gomp */
)
title 'Weibull';

%chekdist(
         data=data2    /* The name of the data set to be used.
                          Default is _last_ */
         ,time=t       /* The name of the time variable  */
         ,cens=cens    /* The name of the censoring variable */
         ,model=expcure /* Model to be fit.  Choices are exp,
                          weibull, lognorm, expcure, and gomp */
         ,pi = .2 to .6 by .1  /* Value(s) for the cure rate */
)
title 'Exp with Cure';
```

Figure 5.2

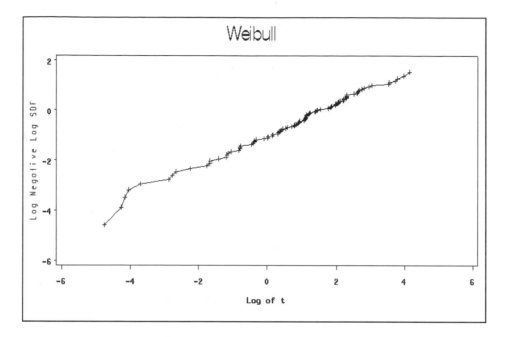

Figure 5.3

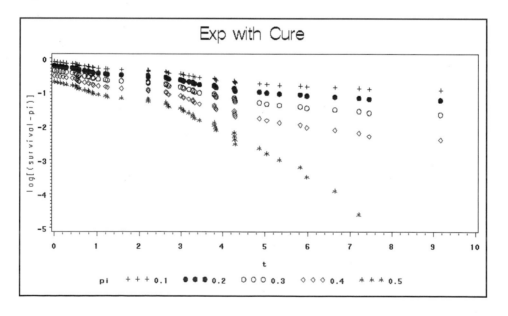

5.17 Other Estimates of Interest

If you assume a model for survival that implies that some patients are cured, then the cure rate is, of course, a critical parameter to estimate. This can be thought of as the probability that a patient entering the study will *not* die from the disease under consideration. Now suppose that probability for a given patient (perhaps based on covariate values) is π. If that patient is alive some time later, then it is reasonable to assume that his or her chances of being cured have been increased. Many investigators simply declare a patient cured when a certain survival time is achieved. Such a declaration is generally based on experience that indicates that patients who survive for that amount of time do not die of the disease. The methods discussed earlier, allow an alternative approach to this question. It's not hard to show that the probability that a patient is cured conditioned on having survived to time *t* is given by $\pi/S(t)$. Replacing S(t) and π by their estimates produces the estimated conditional probability. For example, consider a leukemia patient in the cohort whose survival is modeled in Section 5.10. Using the Gompertz model, that patient has, upon beginning the study, an estimated probability of about 0.60 of not succumbing to the disease. If this patient survives for three years his or her probability of never dying from the disease is now 0.600/0.765, or about 0.784.

Another type of estimate that may be of interest is the survival function for those not cured. For a cohort with survival function S(t) that approaches π as *t* increases, that function is given by $[S(t) - \pi]/(1 - \pi)$. Again, replacement of S(t) and π by their estimates produces the estimated survival function for the non-cures. For example, applying the Gompertz model to the leukemia data, you could estimate that a patient not cured will have a probability of $(0.765 - 0.600)/(1 - 0.600) = 0.412$ of surviving for more than three years.

5.18 Listings of Macros

5.18.1 The Macro PARAMEST

```
%macro paramest(dataset = _last_, vars = t1 t2, method = 2,
                hazard =    , survival = ,init= , alpha = 0.05,
                lower = {. . . . . . . . . .},
                upper = {. . . . . . . . . .},
                pred = x, censval = {0});

/*Remove Observations with Time Values That Are Not Permissible*/

data checked;
     set &dataset;
     if &method=1 and ((&t1 = . and &t2 = .) or &t1 > &t2
     or . < &t1 < 0 or . < &t2 < 0) then delete;
     if &method=2 and (&t1 < 0 or &t2 = . ) then delete;

/* to get rid of previous data sets */

data survival;
     set _null_;
data x;
     set _null_;

proc iml;
b = &upper;
     a = &lower;
     con = a//b;
     use checked;
     read all var {&vars} into vars;
     nvars = ncol(vars);
```

```
        ncovs = nvars - 2;
        nobs = nrow(vars);
        times = vars[, 1:2];

/*  convert to method 1 for time and censoring data */

if &method = 1 then do i=1 to nobs;
    if sum((times[i,2] = &censval)) >0 then times[i,2] = .;
    else times[i,2] = times[i,1];
    end;

/* module to calculate log likelihood  */

        start loglik(theta) global (times,vars,nobs,nvars);
        LL=0;
        do i=1 to nobs;
   /*  get covariates  */

            if nvars > 2 then x = vars[i,3:nvars];

    /*   right censored time */

            if (times[i,1] ^= .) & (times[i,2] = . ) then do;
            t = times[i,1];
            LL = LL + log(&survival);
            end;

    /* left censored time */

        if (times[i,1] = .) & (times[i,2] ^= .) then do;
            t = times[i,2];
            LL = LL + log(1 - &survival);
            end;

    /* interval censored time */

    if (times[i,1] ^= .) & (times[i,2] > times[i,1]) then do;
            t = times[i,1];
            temp = &survival ;
            t = times[i,2];
            y = temp - &survival ;
            LL = LL + log(y);
            end;

    /* uncensored time */

    if times[i,1] = times[i,2] then do;
            t=times[i,1];
            LL = LL + log(&hazard) + log(&survival);
            end;
    end;
    return(LL);
    finish loglik;
    theta0= &init`;
    nparams = ncol(&init);
    con = con[, 1:nparams];
    optn = {1 0};

/*  call optimization function */

    call nlptr(rc,thetares,"loglik",theta0,optn,con,,,,,);
    thetaopt=thetares`;
    maxll=loglik(thetaopt);

/*  rc is return code  - negative means failed to converge  */

    if rc < 0 then
    print "Iteration failed to converge.  Estimates are  unreliable.";
    if rc > 0 then do;
            print "Successful Convergence";
            print maxll " Is Maximum Loglikelihood.";
            end;
```

```
/*  module to calculate first derivs (deriv) and second derivs (h) */

    call nlpfdd(LL,deriv,h,"loglik", thetaopt);

/* get covariance matrix and standard errors of estimates */

    cov = -inv(h);
    setheta=sqrt(vecdiag(cov));
    theta=thetaopt;
    use &pred;
    read all var _all_ into values;
    n = nrow(values);
    survival = j(1,n,0);
    sesurv = j(1,n,0);
    covplus1 = ncovs + 1;

/* calculate survival function for t and covariates in pred dataset,
as well as standard error using delta method */

    do i = 1 to n;
          if ncovs > 0 then x = values[i,2:covplus1];
          t = values[i,1];
          start surv(theta) global (i, t, x);
          surv = &survival;
          return(surv);
          finish surv;
          call nlpfdd(s,deriv,hess,"surv", theta);
          survival[i] = s;
          sesurv[i] = sqrt(deriv*cov*deriv');
          end;
    survival = survival`;
    sesurv = sesurv`;
    create thetas from theta[colname = 'theta'];
    append from theta;
    create setheta from setheta[colname = 'stderr'];
    append from setheta;
    create cov from cov;
    append from cov;
    create survival from survival[colname = 'survival'];
    append from survival;
    create sesurv from sesurv[colname = 'stderr'];
    append from sesurv;
data thetas;
    merge thetas setheta;
    c = probit(1 - &alpha/2);

/*  (1 - alpha)100% CI */

    lower = theta - stderr*c;
    upper = theta + stderr*c;
proc print data = thetas;
    var theta stderr lower upper;
    title 'Parameter Estimates';
run;
proc means noprint n data = cov;
    var col1;
    output out = out n = nparams;
run;
data;
    set out;
    call symput('n', nparams);
run;
data names;
%do i = 1 %to &n;
    name = "theta&i";
    output;
    %end;
run;
data cov;
merge names cov;
proc print data= cov noobs label ;
```

```
%do i = 1 %to &n;
   label col&i = "theta&i";
   %end;
   label name = 'Cov';
   title 'Estimated Covariance Matrix';
run;

/* merge survival estimates and stderrors with pred dataset */

data table;
   merge &pred survival sesurv ;
   proc print data = table noobs;
   title 'Estimated Survival Probabilities';
run;
%mend;
```

5.18.2 The Macro CHEKDIST

```
%macro chekdist(data = _last_ , time = , cens = , censvals = 0 ,
model = , pi = ) ;
symbol1 v = plus c = black;
symbol2 v = dot c = black;
symbol3 v = circle c = black;
symbol4 v = diamond c = black;
symbol5 v = star c = black;
%if "&model" = "exp" %then %do;
   proc lifetest data = &data noprint plots = (ls)  ;
   time &time*&cens(&censvals);
   %end;
%if "&model" = "weibull" %then %do;
   proc lifetest data = &data noprint plots = (lls) ;
   time &time*&cens(&censvals);
   %end;
%if "&model" ne "weibull" and "&model" ne "exp" %then %do;
   proc lifetest data = &data noprint outs = out;
   time &time*&cens(&censvals);
   axis1 label = (a = 90);
   %end;
%if "&model" = "lognorm" %then %do;
   data; set out;
   x = log(&time);
   y = -probit(survival);
   label x = 'log(t)';
   label y = '-probit(survival)';
   proc gplot;
   plot y*x /vaxis = axis1;
   %end;
%if "&model" = "expcure" %then %do;
   data; set out;
   do pi = &pi ;
      y = log(survival - pi);
      output;
      end;
   label y = 'log[(survival-pi)]';
   %end;
%if "&model" = "gomp" %then %do;
   data; set out;
   do pi = &pi ;
      y=log(1-log(survival)/log(pi));
      output;
      end;
   label y = 'log[1-log(survival)/log(pi)]';
   %end;
%if "&model" = "gomp" or "&model" = "expcure" %then %do;
   proc gplot;
   plot y*&time = pi /vaxis = axis1;
   %end;
run;
%mend;
```

Appendix A Mathematical Concepts

A.1 A (very) Brief Introduction to Calculus.. 187
A.2 A (very) Brief Introduction to Vectors and Matrices.. 192

A.1 A (very) Brief Introduction to Calculus

A.1.1 The Derivative

Consider the graph of the function $f(x) = x^2$ and the line connecting the point $(1, 1)$ on this graph to a point on the graph a little to the right of $(1, 1)$, say $(1 + \Delta x, (1 + \Delta x)^2)$. The slope of this line is the difference of the y coordinates divided by the difference of the x coordinates; that is, $[2\Delta x + (\Delta x)^2]/\Delta x$. Dividing the numerator and denominator by Δx gives us $2 + \Delta x$. This quantity can be considered the average slope or average rate of change of the curve $y = x^2$ from 1 to $1 + \Delta x$. Alternatively, it is the *average* rate of change of the function $y = f(x)$ from 1 to $1 + \Delta x$. If we let Δx get closer and closer to zero, this average slope gets closer and closer to 2. This limit can be considered the slope of the function $y = x^2$ at $x = 1$ or the *instantaneous* rate of change of the function $y = x^2$ at $x = 1$.

Figure A.1 illustrates these concepts. The dashed line connects the point with coordinates $(1,1)$ to the point with coordinates $(1 + \Delta x, (1 + \Delta x)^2)$ on the graph of $y = x^2$, which is the thick, curved line. Its slope can be thought of as the *average* rate of change of the function $y = x^2$ from $x = 1$ to $x = 1 + \Delta x$. The solid line is the tangent to the graph at the point with coordinates $(1,1)$. Its slope is the *instantaneous* rate of change of the function at $x = 1$, also called the derivative of the function at $x = 1$.

Figure A.1

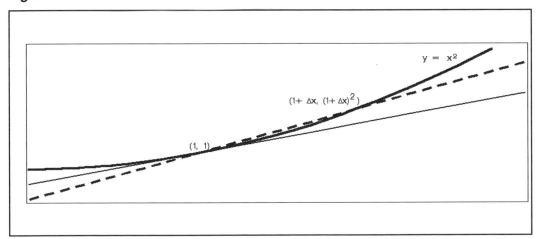

More generally, if y = f(x) is any function, consider the ratio $[f(x + \Delta x) - f(x)]/\Delta x$. This is the average rate of change of the function from x to x + Δx. The limit of this ratio as Δx approaches zero, if the limit exists, is the instantaneous rate of change of f(x) at x. The function that gives us the instantaneous rate of change of f(x) at x is called the derivative of f(x) at x. It is usually denoted by df(x)/dx or f'(x). If the function is written in the form y = f(x), we might write this derivative as dy/dx or y'. The line through the point (x, f(x)) having slope equal to df(x)/dx is called the tangent line to the graph of y = f(x) at that point. A calculus course would spend a lot of time developing formulas and methods to use for finding derivatives of various kinds of functions. We will not do that here. In this book we simply say that a function has a certain derivative. Those who can should confirm that fact for themselves. For those who cannot, it will suffice to think of a derivative as the slope of a tangent line, or the rate of change of a function.

A.1.2 Higher Order and Partial Derivatives

Since the derivative of a function of x is itself a function of x, we can take its derivative as well. This is called the second derivative and we use notations d^2y/dx^2 and y″ to represent it. Of course we can continue with third, fourth, . . . nth derivatives. These are called higher order derivatives. The nth derivative is denoted by d^ny/dx^n or $y^{(n)}$.

Now consider a function of two variables, say y = f(x, u). We can consider derivatives of this function with respect to x (treating u as constant) and with respect to u (treating x as constant). These are called the partial derivatives with respect to x and u respectively and are denoted by $\partial y/\partial x$ and $\partial y/\partial u$. We can also consider mixed higher order partial derivatives. For example, if y = f(x, u), we can take the partial derivative with respect to x and then take the partial derivative of that function with respect to u. The result would be denoted by $\partial^2 y/\partial x \partial u$.

A.1.3 Finding Maximum and Minimum Values of Functions

Consider the function pictured in Figure A.2. Suppose we were interested in finding the value of x that produces the maximum value of f(x). For a reasonably well-behaved function, that would be a value of x at which the tangent line to the graph was horizontal; i.e., has slope equal to zero. Thus a reasonable approach to finding a value of x that maximizes a function f(x) is to find a solution to the equation df(x)/dx = 0. Of course, if we were seeking to minimize the function, we would also look for a solution of df(x)/dx = 0. A word of caution is needed here. A function may have more than one local maximum and minimum. The maximum or minimum you are looking for might be one of them. A value of x for which the derivative is zero may correspond to a minimum or a maximum. It may also not correspond to a maximum or minimum. Finally, functions may have maximums or minimums at values of x for which the derivative does not exist. Nevertheless, when seeking to maximize or minimize a function, it is usually a good idea to start by finding where the derivative is zero.

Now, what about the problem of maximizing or minimizing functions of several variables? The discussion of the previous paragraph has an obvious extension. We find the solution of the system of equations formed by equating all of the partial derivatives to zero. This may be a difficult problem, but we will see ways of dealing with it later.

Figure A.2

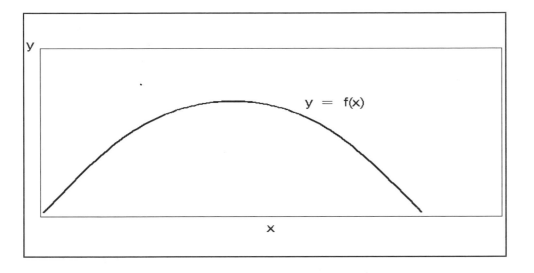

A.1.4 *Definite Integrals*

Consider a function y = f(x) that has a graph that is above the x axis for *x* between *a* and *b* where a < b. We will often need to talk about the area under this graph from *a* to *b*. This area is called the

definite integral of the function y = f(x) from *a* to *b* and is denoted by $\int_a^b f(x)dx$. If the function is

of the form f(x) = cx + d, then the graph is just a straight line, and the area we are talking about is the area of a trapezoid. Such an area is easy to find. For more complex functions, finding the area under the curve may be more difficult. One way to proceed is to consider a partition of the interval from *a* to *b* by a = x_0, x_1, . . ., x_{n-1}, x_n = b where all of the subintervals have the same length, $\Delta x = (b - a)/n$. Now consider the subinterval from x_i to x_{i+1}. The area under the graph over that subinterval can be approximated by the area of a rectangle whose height is f(x_i) and whose width is Δx. Of course, the area of that rectangle is f(x_i)Δx. Figure A.3 illustrates this. The definite integral from *a* to *b*; i.e., the area under the curve from *a* to *b*, can be approximated by the sum of the areas

of all of these rectangles, $\sum_{i=0}^{n-1} f(x_i)\Delta x$. As the number of these subintervals increases, Δx gets closer

to zero and the rectangles get skinnier. The limit of the sum described above as *n* increases is

written $\lim_{n\to\infty} \sum_{i=0}^{n-1} f(x_i)\Delta x$ and is defined to be the definite integral of the function y = f(x) from *a* to *b*,

or $\int_a^b f(x)dx$.

Of course, this discussion raises two important questions: Does the limit of the sum of these areas of rectangles actually exist? and How do we find it when it does exist? The answer to the first question is that the limit often, but not always, does exist. It exists for the well-behaved functions we will generally be talking about. For the second question, it is often possible to find formulas that enable us to calculate this limit, hence the definite integral, exactly. Sometimes, this cannot be done, however in such cases, we can use approximation methods. Some definite integrals that are particularly useful are found in tables. Many mathematical and statistical software products (including SAS, as we will see later) provide ways to compute them as well.

Figure A.3

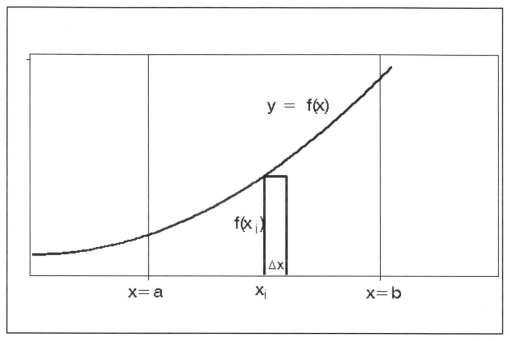

Although it may appear that the derivative and the definite integral are unrelated concepts, there is a very important relationship between them. It is so important that it is often called the Fundamental Theorem of Calculus. Consider a function $y = f(u)$ and create a new function of x, $F(x)$, whose

value, for any value of x is given by $F(x) = \int_{-\infty}^{x} f(u)du$. This function, $F(x)$, has a derivative. In fact,

the Fundamental Theorem of Calculus tells us that $dF(x)/dx = f(x)$. In other words, the definite integral and the derivative operate as inverses of each other. If you do one of them and then do the other, you get back the function you started with.

A.1.5 Exercises

A.1.5.1   Consider the function $f(x) = x^2$. Show that $f'(x) = 2x$.
   Consider the function $f(x) = x^2 + 5x$. Show that $f'(x) = 2x+5$.

A.1.5.2   Consider the function $f(x) = 3x$. Find $\int_{0}^{5} f(x)dx$, $\int_{0}^{8} f(x)dx$, and $\int_{5}^{8} f(x)dx$.
   (Hint: Think about the area of a triangle.)

A.1.5.3   a) Draw the graph of a function having a minimum where the derivative equals zero.
   b) Draw the graph of a function which has several values for which the
      derivative is zero.
   c) Draw the graph of a function with a value having a derivative
      equal to zero without being a maximum or minimum.

A.1.6 The Exponential and Logarithmic Functions

Let *a* be any positive number. You are probably familiar with the notation a^n where *n*, called an exponent, is a positive integer. Although we won't go through the process here, this concept can be extended to exponents that are any real numbers. The function $f(x) = a^x$ is often called an exponential function with base *a*. It turns out that one particular value of the base generates the exponential function that is most useful in mathematics and statistics. This value, called *e*, (after Leonard Euler, a great eighteenth-century Swiss mathematician) is an irrational number, so a terminating or repeating decimal can't represent it. To three decimal places, its value is about 2.718. Because this is such an important base for an exponential function, whenever we refer to the *exponential function*, we mean the exponential function with this base. This function is written as $y = e^x$ or $y = \exp(x)$. It has the following properties:

- $\exp(u + v) = \exp(u)\exp(v)$.
- $\exp(u - v) = \exp(u)/\exp(v)$.
- $\exp(au) = [\exp(u)]^a$.
- If $y = \exp(x)$, then $dy/dx = \exp(x)$.

The fourth property expresses the fact that the exponential function is its own derivative. This is the main reason why the base *e* is so important.

The logarithm function with base *a*, denoted by $y = \log_a(x)$, is the inverse of the exponential function with base *a*. Thus $y = \log_a(x)$ means that $a^y = x$. Here again, the most important base is *e*. Logarithms with base *e* are often called natural logarithms. To distinguish them, authors sometimes denote the logarithm function with base *e* by $\log_e(x)$ or $\ln(x)$. In this book we simply use $\log(x)$ to represent natural logarithms. It follows from the inverse nature of the logarithm and exponential functions that

- $\log(uv) = \log(u) + \log(v)$.
- $\log(u/v) = \log(u) - \log(v)$.
- $\log(u^a) = a\log(u)$.

In addition, the fact that the logarithm and exponential functions are inverses means that $\log[\exp(x)] = x$ and $\exp[\log(x)] = x$ for any value of *x*. Because these two functions are so important, they are among those mathematical functions provided as part of the SAS language. They are discussed further in Appendix C.

A.1.7 Exercises

A.1.7.1 Using a calculator, computer, or appropriate tables, find $\exp(2.1)$, $\exp(.5)$, $\log(34)$, $\log(.25)$, $\log(4)$.

A.1.7.2 *Without* using a calculator, computer, or table, find $\log(1)$, $\log(e)$, $\log(e^3)$, $\exp(0)$, $e^{\log(5.2)}$.

A.2 A (very) Brief Introduction to Vectors and Matrices

A *matrix* is a rectangular array of numbers, often referred to by a capital letter as in

$\mathbf{A} = \begin{pmatrix} 1 & 5 & 2 \\ 3 & 2 & 4 \end{pmatrix}$. This matrix has two rows and three columns. We say that it is a 2×3 matrix. A matrix with only one row is called a *row vector*. A matrix with only one column is called a *column vector*. A matrix with the same number of rows and columns is said to be a *square matrix*.

Matrices have arithmetic operations defined on them. If two matrices, **A** and **B**, have the same dimensions, then their sum and difference are defined as the matrices formed by taking the sums and differences of the corresponding matrix components. For example if $\mathbf{A} = \begin{pmatrix} 1 & 0 & 4 \\ 2 & 3 & 1 \end{pmatrix}$ and $\mathbf{B} = \begin{pmatrix} 2 & 5 & 1 \\ 3 & 4 & 1 \end{pmatrix}$

then $\mathbf{A} + \mathbf{B} = \begin{pmatrix} 3 & 5 & 5 \\ 5 & 7 & 2 \end{pmatrix}$ and $\mathbf{A} - \mathbf{B} = \begin{pmatrix} -1 & -5 & 3 \\ -1 & -1 & 0 \end{pmatrix}$. There is also an operation called multiplication defined for matrices. It is a little more complicated and we won't need to go into how it's done. The components whose row and column numbers are the same are said to be on the main diagonal of the matrix (that's the diagonal going from "northwest" to "southeast"). A square matrix with 1s on the

main diagonal and 0s elsewhere is called an *identity matrix*. For example, the matrix $\mathbf{I} = \begin{pmatrix} 1 & 0 & 0 \\ 0 & 1 & 0 \\ 0 & 0 & 1 \end{pmatrix}$ is

a 3×3 identity matrix. An identity matrix acts like the number 1 in that $\mathbf{AI} = \mathbf{IA} = \mathbf{A}$ if **I** is an identity matrix of the same dimensions as **A**. If **A** and **B** are square matrices of the same dimensions such that $\mathbf{AB} = \mathbf{BA} = \mathbf{I}$ where **I** is an identity matrix, then **A** and **B** are said to be *inverses* of each other. In this case, we write $\mathbf{A} = \mathbf{B}^{-1}$ and $\mathbf{B} = \mathbf{A}^{-1}$. Inverses of matrices act a lot like reciprocals of numbers. One difference is that while all numbers except zero have reciprocals, square matrices do

not necessarily have inverses. For example, the matrix $\begin{pmatrix} 6 & 3 \\ 4 & 2 \end{pmatrix}$ does not have an inverse. Square

matrices that do not have inverses are said to be singular. One reason for using matrices is that they provide a convenient notation for extending results about one variable to results about multiple variables. For many formulas involving operations on numbers, there are analogous formulas involving operations on vectors and matrices. A quotient such as x/y will, when the discussion is extended to multiple variables, often be replaced by the product $\mathbf{XY}^{-1}$ where **X** and **Y** are matrices.

If **A** is a m×k matrix, the transpose of **A**, denoted **A′** is the k×m matrix formed by interchanging the

rows and columns. For example, if $\mathbf{A} = \begin{pmatrix} 4 & 8 & 2 \\ 1 & 3 & 5 \end{pmatrix}$ then $\mathbf{A}' = \begin{pmatrix} 4 & 1 \\ 8 & 3 \\ 2 & 5 \end{pmatrix}$.

Appendix B   Statistical Concepts

B.1   Random Variables 193
B.2   Probability Functions 194
B.3   Discrete Random Variables 194
B.4   Continuous Random Variables 195
B.5   Cumulative Distribution Functions 196
B.6   Exercises 199
B.7   Mean, Variance, and Standard Deviation 199
B.8   Joint Distributions 200
B.9   Conditional Probability and Stochastic Independence 201
B.10   The Delta Method for Two Variables 202
B.11   Parameters and Estimates 202
B.12   Maximum Likelihood Estimation 203
B.13   Likelihood Ratio Tests 206
B.14   Confidence Intervals 207

B.1 Random Variables

We will begin with some of the basic concepts of probability. Consider an experiment that, in some fashion, produces some particular outcome from a set of possible outcomes. The experiment might consist of the toss of a coin with the set of outcomes {Heads, Tails}. It might be the selection of a patient with Hodgkin's disease. The set of possible outcomes is the set of all such patients. Consider a function associating each outcome with a unique real number. In the first example we might associate "Heads" with 1 and "Tails" with 0. In the second we might associate each patient with his or her time from diagnosis until death. Such a function is called a random variable and is generally denoted by a capital letter, such as X or Y. We will use lowercase letters to stand for a particular value of a random variable.

Here we depart from the notation that mathematicians usually use for functions. If o is an outcome, you might expect us to write X(o) = x to express the fact that the experiment resulted in an outcome, o, that the random variable associated with the real number, x. Actually, we say X = x to express this fact. Thus the meaning of the expression X = x can be shown in Figure B.1.

Figure B.1

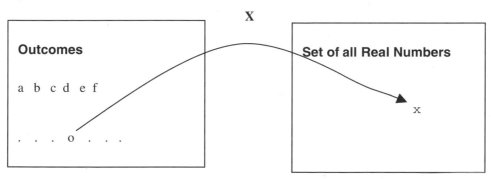

If X and Y are random variables, then if we apply an arithmetic operation or a function to their values, we get another random variable. We will understand expressions such as $2X$, $X + Y$, X^2 to mean the random variable whose value is twice the value of the random variable X, the random variable whose value is the sum of the values of the random variables X and Y, the random variable whose value is the square of the value of the random variable X, and so on.

B.2 Probability Functions

We assume that a random variable, X, is characterized by a probability function that associates a subset of the set of real numbers with a unique number in the interval $[0,1]$. That function will frequently be denoted by Pr, although when more than one random variable is involved in the discussion, we may use subscripts to distinguish them. Thus we will write $\Pr(A) = .3$ or $\Pr_X(A) = .3$ to say that the probability is .3 that the random variable X has a value in the set A. When the subset is an interval we will use a more natural notation such as $\Pr(0 < X < 5)$ or $\Pr(X > 2)$ to represent the probability that the random variable X has a value between 0 and 5 or the probability that the random variable X has a value that exceeds 2.

The function Pr has the following properties:

- $0 \leq \Pr(A) \leq 1$ for any set A.
- $\Pr(\varnothing) = 0$, where $\varnothing$ indicates the null, or empty set.
- If A^c represents the complement of A, then $\Pr(A^c) = 1 - \Pr(A)$.
- If $A \cap B = \varnothing$, then $\Pr(A \cup B) = \Pr(A) + \Pr(B)$.

B.3 Discrete Random Variables

A random variable, X, that can have only integers as its values is said to be a discrete random variable. In that case we can associate with that random variable a function, f_X such that $f_X(i) = \Pr(X = i)$ for any integer i. When clarity permits, we will omit the subscript. This function, f, is called the probability density function, or density, or pdf, of the random variable. The above properties of the probability function immediately give us the following properties for pdf's of discrete random variables:

If f is the pdf of a discrete random variable, then

- $f(i) \geq 0$ for any integer i

- $\sum_{i \in I} f(i) = 1$ where I is the set of all integers.

The notation at the beginning of the second of these properties represents a summation. It is read "the sum of all f(i) where i is in the set of integers." This summation may be finite or infinite. If the random variable X has nonzero probability for a finite number of integers, we can consider the sum to be finite. If it has nonzero probability for an infinite number of integers, then this sum represents an infinite series that must converge—that is, get closer and closer to one. An example of this is a random variable X that takes on positive integer values and for which $\Pr(X = i) = f(i) = 2^{-i}$ for i = 1, 2, 3, ... In this case $\sum_{i \in I} f(i) = 1/2 + 1/4 + 1/8 + 1/16 + \ldots$. After four terms, this sum is .9375.

After eight terms it is about .9961. Continuing, this sum gets closer and closer to one. There is, of course, a more technical definition of this concept, but for now, we will simply say that this sum converges to one. In fact, we would say in this case that $\sum_{i \in I} f(i) = 1$.

B.4 Continuous Random Variables

Now consider a random variable, X, that can take on values in intervals of the form $\{x: a \le x \le b\}$ where a and b are real numbers. If there exists a function f_x such that $\Pr(a \le X \le b)$ equals the area under the graph of $y = f_x(x)$ between a and b, then X is said to be a continuous random variable and f_x is called its probability density function, or density, or pdf. As discussed in Appendix A, the area described above is called the definite integral of $f_x(x)$ from a to b, and it is denoted by $\int_a^b f_X(u)du$.

Here again, we will drop the subscript when no confusion is possible. It follows that such a function must be nonnegative and that $\int_{-\infty}^{\infty} f_X(u)du = 1$. According to this definition, the probability that a continuous random variable takes on a value between two real numbers, a and b, can be thought of geometrically as the area under the curve of the random variable's density and above the horizontal axis between a and b. This is illustrated in Figure B.2.

Figure B.2

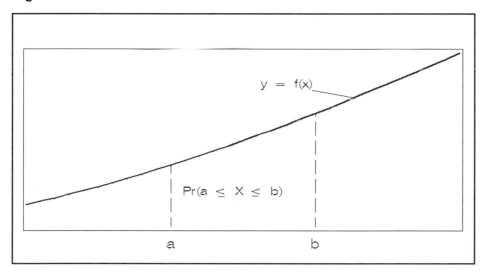

It may seem strange to use the phrase "probability density function" to refer to two apparently different concepts depending on whether a random variable is discrete or continuous. Some authors use "probability mass function" when referring to a discrete random variable and reserve "probability density function" for continuous random variables. Others use "probability density function" for both. I will follow this latter approach. This will not cause any problems. Although the value of a pdf is a probability for a discrete random variable and not for a continuous random variable, in the latter case, it resembles a probability in the following sense. If X is a continuous random variable with density $f(x)$, then for any real number x, and small increment, Δx, the probability that X is between x and $x + \Delta x$ can be approximated by $f(x)\Delta x$, the area of the rectangle that approximates the area under the density between x and $x + \Delta x$. This is illustrated in Figure B.3

where the area that is "hatched" one way or crosshatched represents $\Pr(x < X < x + \Delta x)$, while the area that is only "hatched" represents the approximation to that area by $f(x)\Delta x$. Thus, while $f(x)$ is not a probability, it tells us how a random variable's probability is concentrated at a value, x. Many statements about probability density functions will have very similar versions for discrete and continuous functions.

Figure B.3

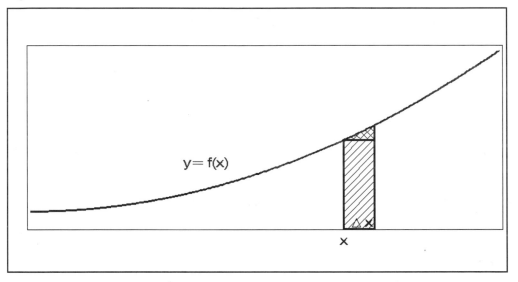

B.5 Cumulative Distribution Functions

If X is a random variable, the cumulative distribution function of X is defined by $F(x) = \Pr(X \leq x)$. Note that this definition applies for both discrete and continuous random variables. If f is the

corresponding pdf, then $F(x) = \displaystyle\sum_{i \leq x} f(i)$ if X is discrete, and $F(x) = \displaystyle\int_{-\infty}^{x} f(u)du$ if X is continuous.

The cumulative distribution function is also called the distribution function or the cdf. Clearly it is nonnegative, increasing (not necessarily strictly), and $F(\infty) = 1$. It is conventional to use corresponding upper- and lowercase letters to represent the cdf and pdf respectively. For a discrete random variable, the pdf can be obtained from the cdf as $f(x) = F(x) - F(x - 1)$. For a continuous random variable $f(x) = dF(x)/dx$ if the derivative of F exists.

B.5.1 Examples

* Consider the random variable, X, which takes on only the two values 0 and 1 with probabilities π and $1 - \pi$ respectively where $0 \leq \pi \leq 1$. X is called a Bernoulli random variable. Its density is given by

$$f(x) = \begin{cases} \pi \text{ if } x = 0 \\ 1 - \pi \text{ if } x = 1 \\ 0 \text{ otherwise} \end{cases}$$

Its distribution function is the step function defined by

$$F(x) = \begin{cases} 0 \text{ if } x < 0 \\ \pi \text{ if } 0 \le x < 1 \\ 1 \text{ if } x \ge 1 \end{cases}$$

If we consider the toss of a coin and let X be the random variable that associates heads and tails with 0 and 1, respectively, then we would consider X to have a Bernoulli distribution with $\pi = .5$ if the coin is fair.

- If n is a positive integer and $0 \le \pi \le 1$, then a binomial random variable has the density

$$f(x) = \begin{cases} \dfrac{n!}{x!(n-x)!}\pi^x(1-\pi)^{n-x} \text{ for } x = 0, 1, 2, \ldots, n \\ 0 \text{ otherwise} \end{cases}$$

The associated cdf is given by

$$F(x) = \sum_{i=0}^{x} \frac{n!}{i!(n-i)!}\pi^i(1-\pi)^{n-i} \text{ for } x = 0, 1, 2, \ldots, n$$

If we think of n tosses of a coin and let X be the number of heads, then we would consider X to be a binomial random variable with $\pi = .5$ if the coin is fair.

- If μ is any real number and $\sigma^2 > 0$ then a normal, or Gaussian, random variable has the density

$$f(x) = \frac{1}{\sqrt{2\pi\sigma^2}}\exp[-\frac{(x-\mu)^2}{2\sigma^2}] \text{ for } -\infty < x < \infty$$

It can be shown, although we won't do it here, that $\int_{-\infty}^{\infty} f(x)dx = 1$.

In this case, the associated cdf

$$F(x) = \int_{-\infty}^{x} \frac{1}{\sqrt{2\pi\sigma^2}}\exp[-\frac{(y-\mu)^2}{2\sigma^2}]dy \text{ for } -\infty < x < \infty \text{ cannot be evaluated exactly.}$$

However, it can be approximated by numerical methods and is tabled extensively for $\sigma^2 = 1$ and $\mu = 0$.

Many naturally occurring random variables such as weights of a group of people, annual amounts of rainfall, and highest temperature on the first day of August are considered normally distributed.

- Let n be any positive integer. The random variable with density given by

$$f(x) = \begin{cases} \dfrac{1}{\Gamma(n/2)2^{n/2}} x^{n/2-1} e^{-x/2} & \text{for } 0 < x < \infty \\ = 0 \text{ elsewhere} \end{cases}$$

is called a chi-square random variable with n degrees of freedom.

Here $\Gamma(x)$ is the gamma function and is given by

$$\Gamma(x) = \int_0^\infty y^{x-1} e^{-y} dy \text{ for } x > 0.$$

This type of random variable is important, not because it occurs in nature, but because it can be shown that calculations in statistics often result in random variables that have, approximately, a chi-square distribution.

- For any real numbers a and b with $a < b$, the random variable with the density given by

$$f(x) = \begin{cases} 0 & \text{if } x < a \\ \dfrac{1}{b-a} & \text{if } a \le x \le b \\ 0 & \text{if } x > b \end{cases}$$

is called a uniform random variable over the interval [a, b]. Its cdf is given by

$$F(x) = \begin{cases} 0 & \text{if } x < a \\ \dfrac{x-a}{b-a} & \text{if } a \le x \le b \\ 1 & \text{if } x > b \end{cases}$$

If we think of a clinical trial that starts on day zero and accrues patients for 180 days, the accrual day of a patient might be thought of as a random variable with a distribution that is uniform over the interval [0, 180].

In each of the previous examples, the densities and distribution functions are not completely specified. Each describes a class of functions of a certain form differing according to the values of certain constants used in their definitions – π in the Bernoulli, π and n in the binomial distribution, μ and σ^2 in the normal distribution, n in the chi-square distribution, and a and b in the uniform distribution. These constants are called parameters of the distributions. Sometimes we are interested in the behavior or properties of random variables with these distributions for various values of the parameters. In such cases we might indicate that by explicitly listing the parameters in the function definition. For example, we might write $f(x, \mu, \sigma^2)$ for the density of a normal random variable with parameters μ and σ^2.

B.6 Exercises

B.6.1 Suppose that X is a binomial random variable with parameters

$\pi = .7$ and n $= 7.$ Find a) $\Pr(3 < X < 5)$, b) $\Pr(X \le 3)$, c) $\Pr(X \ge 4)$.

B.6.2 Let X be a normally distributed random variable with parameters μ and σ^2. Let
$Z = (X - \mu)/\sigma$. Show that Z has a normal distribution with parameters
$\mu = 0$ and $\sigma^2 = 1$. This is why this is the only normal distribution that needs to be tabled. It
is often called the standard normal distribution. Hint: Consider the cdf of Z.

B.7 Mean, Variance, and Standard Deviation

Let X be a random variable with pdf f(x). Let g(X) be any function of X. Then the expected value

of g(X), denoted E[g(X)], is defined as $\sum_i g(i)f(i)$ if X is discrete and $\int_{-\infty}^{\infty} g(x)f(x)dx$ if X is

continuous. If $g(x) \equiv x$ then this becomes $E[X] = \sum_i if(i)$ or $\int_{-\infty}^{\infty} xf(x)dx$. In either case this is called

the mean of X. The Greek letter μ is frequently used for the mean of a random variable.

If μ is the mean of a random variable X, then the expected value of $(X - \mu)^2$ is known as the

variance of X and is often denoted σ^2 or Var[X]. Of course this will be $\sum_i (i - \mu)^2 f(i)$ if X is discrete

and $\int_{-\infty}^{\infty} (x-\mu)^2 f(x)dx$ if X is continuous. The square root of σ^2, denoted σ (naturally) is known as the

standard deviation of X. Note that σ is in the same unit of measurement as the values of X. Of
course, defining a concept doesn't necessarily mean that it always exists. It is not hard to come up
with examples of discrete and continuous random variables for which means and variances do not
exist because the sum or integral shown in this section is not finite.

B.7.1 Exercises

B.7.1.1 Show that for any random variable, X, and constant, a,
a) $E[aX] = aE[X]$
b) $E[a] = a$
c) $E[X + a] = E[X] + a$
d) $Var[X] = E[X^2] - (E[X])^2$ (Note: this provides a convenient alternate way to calculate
variances.)
e) $Var[a] = 0$
f) $Var[aX] = a^2 Var[X]$
g) $Var[X + a] = Var[X]$
(You may do these for X discrete or continuous. The other case will be similar.)

B.7.1.2 Show that for a normally distributed random variable, the parameter μ is the mean. (Hint:
do this first for $\mu = 0$, then apply B.7.1.1 c.)

B.7.1.3 Show that for a pdf of a binomial random variable, the sum over all values is 1. Hint: Remember the binomial formula, $(a + b)^n = ?$. Replace a by π and b by $1 - \pi$. Also show that the mean is $n\pi$ and that the variance is $n\pi (1 - \pi)$.

B.7.1.4 A Poisson random variable has the density $f(x) = e^{-\lambda} \lambda^x/x!$ for $\lambda > 0$ and $x = 0, 1, 2, \ldots$ Find the mean and the variance of a Poisson random variable.

B.7.1.5 An exponential random variable is a continuous random variable with density $f(x) = \lambda e^{-\lambda x}$ for $\lambda > 0$ and $x > 0$. Show that the mean and variance of an exponential random variable are $1/\lambda$ and $1/\lambda^2$ respectively.

B.7.1.6 A Cauchy random variable has the pdf $f(x) = 1/[\pi(1 + x^2)]$ for $-\infty < x < \infty$. Show that this random variable has no mean.

B.7.2 The Delta Method

A type of problem we frequently encounter is to find, or at least approximate, the variance of some continuous function, $g(X)$ of a random variable, X when we know Var[X]. For example, we might want to find the variance of e^X or X^2 when we know the variance of X. A method of doing this is known as the delta method. It is based on the fact that for any continuous function g and real number a, the function $g(x)$ can be written as the infinite series $g(a) + g'(a)(x - a)/1! + g''(a)(x - a)^2/2! + \ldots$, which is called the Taylor series for $g(x)$ about a. It can be shown that, if the function $g(x)$ is continuous, the right side of this equation converges to $g(x)$ as the number of terms increases without bound. By truncating it after some finite number of terms, we get an approximation. A rigorous derivation of the delta method would be beyond the level of this book, but a heuristic justification can be given. Let $\mu = E[X]$ and consider the Taylor series of $g(X)$ about μ, which is given by $g(X) = g(\mu) + g'(\mu)(X - \mu)/1! + g''(\mu)(X - \mu)^2/2! + \ldots$ If we truncate this series after the linear term (i.e., the second term), we get $g(X) \approx g(\mu) + g'(\mu)(X - \mu)$. Now, consider the variances of both sides of this equation, and use the results of Exercise 7.1.1. Then the variance of the constant $g(\mu)$ is zero, the variance of $X - \mu$ is the same as the variance of X, and we get $[g(X)] \approx [g'(\mu)]^2 \text{Var}(X)$. This final result enables us to estimate the variance of a function of X in terms of the variance of X and the derivative of the function.

B.7.3 Exercise

Let X be an exponential random variable with density $f(x) = \lambda e^{-\lambda x}$ for $\lambda > 0$ and $x > 0$. Use the delta method, B.7.1.5, and the first property in A.1.6 of Appendix A to find approximate variances for X^2 and $\exp(X)$.

B.8 Joint Distributions

What we have said about random variables extends quite naturally to vectors of k random variables of the form $\mathbf{X} = (X_1, X_2, \ldots, X_k)$. To keep the notation in this section simple, we restrict our attention to $k = 2$, but the extensions to larger values should be obvious. Consider the set I^2 of all ordered pairs of integers and a function Pr associating subsets of I^2 with real numbers. This function satisfies the properties stated in Section B.2. If there is a bivariate function f which associates subsets of I^2 with real numbers such that $\Pr[(X,Y) \in A] = \sum_{(x,y) \in A} \sum f(x,y)$ and f has the properties

- $0 \le f(x, y)$ for all (x, y) in I^2
- $\displaystyle\sum_{(x,y)\in I^2} \sum f(x,y) = 1$

then (X, Y) said to be a discrete bivariate random variable and f is its probability density function. The associated cumulative distribution function is given by $F(x, y) = \displaystyle\sum_{i \le x} \sum_{j \le y} f(i, j)$. For continuous bivariate random variables, we simply replace the double summations with double integrals. In this case the probability function, Pr, associates subsets of R^2, the set of all ordered pairs of real numbers, with nonnegative numbers less than or equal to one and there is a function f defined on R^2 such that $Pr[(X, Y) \in A] = \displaystyle\iint_{(x, y) \in A} f(x, y)dxdy$. Of course, f must be nonnegative and its integral over R^2 must be one. The bivariate distribution function is defined by $F(x, y) = \displaystyle\int_{-\infty}^{y} \int_{-\infty}^{x} f(u, v)dudv$.

If $\mathbf{X} = (X, Y)$ is a bivariate random variable, then $E[\mathbf{X}]$ is defined as the vector $(E[X], E[Y])$. If $\mathbf{X}$ has density $f(x,y)$ and $g(x,y)$ is any bivariate function, then $E[g(X,Y)]$ is defined as

$\displaystyle\sum_{X\in I} \sum_{Y\in I} g(X,Y)f(X,Y)$ if X and Y are discrete and as $\displaystyle\int_{-\infty}^{\infty} \int_{-\infty}^{\infty} g(x,y)f(x,y)dxdy$ if X and Y are continuous.

Given a bivariate density function, the densities of each of the component univariate random variables can be obtained by summing (in the discrete case) or integrating (in the continuous case) over the other variable. Specifically, if $f(x, y)$ is a bivariate density, the density of X, $f_X(x)$, is given

by $f_X(x) = \displaystyle\sum_{y} f(x, y)$ in the discrete case and $f_X(x) = \displaystyle\int_{-\infty}^{\infty} f(x, y)dy$ in the continuous case. The

densities of X and Y are referred to as the marginal densities associated with the joint density of X and Y.

If (X, Y) is a bivariate random variable, then $E[X]$, $E[Y]$, $Var(X)$, and $Var(Y)$ refer to the means and variances of the random variables having the associated marginal distributions. In addition, we define the covariance of X and Y as $E[(X - E[X])(Y - E[Y])]$. Note that the variance of X is the covariance of X with itself.

B.9 Conditional Probability and Stochastic Independence

Let X and Y be random variables having a bivariate density $f(x, y)$ and marginal densities $f_X(x)$ and $f_Y(y)$. Now let x be some fixed value such that $f_X(x) > 0$ and consider $f(x, y)/f(x)$. This expression defines a function (of y) that is easily seen to satisfy the properties of a pdf. We will denote this pdf by $f(y|x)$, which will be read "f of y conditioned on x" or "f of y given x." Thus by definition, $f(y|x) = f(x, y)/f_X(x)$. It follows that $f(x, y) = f_X(x)f(y|x)$ for all x and y. If it happens that $f(y|x) = f_Y(y)$ for all x and y, then $f(x, y) = f_X(x)f_Y(y)$ for all x and y. In this case X and Y are said to be stochastically independent (or simply independent). Note that this discussion applies to both discrete and continuous random variables.

B.9.1 Exercise

Show that if X and Y are random variables and a and b are constants then
1) $E[X + Y] = E[X] + E[Y]$
2) $Var(X + Y) = Var(X) + Var(Y) + 2Cov(X,Y)$
3) $Cov(aX, bY) = abCov(X, Y)$
4) $Cov(X + a, Y + b) = Cov(X, Y)$
5) If X and Y are independent, then $E[XY] = E[X]E[Y]$
6) If X and Y are independent, then $Cov(X,Y) = 0$ (so $Var(X + Y) = Var(X) + Var(Y)$).
Hint: Do these either for X and Y discrete random variable or X and Y continuous random variable. The other case will be similar.

B.10 The Delta Method for Two Variables

The delta method, as discussed earlier, can be extended to functions of two variables to provide a method of approximating $Var[g(X, Y)]$ where X and Y are random variables with means μ_X and μ_Y, respectively. Again, only a rather simplified argument will be given here. The Taylor series for $g(X, Y)$ about (μ_X, μ_Y), truncated after the linear terms, can be written $g(X, Y) \approx g(\mu_X, \mu_Y) + (X - \mu_X) \partial g(\mu_X, \mu_Y)/\partial X + (Y - \mu_Y) \partial g(\mu_X, \mu_Y)/\partial Y$. Using the results of B.9.1.1, we obtain
$Var[g(X, Y)] \approx [\partial g(\mu_X, \mu_Y)/\partial X]^2 Var(X) + [\partial g(\mu_X, \mu_Y)/\partial Y]^2 Var(Y) + 2[\partial g(\mu_X, \mu_Y)/\partial X][\partial g(\mu_X, \mu_Y)/\partial Y]Cov(X, Y)$.

B.11 Parameters and Estimates

Let us return to the set of outcomes for an experiment and a random variable, X, defined on this set of outcomes. The density function, f(x), of X associates probabilities with these outcomes. A random sample of size n is a set of independent random variables $X_1, X_2, \ldots, X_n$ each having the same pdf, f(x), as X. If this book was about probability, we would be interested in answering questions about $X_1, X_2, \ldots, X_n$ given information about f(x). Since this book is about statistics, we are instead interested in answering questions about f(x) given information about $X_1, X_2, \ldots, X_n$. Often we are willing to assume that f(x) is a density of a certain type with the value of a parameter (or parameters) unknown. In that case we are often interested in answering questions about the parameter(s) using the information contained in the random sample. Here are some questions we might want to ask about parameters of a distribution:

- What is a good estimate of the value of a parameter?
- Do two distributions have the same values for their parameter(s)?
- How good is a parameter estimate? That is, what can be said for how far it might be from the true parameter value?

Before we discuss a general method of parameter estimation, it might be a good idea to consider some desirable properties of any estimation method.

- There should be a straightforward algorithm for calculating an estimate from a random sample. It should be something we can do, perhaps with the aid of a computer and some software.
- Since the estimate is the value of some function of the random sample and the random sample is a set of random variables, the estimate is actually a value of a random variable. It would be nice to know something about the distribution of that random variable. Then we could make probability statements about the estimate.

- The estimated value of the parameter probably won't equal the true value of the parameter. But it would be nice if "on the average" such estimates equaled, or at least were close to, the true value. An estimate (which is a random variable) whose mean is the true value of the parameter being estimated is said to be unbiased. If the mean is close to the true value when the sample size is large, the mean is said to be consistent.

This is a good place to mention some common notation used for parameters and their estimates. We often use Greek letters to represent parameters. The corresponding Latin letter is often used for its estimate. For example, b, s, and r might be used for the estimates of parameters β, σ, and ρ respectively. Another common notation is to use a "hat" over the name of a parameter to indicate its estimate. Thus $\hat{\theta}$ might be used for an estimate of θ.

B.12 Maximum Likelihood Estimation

Consider a random variable having the Bernoulli distribution as described in Section B.5.1 with unknown parameter, π. Suppose we have a random sample of size 6 with values $x_1, x_2, \ldots, x_6$. Now those values are all either 0 or 1. Suppose four of them are 0 and two are 1. Then the joint probability of this sample is called the likelihood of this sample and is given by

$L(\pi) = \displaystyle\prod_{i=1}^{6} f(x_i) = \pi^4 (1 - \pi)^2$. The notation reminds us that the value of the likelihood depends

upon the value of π. Now it seems only reasonable that a good choice for an estimate of π would be a value that makes the probability of what actually happened as large as possible. Thus we might choose that value of π that maximizes $L(\pi)$ as the estimator of π. If we plot this function we get the graph in Figure B.4.

Figure B.4

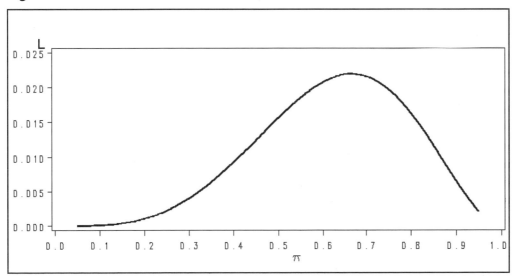

Note that the likelihood apparently is maximized by some value of π between 0.6 and 0.7. But we can do better than that. First of all, maximizing any function is equivalent to maximizing its logarithm. This is seen in Figure B.5, where $\log L(\pi) = 4\log(\pi) + 2\log(1 - \pi)$.

Figure B.5

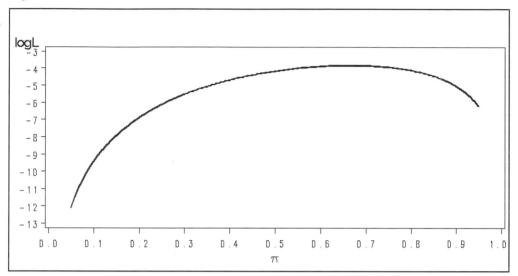

Recalling the discussion in Appendix A, we can maximize $L(\pi)$ by finding the value of π for which $d\log L(\pi)/d\pi = 0$. The derivative of $\log L(\pi)$ with respect to π is $4/\pi - 2/(1 - \pi)$. Thus we can find the value of π that maximizes the likelihood by solving the equation $4/\pi - 2/(1 - \pi) = 0$. The solution is easily found to be 2/3. We refer to 2/3 as the maximum likelihood estimator (or MLE) of π. Of course, we are hardly surprised by this result. After all, with four zeroes and two ones we would have estimated the probability of zero to be 2/3 without all of this fancy stuff! Nevertheless, it is comforting when our method produces that result that we feel we ought to get in a simple case such as this. It instills some confidence that it might work in more complex cases.

Now if a random variable is continuous, the likelihood is not a probability. Nevertheless, recall that $f(x)\Delta x$ is approximately the probability that the random variable has a value in the vicinity of x (specifically, between x and x + Δx). Thus the value of a parameter, θ, that maximizes the

likelihood defined by $L(\theta) = \prod_{i=1}^{n} f(x_i, \theta)$ makes sense as an estimate of θ in this case as well. Of

course, the solution of the equation formed by equating the derivative to zero may not be as easy as it was in the previous example. In fact, it may not be possible to find an exact solution to the equation. When this happens we must rely on one of many methods of approximation. The best-known method is known as the Newton (or Newton-Raphson) method. To find an approximate solution of $g(\theta) = 0$, start with some initial estimate of a solution, θ_0. Then define

$\theta_1 = \theta_0 - g(\theta_0)/g'(\theta_0)$ where $g'(\theta_0)$ is the derivative with respect to θ evaluated at θ_0. Repeat this

process, letting $\theta_2 = \theta_1 - g(\theta_1)/g'(\theta_1)$ etc. If the function is "well behaved" in the vicinity of the

solution, the sequence $\theta_0, \theta_1, \ldots$ will converge to a solution, $\hat{\theta}$. In practice, we would end the process when two consecutive iterates differ by less than some small, preassigned value or when $g(\theta_i)$ is sufficiently close to 0.

When we are maximizing the logarithm of a likelihood, the function $g(\theta)$ referred to earlier is the derivative of the loglikelihood, so $g'(\theta)$ is the second derivative of the loglikelihood. We will see later that this second derivative plays another important role.

A word of caution is needed here. Often the density function whose parameter is being estimated imposes limits on the set of permissible values for that parameter. For example, the parameter, π, of the binomial distribution must satisfy $0 < \pi < 1$ and the parameter σ^2 of the normal distribution must satisfy $\sigma^2 > 0$. The set of all possible values for the parameter is called its parameter space. In such cases, we must be careful to maximize the likelihood only over the parameter space. Allowing the maximization process to consider values outside this parameter space can have unpredictable results. This is of particular concern when using existing software.

Another word of caution. There may be several values of the parameter that cause the derivative of the loglikelihood to be zero. This can happen for values of the parameter associated with local maxima and at values associated with local minima. Thus we may need to look more carefully at the loglikelihood, especially if setting the derivative equal to zero yields an equation with more than one solution. It might be a good idea to draw the graph of the likelihood of loglikelihood.

Although it is certainly possible to describe situations in which maximum likelihood estimators do not exist, or exist but are not very good, or are very difficult to find, these situations are the exceptions. Generally MLEs can be found (although perhaps you will need a computer and good software, as seen in the Appendix C). Furthermore, under certain regularity conditions, MLEs should have the following desirable properties:

- Recall that the MLE of a parameter is a random variable. That random variable has, asymptotically, a normal distribution. This means, roughly, that as the sample size gets larger, the distribution of the MLE gets closer and closer to that of a normal random variable.

- The mean of that normal distribution approaches the parameter value as the sample size increases. In other words, MLEs are consistent estimates.

- The variance of a MLE can be approximated by $-[d^2\log L(\hat{\theta})/d\theta^2]^{-1}$; that is the negative of the reciprocal of the second derivative of the loglikelihood, evaluated at the MLE. Recall that this is the second derivative that is needed in the Newton-Raphson method.

These properties allow us to say something about the precision of our estimate of the parameter, to write approximate confidence intervals for it, and to perform hypothesis tests concerning it.

Of course, as seen in the previous examples, a density function might have more than one parameter. Our discussion can be extended to the case of multiple parameters. Suppose that a density function has k parameters $\theta_1, \theta_2, \ldots, \theta_k$. We think of them collectively as a vector $(\theta_1, \theta_2, \ldots, \theta_k)$. If we want to think of that vector as a column vector rather than a row vector, we can write it as $(\theta_1, \theta_2, \ldots, \theta_k)'$. We will use bold symbols for vectors. Thus the vector of parameters might be written as the column vector $\boldsymbol{\theta} = (\theta_1, \theta_2, \ldots, \theta_k)'$. Now the parameter space is a k-dimensional subset of the set of all k-tuples of real numbers. We define the MLE of $\boldsymbol{\theta}$ to be the vector of values of $\theta_1, \theta_2, \ldots, \theta_k$ that maximizes the likelihood. Again we usually prefer to maximize the logarithm of the likelihood. One way of finding this vector is to find the values that simultaneously solve the equations $\partial \log L(\boldsymbol{\theta}) / \partial \theta_i = 0$ for $i = 1, 2, \ldots, k$. This can be a difficult problem. The Newton-Raphson method generalizes to systems of equations in the following way. Let the vector $\boldsymbol{\theta}_0$ be an initial estimate of the solution. Let $G(\boldsymbol{\theta})$ be the k-dimensional row vector in which the ith element is the partial derivative of the loglikelihood with respect to θ_i. Let $H(\boldsymbol{\theta})$ be the $k \times k$ array, or matrix, in which the ith row jth column element is the second partial derivative of the loglikelihood with respect to θ_i and θ_j. G and H are called the gradient and hessian, respectively, of the system of equations. Then $\boldsymbol{\theta}_1 = \boldsymbol{\theta}_0 - G(\boldsymbol{\theta}_0)\left[H(\boldsymbol{\theta}_0)\right]^{-1}$ will, under reasonable conditions, be a better estimate. The $[H(\boldsymbol{\theta}_0)]^{-1}$ is the inverse of the matrix $H(\boldsymbol{\theta}_0)$ and the indicated multiplication and subtraction are operations on vectors and matrices. The sequence defined by $\boldsymbol{\theta}_{n+1} = \boldsymbol{\theta}_n - G(\boldsymbol{\theta}_n)\left[H(\boldsymbol{\theta}_n)\right]^{-1}$ will generally converge to a solution, which we will write as $\hat{\boldsymbol{\theta}}$. Note that this is a direct extension of the technique described earlier for a single parameter.

The process described earlier can require a huge amount of computation. Fortunately, modern software can do that computation for us. We will see in Appendix C a way to find MLEs using SAS.

The MLE for a vector of parameters has properties that generalize the properties already stated for the one-parameter case as well. Specifically

- $\hat{\theta}$ is a multivariate random variable whose joint distribution is multivariate normal.
- The mean vector of that random variable approaches θ as the sample size increases.
- The ith row, jth column element of $-[H(\hat{\theta})]^{-1}$ is an approximation of the covariance of the ith and jth elements of $\hat{\theta}$. In particular the ith diagonal element is an approximation of the variance of the ith element of $\hat{\theta}$.

Maximum likelihood estimators have another property that is very useful. We are sometimes interested in the properties of functions of a parameter or parameters. Of course, such functions are themselves random variables; so, we might ask about their (asymptotic) distributions. It can be shown that a continuous function of a MLE is itself a MLE. Hence a parameter created by applying a continuous function to a MLE has all of the properties listed earlier.

B.13 Likelihood Ratio Tests

Maximum likelihood estimators lead directly to an important class of hypothesis tests. Consider a likelihood $L(\theta)$ where θ is a k-dimensional vector. Thus the parameter space has dimension k. A null hypothesis typically makes some specification about the vector θ that reduces the dimensionality of the parameter space. For example, if the null hypothesis states that two of the parameters are equal, it reduces the dimensionality of the space by one. If it specifies values for j of the k parameters, it reduces the dimensionality of the parameter space by j. Let L_Ω be the value of likelihood maximized over the entire parameter space. Let L_ω be the value of the likelihood maximized over the subset defined by the null hypothesis. Both L_ω and L_Ω are positive, and L_ω must be smaller than L_Ω because it is a value of the likelihood maximized over a subset of the space over which L_Ω is maximized. Intuitively, it would seem that the ratio, $\Lambda = L_\omega/L_\Omega$, which must be between zero and one should provide a basis for deciding whether or not to reject the null hypothesis. Specifically, if this ratio is near one that tells us that the sample is almost as likely under the null hypothesis as without that restriction. Thus rejection of the null hypothesis is not indicated. On the other hand, if the ratio, Λ, is near zero the sample is not nearly as likely under the null hypothesis as it is without that restriction. In this case rejection of the null hypothesis is called for.

Now, of course, we want to find a cutpoint, C, so that under the null hypothesis, $\Pr[\Lambda < C] = \alpha$ for some preassigned significance level, α. We can do this if we know about the distribution of Λ. Alternatively, we might find a function, g such that $\Lambda < C$ if and only if $g(\Lambda) < g(C)$ or $\Lambda < C$ if and only if $g(\Lambda) > g(C)$ where the distribution of $g(\Lambda)$ is known. In such cases we can use our knowledge of that distribution to perform the hypothesis test. Many familiar tests, including Student's pooled t test and the classical analysis of variance, are of this type.

But when neither of the approaches described earlier are helpful, we have still another alternative. If certain conditions are satisfied, then $-2\log(\Lambda)$ has approximately a chi-square distribution with degrees of freedom equal to the dimension of Ω minus the dimension of ω. If the null hypothesis simply specifies values for j of the k parameters, then the degrees of freedom is j. The statistic $-2\log(\Lambda)$ is often written as $2[\log(L_\Omega) - \log(L_\omega)]$.

B.13.1 Exercises

B.13.1.1 Suppose $f_1(x)$ and $f_2(x)$ are densities of random variables and
$0 < \pi < 1$, and show that $f(x) = \pi f_1(x) + (1 - \pi)f_2(x)$ satisfies the properties of a density.

B.13.1.2 Let $x_1, x_2, \ldots x_n$ be n values of a random variable X having a uniform distribution on the interval [0, b]. Thus $0 \leq x_i \leq b$ for $i = 1, 2, \ldots n$. Show that the method used in the above example does not work to find the MLE of b. What is the MLE of b?

B.14 Confidence Intervals

Once we have computed, by the method of maximum likelihood or by some other method, an estimate for a parameter, θ, we usually like to describe an interval of plausible values for the parameter's true value. Such an interval is called a confidence interval. Recall that an estimate is actually created by mathematical operations on a random sample; hence it is a value of some function of a random sample and thus is itself a value of a random variable. A $(1 - \alpha)100\%$ confidence interval is created by finding values of two other functions of the random sample, L and U, such that $\Pr(L < \theta < U) = 1 - \alpha$. We then say that the interval (L, U) is a $(1 - \alpha)100\%$ confidence interval for θ.

This concept, unfortunately, causes a great deal of confusion. It is commonplace to say something like "There is a probability of $1 - \alpha$ that θ is between L and U." Without getting into arguments about the meaning of such a sentence, it is important to realize that a statement about a confidence interval is not a probability statement about the parameter θ. θ is not a random variable, so we don't make probability statements about it. Rather, it is a probability statement about L and U which are random variables. A better way to describe the situation is to say something like "There is a probability of $1 - \alpha$ that the interval (L, U) contains θ."

If, as is the case with MLEs, an estimate, $\hat{\theta}$, of θ is approximately normally distributed with mean θ, and standard deviation, which is approximated by s, then we have a natural way to form confidence intervals. In this case we can show that $L = \theta - z_{1-\alpha/2}s$ and $U = \theta + z_{1-\alpha/2}s$, where z_x satisfies $\Pr(Z < z_x) = x$ for a standard normal random variable Z, defines the desired confidence interval.

B.14.1 Exercise

Show that if an estimate $\hat{\theta}$ is normally distributed with mean θ and standard deviation s, then $\hat{\theta} \pm z_{1-\alpha/2}s$ are the endpoints of a $(1 - \alpha)100\%$ confidence interval for θ.

Appendix C   SAS Concepts

C.1 DATA Steps and PROC Steps 209
C.2 The DATA Step 209
C.3 The PROC Step 211
C.4 PROC IML 212
C.5 The SAS Macro Language 215

C.1 DATA Steps and PROC Steps

Many simple SAS programs consist of two steps: a DATA step and a PROC (short for *procedure*) step. A *data* step creates a SAS data set or modifies an existing SAS data set. A PROC step then applies a SAS procedure to that data set to accomplish a particular type of task (producing *t* tests, regressions, graphs, descriptive statistics, and so on).

C.2 The DATA Step

Here's an example of a simple DATA step:

```
data mydata;
input patid @8 date_of_birth mmddyy8. @18 date_of_dx
mmddyy8. cancertype $;
/*  Define age at diagnosis.  */
    age_at_dx = (date_of_dx - date_of_birth)/365;
datalines;
21375   03/05/56   06/29/98   HD
36534   09/16/45   12/04/99   NHL
41224   11/17/62      .       MEL
;
```

The DATA statement in the first line tells SAS that we are starting a DATA step and provides a name for the data set to be created. Providing the name is optional. If you don't provide a name, SAS uses what is called the DATAn convention. It names the first such data set Data1, the second Data2, and so on. The INPUT statement provides the names of the variables being input in this step. Note that, beginning with Version 7 of SAS, it is possible to use long variables names. Previous versions require that variable names have no more than eight characters. Names can include letters (case is immaterial), underscores, and the digits 0 – 9. The first character in the variable name must not be a digit.

The MMDDYY8. format tells SAS that the preceding variable has an eight-character date format. The @n notation gives the starting columns of the values. The dollar sign *($)* means that the previous variable, in this case Cancertype, represents a character string, rather than a number.

Any characters that you type between /* and */ are ignored by SAS. To some programmers, particularly beginners, this means that there is no point in typing anything that SAS will ignore. More experienced programmers, however, use this feature to include comments, also called internal documentation, in a program. This facilitates the process of correcting errors. It also helps others who may "inherit" your program and need to modify it later.

The assignment statement in the next line defines a new variable, Age_at_dx, as the result of subtracting variable values. The reason this statement makes sense is that, in SAS, dates are stored as numbers—the number of days before or after January 1, 1960. For example, 03/05/56 is stored as –1397 and 06/29/98 as 14059. Thus, the difference defined by `date_of_dx - date_of_dx` is the number of days between these dates. Dividing by 365 converts this value to years. This is done for every observation. An assignment statement looks like an algebraic equation, but it has a different meaning. It tells the program to perform the calculation indicated to the right of the equal sign and to assign the result to the variable that is to the left of the equal sign. For example, the statement `x = x + 1;` would not make sense as an algebraic equation. In a SAS data set it makes perfectly good sense. It instructs the program to increase the value of *x* by one.

SAS provides a large number of functions that can be used in expressions on the right side of assignment statements (and elsewhere). For example, the statements `u = tan(y);` and `v = exp(z);` create new variables *u* and *v* whose values are the values of the tangent of y and e^z respectively.

Because many probability density functions and cumulative distribution functions are difficult to calculate, SAS provides a large collection of functions for that purpose as well. These functions are documented in the SAS Language Reference. Twenty-two densities and distribution functions are available in Version 9. Inverses of distribution functions are also frequently needed. SAS provides seven of them in Version 9.

The DATALINES statement tells SAS that the data follow. Incidentally, the CARDS statement can be used instead. This statement name dates from the days when the data would be on IBM punch cards. Note the decimal point used for the value of Date_of_dx in the third observation. That indicates a missing value.

The data set created by these statements will last for the duration of the SAS session. When you end your SAS session, it will be gone. If you want to make it permanent, give the data set a two-part name. Before you do that, submit a LIBNAME statement. It has this form:

```
LIBNAME name 'path';
```

Here *name* is a name that you provide and *path* is a subdirectory or folder, based on your system's conventions. For example, on a PC running under Windows, this might be

```
libname mydata 'c:\sasdatasets';
```

where **c:\datasets** is a subdirectory (or folder) on your hard disk.

If we follow this statement with a DATA step that starts with `data mydata.cancer;` the data set created will be stored, after the SAS session has ended, in the subdirectory **c:\sasdatasets**. It will have the name Cancer.*ext* where *ext* depends on the system and SAS version. For Versions 7, 8, and 9 in the Windows PC environment, the extension is SAS7BDAT.

If we want to use this data set later, we can use the LIBNAME statement that we discussed earlier. We can then start a DATA step with

```
data newdata;
set mydata.cancer;
```

This initializes the new data set Newdata as the previously created data set Mydata.cancer. No INPUT statement, DATALINES statement, or data are needed. However, we can have assignment statements that create new variables and modify old ones.

The previous discussion is meant to provide only a brief introduction to the DATA step for those readers new to SAS. In fact, the DATA step is an extremely rich programming language with loops, conditional statements, arrays, and so on. We can't discuss all of this here, but you will see examples of the capabilities of the DATA step in programs presented elsewhere in this book. For a more complete discussion of the DATA step, see one of the excellent BBU books on the subject (Cody 1996; DiIorio 1991; Scerbo et. al. 2001).

C.3 The PROC Step

The PROC step starts with a PROC statement. It has the form

```
PROC procname (options);
```

Here *procname* is the name of one of the SAS procedures in one of the SAS products installed on your computer. Most SAS procedures have several options you can choose to specify some details of how the procedure is performed. These options will generally have defaults that are often acceptable to the user. One such option is the name of the data set to which the procedure is to be applied. The default is the last data set defined. There are usually several additional statements that can be used to further specify details concerning how the procedure is performed and what results are printed in the output.

One frequently used procedure is `PROC PRINT`. As the name implies, it is used to print a data set. If you follow the DATA step of the previous section with the statement

```
proc print; run;
```

you will get the following output:

```
                              The SAS System

                       date_of_     date_                         age_at_
        Obs    patid     birth      of_dx      cancertype          dx

         1     21375     -1397      14059         HD             42.3452
         2     36534     -5220      14582         NHL            54.2521
         3     41224      1051        .           MEL               .
```

Incidentally, the need for the RUN statement depends on what system you are using and whether you are working in interactive or batch mode. In the Windows PC environment, when you are working interactively, the beginning of each step causes the previous step to run. However, the final step will not run unless the RUN statement is used.

Note that the values of Date_of_birth and Date_of_dx look strange to us. Recall what was said earlier about their being stored as numbers. If you want them printed in a more familiar format, specify one of several date formats. For example, if you use

```
proc print; format date_of_birth date_of_dx date9. ;
```

you will get the following output:

```
                            The SAS System

                    date_of_        date_                    age_at_
      Obs    patid     birth        of_dx    cancertype        dx

       1     21375   05MAR1956    29JUN1998      HD          42.3452
       2     36534   16SEP1945    04DEC1999      NHL         54.2521
       3     41224   17NOV1962        .          MEL            .
```

C.4 PROC IML

PROC IML is an extremely useful SAS tool. IML is an acronym for interactive matrix language. As this suggests, IML is a programming language, imbedded within SAS, which works with matrices, rather than only with numbers. For example, in IML the variable x might represent a 1×5 row vector and v might represent a 5×5 matrix. Then the statement

```
u = x*inv(v)*x';
```

would cause the program to multiply x by the inverse of v, multiply the result by the transpose of x, and then assign the resultant value to the variable u. You won't need to understand PROC IML to learn the material in the rest of this book. However, we will provide several SAS programs that use PROC IML and that you may find useful. Those interested in learning methods of writing programs to implement mathematical and statistical methods might want to study them and learn to write their own PROC IML programs. By the way, PROC IML is a separately licensed product and is not installed with SAS on all computers. Since this book uses it extensively you might want to check this and make sure it is installed on the computer you will be using.

C.4.1 The Quad Subroutine

PROC IML also includes several subroutines that perform calculations that might otherwise require considerable programming. One of them, Quad, provides estimates of definite integrals. Here's a simple example.

The Gumbel distribution has the density $f(x) = \exp[x - \exp(x)]$ for $-\infty < x < \infty$. Here is a SAS program that uses Quad to calculate a value of the corresponding distribution function

$$F(1) = \Pr(\ X \le 1) = \int_{-\infty}^{1} e^{x - e^x}\, dx.$$

```
proc iml;
 /* Define the Gumbel pdf as the integrand */
  start f(x);
      v = exp(x-exp(x));
      return(v);
  finish;

  /* Define limits of integration to be -infinity to 1, call QUAD, and
     print results*/
  a={.m 1};
  call quad(z,"f",a);
  print z[format = 8.6];
  run;
```

The output is simply

```
                        The SAS System

                 Z

                 0.934012
```

The code that begins with `start` f(x); and ends with `finish`; is used to define a function. In this case it is the function to be integrated. The vector **a** gives the limits of the integration. The .M means -∞. Note that the call to the Quad subroutine takes three arguments. The first is the name of the matrix (in this case 1 x 1) of results of the call to Quad. The second is the name of the integrand, which is defined earlier. The third is the name of the row vector that gives the limits of integration. The next statement causes the results to be printed.

C.4.1.1 Exercise

Modify the program in the previous section to find $\int_{1}^{4} \exp(x^2)dx$.

C.4.2 Optimization Routines

In Appendix A we discussed the problem of finding values of a variable (or variables) that maximize or minimize the value of a function. In Appendix B we showed that being able to do this could be very useful in statistical analysis (when you need to compute a maximum likelihood estimate). Here we show how this can actually be done using SAS/IML. SAS/IML has ten routines that can maximize or minimize functions. Most are variants of the Newton-Raphson method described in Appendix A. Fortunately, we don't need to understand the details of how a method works to use it. Here is an example in which we find MLEs from a random sample.

If $\lambda > 0$ and $\gamma > 0$, then the function defined by f(x) = $\lambda\gamma x^{\gamma-1} \exp(-\lambda x^\gamma)$ for x $\geq$ 0 is the density for a random variable having the Weibull distribution. This distribution is sometimes used to describe the lifetimes of industrial products or humans with a disease. For $\gamma = 1$, it becomes an exponential random variable. Suppose we have a random sample, $x_1, x_2, \ldots x_{100}$, of 100 lifetimes that we feel are described by this distribution for some λ and γ that we wish to estimate. The log likelihood is given by $\text{LogL}(\lambda,\gamma) = 100[\log(\lambda) + \log(\gamma)] + (\gamma - 1)\sum_{i=1}^{100} \log(x_i) - \lambda\sum_{i=1}^{100} x_i^\gamma$. The MLEs of λ and γ are the values of λ and γ that maximize this function.

Assume that the lifetimes are in a SAS data set named Times as a variable named Time. Here is a SAS/IML program to find the MLEs of λ and γ:

```
/* Invoke IML */
proc iml;
/* establish constraints, lambda > 0 and gamma > 0 */
con = {.001 .001, . .};
/*  convert data set to matrix xmatrix */
use times;
read all var {time} into xmatrix;
/*  define loglikelihood function */
start loglik(theta)  global (xmatrix);
lambda = theta[1];
gamma = theta[2];
sum1 = 0;
sum2 = 0;
LL = 100*(log(lambda) + log(gamma));
do i = 1 to 100;
x = xmatrix[i,1];
sum1 = sum1 + log(x);
sum2 = sum2 + x**gamma;
end;
LL = LL + (gamma - 1)*sum1 - lambda*sum2;
return(LL);
finish loglik;
/*  options: first component specifies maximization second
    controls amount of printout */
optn = {1 2};
a = {0 0};
/*  find initial feasible values, theta0 */
call nlpfea(theta0, a, con);
/* invoke optimization program to find MLE, thetares */
call nlpnra(rc, thetares,"loglik",theta0 ,optn, con ,,,,,);
/*  find Hessian h */
call nlpfdd(f, g, h, "loglik", thetares);
/* find covariance matrix of parameter estimates and print it */
cov = -inv(h);
print cov;
run;
```

Con is a 2×2 matrix whose first row, (.001, .001), gives the lower bounds for the parameters. By establishing these lower bounds for the parameters we prevent the program from considering non-positive values of the parameters. The (. .) for the second row means that the upper bounds for both parameters are infinite. PROC IML works with matrices, not data sets. Thus, we need to convert the data set, Times, to a matrix named XMATRIX. The parameter values for λ and γ are contained in the vector, Theta. The function loglik is used to compute the loglikelihood function as a function of Theta. The vector Optn provides certain options to the program. The 1 for the first component causes the LOGLIK function to be maximized; 0 would be used for minimization. The second component controls the amount of output. A value of 0 suppresses all output and 5 gives us the most verbose output. The value of 2 gives us what we need. Other options, which are not needed here, can also be used. The module NLPFEA finds a feasible first estimate for the parameters. One of its arguments, A, is simply a vector of the appropriate dimension. The vector Theta0 is output from this module and used in the module NLPNRA (which stands for nonlinear programming – Newton Raphson Algorithm) that follows. The use of NLPFEA frees us from the need of finding an initial estimate ourselves, but using it can increase the amount of CPU time required. As an alternative, we can provide the initial estimate. (You can notice throughout this book that I tend to prefer saving my time to saving CPU time.) The NLPNRA module implements the Newton-Raphson method, which produces the MLEs as the vector Thetares. Part of the output is a return code, called rc, which provides information about the iteration. If it fails, the value of this code gives the reason. The possible values of rc and their meanings are given in the documentation for PROC IML. Note that we did not have to provide first or second derivatives. That is because the module NLPNRA can estimate them using finite difference methods if they are not provided. This increases the CPU time for the program, but saves a lot of work for the programmer. The module NLPFDD computes F, the value of the function being maximized, G, the vector of partial derivatives (called the gradient vector), and H, the matrix of second partial derivatives (called the Hessian), at the vector value, Thetares. Finally, the negative of the inverse of H gives us the approximate covariance matrix of the parameter estimates.

Here is part of the output from this program. I've omitted some output that gives information about the iteration.

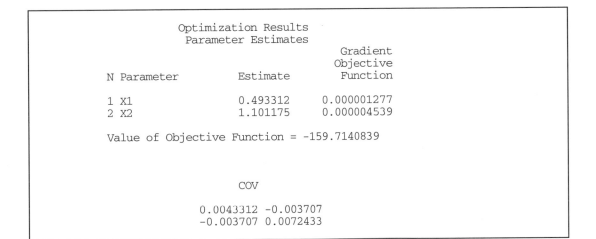

```
                    Optimization Results
                    Parameter Estimates
                                             Gradient
                                             Objective
         N Parameter         Estimate        Function

         1 X1                0.493312        0.000001277
         2 X2                1.101175        0.000004539

         Value of Objective Function = -159.7140839



                         COV

              0.0043312  -0.003707
             -0.003707   0.0072433
```

This output tells us that the MLEs of λ and γ are 0.493312 and 1.101175, respectively. The variances of these MLEs are 0.0043312 and 0.0072433, respectively. The maximum value of the loglikelihood is -159.7140839.

C.5 The SAS Macro Language

The previous SAS program works fine for one specific problem of maximum likelihood estimation. But suppose we anticipated needing to solve problems like this frequently for a variety of density functions. We could, of course, go through the program each time, making changes that are necessary; but this would be quite cumbersome. We might also want to produce a program that others could use easily for any density function. What we would like is a sort of program template, or subroutine, into which we, or others, could simply plug in a few items to solve a particular maximum likelihood estimation problem. The SAS macro language provides a way of doing this.

The SAS macro language is a preprocessing language that enables SAS to write conventional SAS code. When SAS attempts to run a program, it first looks for elements of the macro language. If it sees any, it writes the SAS program as directed by the macro statements. It then processes the resultant SAS program. A SAS macro has the following form:

```
%MACRO macro-name(var-1 =    , var-2 = ,    . . . var-k = );
            .
            .
            .               &var-i       .      .      .
            .
            .                     &var-j    .    .
            .
%MEND;
```

The macro is invoked by a statement of the form

```
%macro-name(var-1 = text-1, var-2 = text-2,  .  .  .  var-k = text-k);
```

The arguments of the macro are called macro variables. The power of this capability is enhanced by the fact that the values of the macro variables are not simply numbers or character strings, but are pieces of text that, when inserted in the macro, become part of the SAS program that is created. Every occurrence of &*var-1* in the macro gets replaced by *text-1*, every occurrence of &*var-2* gets replaced by *text-2*, and so on. The SAS program that finds the MLEs of the parameters of the Weibull density can be generalized by the following macro.

```
%macro mle(dataset = _last_, n =  , varname = , lower = , upper = ,
logpdf =  );
proc iml;
/*  convert data set to matrix xmatrix */
use &dataset;
read all var {&varname} into xmatrix;
/*  define loglikelihood function */
start loglik(theta)  global (xmatrix);
LL = 0;
do i = 1 to &n;
x = xmatrix[i,1];
LL = LL + &logpdf;
end;
return(LL);
finish loglik;
/*  options: first component specifies maximization
    second argument controls amount of printing */
optn = {1 2};
con = &lower//&upper;
k = ncol(con);
a = j(1,k,0);
/*  find intitial feasible values, theta0 */
call nlpfea(theta0, a, con);
/* invoke optimization program to find MLE, thetares */
call nlpnra(rc, thetares,"loglik",theta0 ,optn, con ,,,,,);
/*  find Hessian, h */
call nlpfdd(f, g, h, "loglik", thetares);
/* find covariance matrix of parameter estimates and print it */
cov = -inv(h);
print  cov;
run;
%mend;
```

The macro MLE takes six arguments:

dataset   is the data set to be used. The last data set created is the default.

varname   is the name of the variable in the data set.

n   is the number of observations in the data set. The astute reader will probably notice that we could have had the program find this value instead of providing it.

lower and upper   are the lower bounds and upper bounds of the parameters.

Finally *logpdf* is the logarithm of the density. The parameters must be called *theta[1]*, *theta[2]*, and so on, and the variable must be called *x*. To solve the MLE problem of the previous example, we invoke the macro with the statement

```
%mle(dataset = times,varname = time, n = 100,
lower = {.001 .001}, upper = {  .  .},
logpdf = log(theta[1]) + log(theta[2]) + (theta[2] - 1)*log(x) -
theta[1]*x**theta[2]);
```

The macro now generates a SAS program in which every instance of &dataset is replaced by times, &varname is replaced by Time, &n is replaced by 100, &lower is replaced by {.001 .001}, &upper is replaced by {. .}, and &logpdf is replaced by log(theta[1]) + log(theta[2]) + (theta[2] - 1)*log(x) - theta[1]*x**theta[2]. The results are identical to what we saw earlier.

As with PROC IML, it will not be necessary for you to be able to write macros to understand the material presented in this book. Several macros, written to do some things that are useful, will be presented and discussed; but you will not have to understand how they work in order to use them.

Here's a suggestion that you might consider. The SAS macro language is extremely powerful. By mastering it, a SAS programmer graduates to a new level of capability. It's not easy, so if you are a casual SAS user, you may not want to bother with it. But if you plan to become a serious SAS programmer and have not yet dealt with macros, you might want to begin to do so. This book will not serve as a tutorial on the macro language. Two excellent BBU books on the macro language are by Carpenter (1998) and Burlew (1998). However, the macros in this book introduce the subject.

References

Altman, D. G., B. Lausen, W. Sauerbrei, and M. Schumacher. 1994. "Dangers of Using 'Optimal' Cutpoints in the Evaluation of Prognostic Factors." *Journal of the National Cancer Institute* 86:829-835.

Bowman, L. C., R. P. Castleberry, A. B. Cantor, V. V. Joshi, S. Cohn, E. Smith, A. L.Yu, G. M. Brodeur, F. Hayes, and A. Look. 1997. "Genetic Staging of Unresectable or Metastatic Neuroblastoma in Infants: A Pediatric Oncology Group Study." *Journal of the National Cancer Institute* 89:373-377.

Breslow, N. 1970. "A Generalized Kruskal-Wallis Test for Comparing K Samples Subject to Unequal Patterns of Censorship." *Biometrika* 57:579-594.

Breslow, N. E. 1974. "Covariance Analysis of Censored Survival Data." *Biometrics* 30:89-99.

Burlew, Michele M. 1998. *SAS Macro Programming Made Easy.* Cary, NC: SAS Institute Inc.

Cantor, A. B. 1994. "A Test of the Association of a Time-Dependent State Variable to Survival." *Computer Methods and Programs in Biomedicine* 46:101-105.

Cantor, A. B., and J. J. Shuster. 1992. "Parametric versus Non-Parametric Methods for Estimating Cure Rates Based on Censored Survival Data." *Statistics in Medicine* 11:931-937.

Cantor, A. B. 1992. "Sample Size Calculations for the Log Rank Test: A Gompertz Model Approach." *Journal of Clinical Epidemiology* 45:1131-1136.

Cantor, A. B. 2001. "Projecting the Standard Error of the Kaplan-Meier Estimator." *Statistics in Medicine* 20:2091-2097.

Cantor, A. B., and J. J. Shuster. 1994. "Re: Dangers of Using 'Optimal' Cutpoints in the Evaluation of Prognostic Factors." Letter. *Journal of the National Cancer Institute* 86:1798-1799.

Carpenter, Art. 1998. *Carpenter's Complete Guide to the SAS Macro Language.* Cary, NC: SAS Institute Inc.

Cassell, David. 2002. "A Randomization-Test Wrapper for SAS PROCs." *Proceedings of the Twenty-seventh Annual SAS Users Group International Conference*, Orlando, FL, paper number 251-27.

Cody, Ron. 1996. *The SAS Workbook.* Cary, NC: SAS Institute Inc.

Cox, D. R. 1972. "Regression Models and Life Tables." *Journal of the Royal Statistical Society, B* 34:187-220.

Crowley, J. 1974. "Asymptotic Normality of a New Non-Parametric Statistic for Use in Organ Transplant Studies." *Journal of the American Statistical Association* 69:1006-1011.

DiIorio, Frank C. 1991. *SAS Applications Programming: A Gentle Introduction.* Belmont, CA: Duxbury Press.

Gamel, J. W., R. L. Vogel, P. Valagussa, and G. Bonadonna. 1994. "Parametric Survival Analysis of Adjuvant Therapy for Stage II Breast Cancer." *Cancer* 74:2483-2490.

Garg, M. L., B. R. Rao, and C. K. Redmond. 1970. "Maximum Likelihood Estimation of the Parameters of the Gompertz Survival Function." *Applied Statistics* 19:152-159.

Gehan, E. A. 1965. "A Generalized Wilcoxon Test for Comparing Arbitrarily Singly-Censored Samples." *Biometrika* 52:203-223.

Gehan, E. A., and M. M. Siddiqui. 1973. "Simple Regression Methods for Survival Time Studies." *Journal of the American Statistical Association* 68:848-856.

George, S. L., and M. M. Desu. 1974. "Planning the Size and Duration of a Clinical Trial Studying the Time to Some Critical Event." *Journal of Chronic Diseases* 27:15-24.

Goldman, A. I. 1984. "Survivorship Analysis When Cure Is a Possibility: A Monte Carlo Study." *Statistics in Medicine* 3:153-163.

Gompertz, B. 1825. "On the Nature of the Function Expressive of the Law of Human Mortality, and on the New Mode of Determining the Value of Life Contingencies." *Philosophical Transactions of the Royal Society, Series A* 115:513-580.

Gray, R. J., and A. A. Tsiatis. 1989. "A Linear Rank Test for Use When the Main Interest Is in Cure Rates." *Biometrics* 45:899-904.

Greenwood, M. 1926. "The Natural Duration of Cancer." *Reports on Public Health and Medical Subjects* (London: Her Majesty's Stationary Office) 33:1-26.

Hall, W. J., and J. A. Wellner. 1980. "Confidence Bands for a Survival Curve from Censored Data." *Biometrika* 97:133-143.

Harrington, D. P., and T. R. Fleming. 1982. "A Class of Rank Test Procedures for Censored Survival Data." *Biometrika* 69:553-566.

Haybittle J. 1959. "The Estimation of the Proportion of Patients Cured after Treatment for Cancer of the Breast." *British Journal of Radiology* 32:725-733.

Hsieh, F. Y., and P. W. Lavori. 2000. "Sample-Size Calculation for the Cox Proportional Hazards Regression Model with Nonbinary Covariates." *Controlled Clinical Trials* 21:552-560.

Kalbfleisch, J. D., and R. L. Prentice. 1980. *The Statistical Analysis of Failure Time Data.* New York: Wiley.

Kalish, Leslie A. 2000. "SAS Macros for Proportional Hazards Models with Time-Varying Covariates." *Controlled Clinical Trials* 21, no. 2S (April): 90S.

Kaplan, E. L., and P. L. Meier. 1958. "Nonparametric Estimation from Incomplete Observations." *Journal of the American Statistical Association* 53:457-481.

Lachin, J. 1981. "Introduction to Sample Size Determination and Power Analysis for Clinical Trials." *Controlled Clinical Trials* 2:93-113.

Lakatos, E. 1988. "Sample Sizes Based on the Log-Rank Statistic in Complex Clinical Trials." *Biometrics* 44:229-241.

Laska, E. M., and M. J. Meisner. 1992. "Nonparametric Estimation and Testing in a Cure Model." *Biometrics* 48:1223-1234.

Lee, E. T., M. M. Desu, and E. A. Gehan. 1975. "A Monte Carlo Study of the Power of Some Two-Sample Tests." *Biometrika* 62:425-432.

Liu, P. Y., and S. Dahlberg. 1995. "Design and Analysis of Multi-Arm Clinical Trails with Survival Endpoints." *Controlled Clinical Trials* 16:119-130.

Look, A. T., F. A. Hayes, J. J. Shuster, E. C. Douglass, R. P. Castleberry, L. C. Bowman, E. I. Smith, and G. M. Brodeur. 1991. "Clinical Relevance of Tumor Cell Ploidy and N-myc Gene Amplification in Childhood Neuroblastoma: A Pediatric Oncology Group Study." *Journal of Clinical Oncology* 9:581-591.

Makuch, R. W., and R. M. Simon. 1982. "Sample Size Requirements for Comparing Time-to-Failure among k Treatment Groups." *Journal of Chronic Diseases* 35:861-867.

Mantel, N., and D. Byar. 1974. "Evaluation of Response Time Data Involving Transient States: An Illustration Using Heart-Transplant Data." *Journal of the American Statistical Association* 69:81-86.

Mantel, N. 1966. "Evaluation of Survival Data and Two New Rank Order Statistics Arising in Its Consideration." *Cancer Chemotherapy Reports* 50:163-170.

Mantel, N., and W. Haenszel. 1959. "Statistical Aspects of the Analysis of Data from Retrospective Studies of Disease." *Journal of the National Cancer Institute* 22:719-748.

Mehta, C. R., and N. R. Patel. 1983. "A Network Algorithm for Performing Fisher's Exact Test in **rxc** Contingency Tables." *Journal of the American Statistical Association* 78:427-434.

Miller, R. G. 1981. *Survival Analysis.* New York: Wiley.

Miller, R. G. 1983. "What Price Kaplan-Meier." *Biometrics* 39:1077-1081.

Nair, V. N. 1984. "Confidence Bands for Survival Functions with Censored Data: A Comparative Study." *Technometrics* 26:265-275.

Nelson, W. 1969. "Hazard Plotting for Incomplete Failure Data." *Journal of Quality Technology* 1:27-25.

Oakes, D. 1993. "A Note on the Kaplan-Meier Estimator." *The American Statistician* 47:39-40.

Olsen, O., and P. C. Gotzsche. 2001. "Cochrane Review on Screening for Breast Cancer with Mammography." *Lancet* 358:1340-1342.

Peto, R. 1973. "Experimental Survival Curves for Interval-Censored Data." *Applied Statistics* 22:86-93.

Peto, R., and J. Peto. 1972. "Asymptotically Efficient Rank Invariant Test Procedures (with Discussion)." *Journal of the Royal Statistical Society, A* 135:185-206.

Peto, R., M. C. Pike, P. Armitage, N. E. Breslow, D. R. Cox, S. V. Howard, N. Mantel, K. McPherson, J. Peto, and P. G. Smith. 1977. "Design and Analysis of Randomized Clinical Trials Requiring Prolonged Observation of Each Patient: II. Analyses and Examples." *British Journal of Cancer* 35:1-39.

Pocock, S. J, T. C. Clayton, and D. G. Altman. 2002. "Survival Plots of Time-to-Event Outcomes in Clinical Trials: Good Practice and Pitfalls." *Lancet* 359:1686-1689.

Prentice, R. L. 1978. "Linear Rank Tests with Right Censored Data." *Biometrika* 65:167-179.

Prentice, R. L., and P. Marek. 1979. "A Qualitative Discrepancy between Censored Data Rank Tests." *Biometrics* 35:861-867.

Reid, N. M. 1981. "Influence Functions for Censored Data." *Annals of Statistics* 9:78-92.

Riley, W. J., N. K. Maclaren, J. P. Krischer, R. P. Spillar, J. H. Silverstein, D. A. Schatz, S. Schwartz, J. Malone, S. Shah, C. Vadheim, and J. I. Rotter. 1990. "A Prospective Study of the Development of Diabetes in Relatives of Patients with Insulin Dependent Diabetes." *New England Journal of Medicine* 323:1167-1172.

Rubenstein, L. V., M. H. Gail, and T. J. Santner. 1981. "Planning the Duration of a Comparative Clinical Trial with Loss to Follow-up and a Period of Continued Observation." *Journal of Chronic Diseases* 34:469-479.

Sander, J. M. 1975. "Asymptotic Normality of Linear Combinations of Functions of Order Statistics with Censored Data." *Technical Report #8,* Division of Biostatistics, Stanford University, Stanford, CA.

SAS/STAT Software *Changes and Enhancements through Release 6.11.* Cary, NC: SAS Institute Inc., 813-814.

SAS/STAT User's Guide, Version 8. Cary, NC: SAS Institute Inc.

Scerbo, Marge, Craig Dickstein, and Alan Wilson. 2001. *Health Care Data and the SAS System.* Cary, NC: SAS Institute Inc.

Shapiro, S., W. Venet, P. Strax, and L. Venet. 1988. *Periodic Screening for Breast Cancer: The Health Insurance Plan Project and Its Sequelae, 1963-1986.* Baltimore: Johns Hopkins University Press.

Shih, J. H. 1995. "Sample Size Calculation for Complex Clinical Trials with Survival Endpoints." *Controlled Clinical Trials* 16:395-407.

Shuster, J. J. 1992. *Handbook of Sample Size Guidelines for Clinical Trials.* Boca Raton: CRC Press.

Sposto, R., and H. N. Sather. 1985. "Determining the Duration of Comparative Clinical Trials While Allowing for Cure." *Journal of Chronic Diseases* 38:683-690.

Tarone, R., and J. Ware. 1977. "On Distribution-Free Tests for Equality of Survival Distributions." *Biometrika* 64:156-160.

Turnbull, B. W. 1976. "The Empirical Distribution Function from Arbitrarily Grouped, Censored and Truncated Data." *Journal of the Royal Statistical Society, B* 38:290-295.

Index

A

accelerated failure time model 16, 155, 163

actuarial life table 20-22

ALPHA= option
    BASELINE statement (PHREG procedure)
      139
    LIFETEST procedure 28
    MODEL statement (PHREG procedure) 126
    SURVIVAL statement (LIFETEST procedure)
      29

assumptions in survival analysis 16

average rate of change 187

B

bascline cumulative hazard 116

baseline hazard function 112
    See also PHREG procedure

BASELINE statement, PHREG procedure
    138-141
    ALPHA= option 139
    COVARIATES= option 139
    NOMEAN option 139

Bernoulli random variables 196

BEST= option, MODEL statement (PHREG) 127

beta coefficients for Cox regression, estimating
    112-117

binomial random variables 197

breast cancer data (example) 2
    FREQ procedure for stage distribution 68
    LINRANK macro to compare distributions
      67-73
    log rank and Gehan tests 60-64

Breslow test
    See Gehan test

BY statement, PHREG procedure 125

C

calculus, introduction to 187-191

calendar time 5-6

categorical variables with more than two values
    114-115

cause-specific deaths 2

cdf (cumulative distribution function) 9, 196

censoring 2, 154
    See also interval censoring
    See also Kaplan-Meier estimator
    See also left censoring
    right censoring 2-3

CHEKDIST macro 180-183, 186

chi-square random variables 198

Clark level of melanoma data (example)
    comparing groups 173-176
    interaction considerations 122-123
    multivariate analysis 120-122
    stratification 123-125
    survival function estimation 139-141
    univariate analysis 118-120

column vectors 192

comments in SAS code 209

comparing survival distributions, nonparametric
  methods
    See nonparametric comparisons of survival
      distributions

conditional cure probability 183

conditional power 92-95

conditional probability 201

conditional survival for time interval 20

CONDPOW macro 94-95, 107-109

CONFBAND= option, SURVIVAL statement
    (LIFETEST) 29

confidence intervals 25, 207

CONFTYPE= option, SURVIVAL statement
    (LIFETEST) 29

continuous covariates 133-134

continuous random variables 195-196

CONTROL= option, OUTPUT statement
    (LIFEREG) 160

controlling standard error 37-39

conversion to IDDM among children (example)
    82-83

correlated covariates 131

covariates
    continuous covariates 133-134
    correlated covariates 131
    cutpoints on continuous covariates 133-134
    dichotomous covariates 133-134
    grouping 132-133, 173-176
    interaction among 114, 122-123
    prescreening 132

covariates (*continued*)
    scaling date-based covariates 115
    time-dependent covariates 134-136

covariates and proportional hazards regression 114
    See also proportional hazards regression
    categorical variables with more than two values
      114-115
    cutpoints on continuous covariates 133-134
    effects on survival function parameters
      176-178
    interactions among 114, 122-123
    model-building considerations 131-134
    scaling 115
    time-dependent 134-136

COVARIATES= option, BASELINE statement
    (PHREG) 139

COVOUT option, OUTEST statement (PHREG)
    149

Cox regression
    See proportional hazards regression (Cox
      regression)

cumulative distribution functions (cdf) 9, 196

cumulative hazard function 10

cure models 13

cure probability, conditional 183

cure rate estimation 10

cutpoints on continuous covariates 133-134

D

DATA step 209-211

DATALINES statement 210

DATASET= option, PARAMEST macro 164

date-based covariates, scaling 115

definite integrals 189-190

delta method 200-201

density function 9
    for subinterval midpoints 22

derivatives (calculus) 187-188

DETAILS option, MODEL statement (PHREG)
    127

deviance residual 144

DFS time after tumor removal (example) 127-131
    comparing parametric distributions 159
    LIFEREG procedure (example) 156-158
    PARAMEST macro 166-169
    quantile and survival function estimates
      160-163

diabetes, insulin-dependent, among children
    (example) 82-83

dichotomous covariates 133-134

discrete random variables 194

disease-free time after tumor removal
    See DFS time after tumor removal (example)

distribution functions, cumulative 9, 196

E

early stopping based on conditional power 92-95

effective number at risk 20

estimated distribution function 19

estimating parameters 202-203

estimation by models 111-112

exponential distribution
    calculus of exponential functions 191
    compared with other parametric distributions
      159
    graphical checks of parametric methods
      179-182

exponential function 11
    stepwise (piecewise) exponential model 13

F

Fisher's Exact Test 74

FREQ procedure
    breast cancer data (example) 68
    permutation tests 73-74

fully parametric methods 15

functions, maximum/minimum value of 188

Fundamental Theorem of Calculus 190

G

gamma model, compared with other parametric
    distributions 159

Gaussian random variables 197

Gehan test 58
    See also LIFETEST procedure
    breast cancer data (example) 60-64
    permutation and randomization tests 75-78
    power analysis example 89-91

generalized Wilcoxon test
    See Gehan test

Gompertz function 13-14
    graphical checks of parametric methods 180

graphing
  checking parametric methods 179-183
  survival function, proportional hazards
    regression 141-143
Greenwood's formula 23-24
  variance projections 38
  variance projections, KMPLAN macro for
    39-42
grouping covariates 132-133
  comparing groups 173-176
grouping variables with more than two values
  114-115
Gumbel distribution 212

H

Harrington and Fleming weights 58, 66
hazard function 9-10
  assumptions in survival analysis 16
  baseline cumulative hazard 116
  baseline hazard function 112
  complex expressions for 179
  cumulative 10
  for subinterval midpoints 22
hazard ratio 112-113
higher-order derivatives 188
hypothesis tests of survival function 24

I

ICE macro
  interval censoring 43-44
  leukemia survival data 45-48
IDDM, children with (example) 82-83
identity matrices 192
IML procedure 212-215
  optimization routines with 213-215
  Quad subroutine 212
imputing missing values, proportional hazards
  regression 148-150
INPUT statement 209
instantaneous rate of change 187
insulin-dependent diabetes mellitus (example)
  82-83
integrals (calculus) 189-190
interactions among covariates 114
  ulceration of melanoma data (example)
    122-123

intercept parameter, accelerated failure time model
  155
interval censoring 2, 42-48, 154
  allowing for, LIFEREG procedure 156
  ICE macro 43-44
  leukemia survival data (example) 45-48
  representation of 3
inverses, matrix 192

J

joint distributions 200-201

K

Kaplan-Meier estimator 17-20
  See also LIFETEST procedure
  controlling standard error 37-42
  KMPLAN macro 39-42
  KMPLOT macro 35-36, 51-52
  KMTABLE macro 32-35, 48-50
  left-continuous version 58, 66
  projected standard error 37-39
  shortcomings of 25-27
  variance of 23-24, 38, 39-42
KMPLAN macro 39-42
KMPLOT macro 35-36, 51-52
KMTABLE macro 32-35, 48-50

L

left censoring 2, 154
  allowing for, LIFEREG procedure 156
  representation of 3
left-continuous version of Kaplan-Meier estimator
  58, 66
leukemia survival data (example)
  See pediatric leukemia survival data (example)
LIBNAME statement 210
life table method 20-22
LIFEREG procedure 153, 156
  allowing for censoring 156
  comparing groups 173-176
  DFS time after tumor removal (example)
    156-158
  MODEL statement 156, 160
  OUTPUT statement 160
  parameters of 163
  quantile and survival function estimates
    160-163

LIFETEST procedure 27-32, 59-64
  ALPHA= option 28
  breast cancer data (example) 60-64, 67-73
  checking proportional hazards assumption
    113-137
  example 29-32
  leukemia survival data (example) 29-32
  LINRANK macro vs. 66
  macro alternatives to 32-36
  METHOD= option 28
  NINTERVAL= option 28
  NOPRINT option 136
  OUTS= option 28
  OUTSURV= option 28
  PLOTS= option 27, 136
  STRATA statement 59-60
  SURVIVAL statement 29
  SYMBOL statement 60
  syntax 27-29
  TIME statement 27
  TIMELIST= option 28
  WIDTH= option 28
likelihood ratio tests 206
LINRANK macro 66-73, 95-100
  breast cancer data (example) 67-73
  LIFETEST procedure vs. 66
log rank statistic 54-57
  See also LIFETEST procedure
  breast cancer data (example) 60-64
  effects of covariates on survival function
    parameters 178
  more than two groups 56-57
  permutation and randomization tests 75-78
  weighted sums 57-59
logarithmic functions, calculus of 191
lognormal distribution, checking graphically 180

M

macro language 215-217
macro variables 216
macros
  See also LINRANK macro
  See also PARAMEST macro
  as alternatives to LIFETEST procedure 32-36
  CHEKDIST 180-183, 186
  CONDPOW 94-95, 107-109
  ICE 43-48
  KMPLAN 39-42
  KMPLOT 35-36, 51-52
  KMTABLE 32-35, 48-50
  MANTBYAR 80-83, 105-107

MLE 216-217
  PERM_GEN 76-78, 101
  permutation tests with 75-78
  PHPLOT 141-143, 150-151
  PHPOW 146-148, 151-152
  RAND_GEN 76-101
  SAS macros 215-217
  SURVPOW 84, 86-92, 103-105
  TEST 77, 102
mammography data (example) 2
  log rank and Gehan tests 60-64
MANTBYAR macro 80-83, 105-107
Mantel-Byar method 79-83
Mantel-Haenszel statistic
  See log rank statistic
martingale residual 144
matrices 192
maximum likelihood estimation (MLE) 203-206
  Cox regression coefficients 116-117
  likelihood ratio tests 206
  MLE macro 216-217
maximum values of functions 188
mean of random variables 199
melanoma data, Cox regression (example)
  comparing groups 173-176
  interaction considerations 122-123
  multivariate analysis 120-122
  stratification 123-125
  survival function estimation 139-141
  univariate analysis 118-120
melanoma removal and DFS time
  See DFS time after tumor removal (example)
METHOD= option
  LIFETEST procedure 28
  PARAMEST macro 164
MI procedure 132, 148-150
MIANALYZE procedure 132, 148-150
minimum values of functions 188
missing values, imputing in Cox regression
  148-150
mixture models 13
MLE
  See maximum likelihood estimation
MLE macro 216-217
model-based estimation 111-112
model building, proportional hazards regression
  131-134
  DFS time after tumor removal (example)
    127-130

PHREG options for 126

MODEL statement, LIFEREG procedure 156, 160

MODEL statement, PHREG procedure 117-118, 126-127
   ALPHA= option 126
   BEST= option 127
   DETAILS option 127
   RISKLIMITS option 126
   SELECTION= option 126
   SLENTRY= option 126, 132
   STOP= option 126

multiple testing problem 132

multivariate analysis with PHREG procedure (example) 120-122

N

natural logarithms, calculus of 191

Newton-Raphson method 214

NINTERVAL= option, LIFETEST procedure 28

NLPFDD module 215

NLPFEA module 214

NLPNRA module 214

NLPTR subroutine, PARAMEST macro 164

NOMEAN option, BASELINE statement 139

non-cause-specific deaths 2

nonparametric approaches to survival data
   See also Kaplan-Meier estimator
   See also LIFETEST procedure
   See also parametric approaches to survival data
   controlling standard error 37-39
   parametric methods vs. 4, 15

nonparametric comparisons of survival distributions 53-109
   See also Kaplan-Meier estimator
   LIFETEST procedure for 59-64
   LINRANK macro 66-73
   log rank statistic 54-57
   Mantel-Byar method 79-83
   permutation and randomization tests 73-78
   power analysis 84-92
   stratified analysis 65-66
   study termination based on conditional power 92-95
   trend tests 64-65
   weighted sums 57-59

NOPRINT option, LIFETEST procedure 136

normally distributed random variables 197

O

one-sample tests of parameters 176

optimization routines with IML procedure 213-215

organ transplants data (example) 79-83

OUT= option
   OUTPUT statement (PHREG) 144
   SURVIVAL statement (LIFETEST) 29

OUTEST statement, PHREG procedure 149
   COVOUT option 149

OUTPUT statement, LIFEREG procedure 160
   CONTROL= option 160

OUTPUT statement, PHREG procedure 144
   OUT= option 144

OUTS= option, LIFETEST procedure 28

OUTSURV= option, LIFETEST procedure 28

P

p-value, discrepancies with 64

PARAMEST macro 153, 163-166, 183-186
   comparing groups 173-176
   complex expressions for survival and hazard functions 179
   DATASET= option 164
   DFS time after tumor removal (example) 166-169
   effects of covariates on survival function parameters 176-178
   leukemia survival data (example) 169-172
   METHOD= option 164
   NLPTR subroutine 164

parameters and parameter estimation 202-203
   confidence intervals 25, 207

parametric approaches to survival data 153-183
   See also LIFEREG procedure
   See also nonparametric approaches to survival data
   See also PARAMEST macro
   accelerated failure time model 155
   comparing groups and group parameters 173-175
   comparing models 159
   complex expressions for survival and hazard functions 179
   effects of covariates on parameters 176-178
   graphical checks 179-183
   nonparametric methods vs. 4, 15

parametric approaches to survival data (*continued*)
　one-sample tests 176
　quantile and survival function estimates
　　160-163
　semiparametric vs. fully parametric 15

partial derivatives 188

partial likelihood estimation of Cox regression
　coefficients 117
　stratification 123-125

pdf (probability density function) 194-195

pediatric leukemia survival data (example)
　effects of covariates on survival function
　　parameters 177
　ICE macro 45-48
　LIFETEST procedure 29-32
　PARAMEST macro 169-172

PERM_GEN macro 76-78, 101

permutation tests 73-74
　Gehan test 75-78
　log rank statistic 75-78
　macros for 75-78

Peto's formula 24
　standard error projections 37-38
　standard error projections, KMPLAN macro for
　　39-42

PHPLOT macro 141-143, 150-151

PHPOW macro 146-148, 151-152

PHREG procedure 117-131
　See also proportional hazards regression
　BASELINE statement 138-141
　BY statement 125
　checking proportional hazards assumption 137
　DFS time after tumor removal (example)
　　127-131
　grouping covariates 132-133
　grouping covariates, comparing groups
　　173-176
　imputing missing values 148-150
　MODEL statement 117-118, 126-127
　multivariate analysis (example) 120-122
　OUTEST statement 149
　OUTPUT statement 144
　residuals, producing 144
　SIMPLE option 126
　time-dependent covariates 134-136
　univariate analysis (example) 118-120
　WHERE statement 125

piecewise exponential model 13

PLOTS= option, LIFETEST procedure 27, 136

positive cure rate example
　See pediatric leukemia survival data (example)

power analysis 84-92
　conditional power 92-95
　Gehan test 89-91
　sample size and 84
　selecting power for proportional hazards
　　regression 145-148

prescreening covariates 132

PRINT procedure 211

probability, conditional 201

probability density function (pdf) 194-195

probability functions 194

probability mass function 195

Proc-StatXact product 75

PROC steps 211

product limit method
　See Kaplan-Meier estimator

projected standard error of Kaplan-Meier estimator
　37-39
　KMPLAN macro for 39-42

proportional hazards assumption 16, 58
　checking with PHREG procedure 137
　validity of 113, 136-138

proportional hazards regression (Cox regression)
　112-150
　See also covariates and proportional hazards
　　regression
　See also PHREG procedure
　See also tumor data, Cox regression (example)
　DFS time after tumor removal (example)
　　127-131
　estimating beta coefficients 112-117
　hazard ratio vs. survival function 113
　imputing missing values 148-150
　melanoma data, interaction considerations
　　122-123
　melanoma data, multivariate analysis 120-122
　melanoma data, stratification 123-125
　melanoma data, survival function estimation
　　139-141
　melanoma data, univariate analysis 118-120
　model-building considerations 126, 127-130,
　　131-134
　partial likelihood estimation 117
　power and sample size selection 145-148
　residuals 143-144
　stratification 123-125
　survival function estimates 116, 138-141
　survival function estimates, graphing
　　141-143

time-dependent covariates 134-136
validity of assumption behind 113, 136-138
prostate cancer treatment (example) 87-92

Q

Quad subroutine, IML procedure 212
quantile estimates, LIFEREG procedure for 160-163

R

RAND_GEN macro 76-101
random variables 3, 193
Bernoulli 196
binomial 197
chi-square 198
conditional probability and stochastic independence 201
continuous 195-196
discrete 194
Gaussian 197
joint distributions 200-201
mean of 199
normally distributed 197
parameters and parameter estimation 202-203
standard deviation of 199
uniformly distributed 198
variance of 199
randomization tests 75-78
rate of change 187
residuals in proportional hazards regression 143-144
right censoring 2-3
RISKLIMITS (RI) option, MODEL statement (PHREG) 126
row vectors 192
RUN statement 211

S

sample size
power analysis and 84
reducing standard error 37
selecting for proportional hazards regression 145-148
stratification 65-66
SAS code
comments in 209
variable definitions in 210

scale parameter, accelerated failure time model 155
scaling covariates for proportional hazards regression 115
second derivatives 188
SELECTION= option, MODEL statement (PHREG) 126
semiparametric approaches to survival data 15
See also proportional hazards regression
SIMPLE option, PHREG procedure 126
SLENTRY= option, MODEL statement (PHREG) 126, 132
square matrices 192
stage distribution (example) 68
stage IV prostate cancer treatment (example) 87-92
standard deviation of random variables 199
standard error
controlling 37-39
Kaplan-Meier estimator 37-42
KMPLAN macro 39-42
Peto's formula 37-38
reducing 37
state changes among subjects 79-83
stepwise exponential model 13
stochastic independence 201
STOP= option, MODEL statement (PHREG) 126
STRATA statement, LIFETEST procedure 59-60
stratification 65-66
proportional hazards regression (example) 123-125
study termination based on conditional power 92-95
study time 5-6
subscripts 3
survival data
See also nonparametric approaches to survival data
See also parametric approaches to survival data
characteristics of 1-4
semiparametric approaches 15
survival distributions, comparing nonparametrically
See nonparametric comparisons of survival distributions
survival for time interval, conditional 20
survival function 9
See also Kaplan-Meier estimator
assumptions in survival analysis 16

survival function (*continued*)
    complex expressions for 179
    confidence intervals 25
    estimating in proportional hazards regression
      138-141
    estimating with LIFEREG procedure 160-163
    for those not cured 183
    graphing in proportional hazards regression
      141-143
    hazard ratio vs. 113
    hypothesis tests 24
    proportional hazards model 116
survival function parameters
    See also parametric approaches to survival data
    comparing between groups 175
    effects of covariates 176-178
    one-sample tests of 176
SURVIVAL statement, LIFETEST procedure 29
    ALPHA= option 29
    CONFBAND= option 29
    CONFTYPE= option 29
    OUT= option 29
SURVPOW macro 84, 86-92, 103-105
SYMBOL statement, LIFETEST procedure 60

T

Tarone-Ware weights (example) 89, 92
Taylor series 200
termination of study based on conditional power
    92-95
TEST macro 77, 102
thickness of tumor data (example)
    See tumor data, Cox regression (example)
time, basic concepts of 5-6
time-dependent covariates 134-136
TIME statement, LIFETEST procedure 27
TIMELIST= option, LIFETEST procedure 28
TPHREG procedure 115
transplant data (example) 79-83
transposes, matrix 192
trends in survival differences, testing for 64-65
tumor data, Cox regression (example)
    comparing groups 173-176
    interaction considerations 122-123
    multivariate analysis 120-122
    stratification 123-125
    survival function estimation 139-141
    univariate analysis 118-120

tumor removal and DFS time (example) 127-131
    comparing parametric distributions 159
    LIFEREG procedure (example) 156-158
    PARAMEST macro 166-169
    quantile and survival function estimates
      160-163

U

ulceration of melanoma data (example)
    comparing groups 173-176
    interaction considerations 122-123
    multivariate analysis 120-122
    stratification 123-125
    survival function estimation 139-141
    univariate analysis 118-120
uniformly distributed random variables 198
univariate analysis with PHREG procedure
    (example) 118-120

V

variable definitions in SAS code 210
variables
    See also random variables
    categorical variables 114-115
    grouping 114-115
    macro variables 216
variance of Kaplan-Meier estimator 23-24
    projecting 38
    projecting, KMPLAN macro for 39-42
variance of random variables 199
vectors 192

W

Weibull function 12
    compared to other parametric distributions 159
    effects of covariates on survival function
      parameters 176-177
    graphical checks of parametric methods 179
weighted sums 57-59
WHERE statement, PHREG procedure 125
WIDTH= option, LIFETEST procedure 28
Wilcoxon test, generalized
    See Gehan test
wrapper for randomization tests 75

Call your local SAS office to order these books from Books by Users Press

Advanced Log-Linear Models Using SAS®
by **Daniel Zelterman** ....Order No. A57496

Annotate: Simply the Basics
by **Art Carpenter** ....Order No. A57320

Applied Multivariate Statistics with SAS® Software,
Second Edition
by **Ravindra Khattree**
and **Dayanand N. Naik**...............................Order No. A56903

Applied Statistics and the SAS® Programming Language,
Fourth Edition
by **Ronald P. Cody**
and **Jeffrey K. Smith**.................................Order No. A55984

An Array of Challenges — Test Your SAS® Skills
by **Robert Virgile**.....................................Order No. A55625

Beyond the Obvious with SAS® Screen Control Language
by **Don Stanley** ....Order No. A55073

Carpenter's Complete Guide to the SAS® Macro Language
by **Art Carpenter** ....Order No. A56100

The Cartoon Guide to Statistics
by **Larry Gonick**
and **Woollcott Smith**.................................Order No. A55153

Categorical Data Analysis Using the SAS® System,
Second Edition
by **Maura E. Stokes, Charles S. Davis,**
and **Gary G. Koch** ....Order No. A57998

Client/Server Survival Guide, Third Edition
by **Robert Orfali, Dan Harkey,**
and **Jeri Edwards**......................................Order No. A58099

Cody's Data Cleaning Techniques Using SAS® Software
by **Ron Cody**..Order No. A57198

Common Statistical Methods for Clinical Research with
SAS® Examples, Second Edition
by **Glenn A. Walker**...................................Order No. A58086

Concepts and Case Studies in Data Management
by **William S. Calvert**
and **J. Meimei Ma**......................................Order No. A55220

Debugging SAS® Programs: A Handbook of Tools
and Techniques
by **Michele M. Burlew** ....Order No. A57743

Efficiency: Improving the Performance of Your SAS®
Applications
by **Robert Virgile**.....................................Order No. A55960

A Handbook of Statistical Analyses Using SAS®,
Second Edition
by **B.S. Everitt**
and **G. Der** ....Order No. A58679

Health Care Data and the SAS® System
by **Marge Scerbo, Craig Dickstein,**
and **Alan Wilson** ....Order No. A57638

The How-To Book for SAS/GRAPH® Software
by **Thomas Miron** ....Order No. A55203

In the Know ... SAS® Tips and Techniques From
Around the Globe
by **Phil Mason** ....Order No. A55513

Integrating Results through Meta-Analytic Review Using
SAS® Software
by **Morgan C. Wang**
and **Brad J. Bushman** ....Order No. A55810

Learning SAS® in the Computer Lab, Second Edition
by **Rebecca J. Elliott** ....Order No. A57739

The Little SAS® Book: A Primer
by **Lora D. Delwiche**
and **Susan J. Slaughter** ....Order No. A55200

The Little SAS® Book: A Primer, Second Edition
by **Lora D. Delwiche**
and **Susan J. Slaughter** ....Order No. A56649
(updated to include Version 7 features)

Logistic Regression Using the SAS® System:
Theory and Application
by **Paul D. Allison** ....Order No. A55770

Longitudinal Data and SAS®: A Programmer's Guide
by **Ron Cody** ....Order No. A58176

Maps Made Easy Using SAS®
by **Mike Zdeb** ....Order No. A57495

Models for Discrete Data
by **Daniel Zelterman** ....Order No. A57521

Multiple Comparisons and Multiple Tests Using the SAS®
System Text and Workbook Set
(books in this set also sold separately)
by **Peter H. Westfall, Randall D. Tobias,
Dror Rom, Russell D. Wolfinger,**
and **Yosef Hochberg** ....Order No. A58274

Multiple-Plot Displays: Simplified with Macros
by **Perry Watts** ....Order No. A58314

Multivariate Data Reduction and Discrimination with
SAS® Software
by **Ravindra Khattree**
and **Dayanand N. Naik**..............................Order No. A56902

The Next Step: Integrating the Software Life Cycle with
SAS® Programming
by **Paul Gill** ....Order No. A55697

Output Delivery System: The Basics
by **Lauren E. Haworth** ....Order No. A58087

Painless Windows: A Handbook for SAS® Users
by **Jodie Gilmore** ....Order No. A55769
(for Windows NT and Windows 95)

Painless Windows: A Handbook for SAS® Users,
Second Edition
by **Jodie Gilmore** ....Order No. A56647
(updated to include Version 7 features)

PROC TABULATE by Example
by **Lauren E. Haworth** ....Order No. A56514

Professional SAS® Programmers Pocket Reference,
Second Edition
by **Rick Aster** ....Order No. A56646

Professional SAS® Programmers Pocket Reference,
Third Edition
by **Rick Aster** ....Order No. A58128

Programming Techniques for Object-Based Statistical Analysis
with SAS® Software
by **Tanya Kolosova**
and **Samuel Berestizhevsky** ....Order No. A55869

Quick Results with SAS/GRAPH® Software
by **Arthur L. Carpenter**
and **Charles E. Shipp** ....Order No. A55127

Quick Results with the Output Delivery System
by **Sunil K. Gupta** ....Order No. A58458

Quick Start to Data Analysis with SAS®
by **Frank C. Dilorio**
and **Kenneth A. Hardy**.............................Order No. A55550

Reading External Data Files Using SAS®: Examples Handbook
by **Michele M. Burlew** ....Order No. A58369

Regression and ANOVA: An Integrated Approach Using
SAS® Software
by **Keith E. Muller**
and **Bethel A. Fetterman** ....Order No. A57559

Reporting from the Field: SAS® Software Experts Present
Real-World Report-Writing
Applications...Order No. A55135

SAS® Applications Programming: A Gentle Introduction
by **Frank C. Dilorio** ....Order No. A56193

SAS® for Linear Models, Fourth Edition
by **Ramon C. Littell, Walter W. Stroup,**
and **Rudolf J. Freund** ....Order No. A56655

SAS® for Monte Carlo Studies: A Guide for Quantitative
Researchers
by **Xitao Fan, Ákos Felsővályi, Stephen A. Sivo,**
and **Sean C. Keenan** ....Order No. A57323

SAS® Macro Programming Made Easy
by **Michele M. Burlew** ....Order No. A56516

SAS® Programming by Example
by **Ron Cody**
and **Ray Pass** ....Order No. A55126

SAS® Programming for Researchers and Social Scientists,
Second Edition
by **Paul E. Spector**...................................Order No. A58784

SAS® Software Roadmaps: Your Guide to Discovering
the SAS® System
by **Laurie Burch**
and **SherriJoyce King** ....Order No. A56195

SAS® Software Solutions: Basic Data Processing
by **Thomas Miron**......................................Order No. A56196

SAS® Survival Analysis Techniques for Medical Research,
Second Edition
by **Alan B. Cantor** ....Order No. A58416

SAS® System for Elementary Statistical Analysis,
Second Edition
by **Sandra D. Schlotzhauer**
and **Ramon C. Littell**.................................Order No. A55172

SAS® System for Forecasting Time Series, 1986 Edition
by **John C. Brocklebank**
and **David A. Dickey** ....Order No. A5612

SAS® System for Mixed Models
by **Ramon C. Littell, George A. Milliken, Walter W. Stroup,**
and **Russell D. Wolfinger** ....Order No. A55235

SAS® System for Regression, Third Edition
by **Rudolf J. Freund**
and **Ramon C. Littell**................................Order No. A57313

SAS® System for Statistical Graphics, First Edition
by **Michael Friendly** ....Order No. A56143

The SAS® Workbook and Solutions Set
(books in this set also sold separately)
by **Ron Cody** ....Order No. A55594

Selecting Statistical Techniques for Social Science Data:
A Guide for SAS® Users
by **Frank M. Andrews, Laura Klem, Patrick M. O'Malley,
Willard L. Rodgers, Kathleen B. Welch,**
and **Terrence N. Davidson** ....Order No. A55854

Solutions for Your GUI Applications Development Using
SAS/AF® FRAME Technology
by **Don Stanley** ....Order No. A55811

Statistical Quality Control Using the SAS® System
by **Dennis W. King**....................................Order No. A55232

A Step-by-Step Approach to Using the SAS® System
for Factor Analysis and Structural Equation Modeling
by **Larry Hatcher**......................................Order No. A55129

A Step-by-Step Approach to Using the SAS® System for Univariate and Multivariate Statistics
by **Larry Hatcher**
and **Edward Stepanski** ....Order No. A55072

Step-by-Step Basic Statistics Using SAS®: Student Guide and *Exercises (books in this set also sold separately)*
by **Larry Hatcher** ....Order No. A57541

Strategic Data Warehousing Principles Using SAS® Software
by **Peter R. Welbrock** ....Order No. A56278

Survival Analysis Using the SAS® System: A Practical Guide
by **Paul D. Allison** ....Order No. A55233

Table-Driven Strategies for Rapid SAS® Applications Development
by **Tanya Kolosova**
and **Samuel Berestizhevsky** ....Order No. A55198

Tuning SAS® Applications in the MVS Environment
by **Michael A. Raithel** ....Order No. A55231

Univariate and Multivariate General Linear Models: Theory and Applications Using SAS® Software
by **Neil H. Timm**
and **Tammy A. Mieczkowski** ....Order No. A55809

Using SAS® in Financial Research
by **Ekkehart Boehmer, John Paul Broussard,**
and **Juha-Pekka Kallunki** ....Order No. A57601

Using the SAS® Windowing Environment: A Quick Tutorial
by **Larry Hatcher** ....Order No. A57201

Visualizing Categorical Data
by **Michael Friendly** ....Order No. A56571

Working with the SAS® System
by **Erik W. Tilanus** ....Order No. A55190

Your Guide to Survey Research Using the SAS® System
by **Archer Gravely** ....Order No. A55688

JMP® Books

Basic Business Statistics: A Casebook
by **Dean P. Foster, Robert A. Stine,**
and **Richard P. Waterman** ....Order No. A56813

Business Analysis Using Regression: A Casebook
by **Dean P. Foster, Robert A. Stine,**
and **Richard P. Waterman** ....Order No. A56818

JMP® Start Statistics, Second Edition
by **John Sall, Ann Lehman,**
and **Lee Creighton** ....Order No. A58166

Regression Using JMP®
by **Rudolf J. Freund, Ramon C. Littell,** and **Lee Creighton**
....Order No. A58789

support.sas.com/pubs

*Welcome * Bienvenue *Willkommen *Yohkoso * Bienvenido*

SAS Publishing Is Easy to Reach

Visit our Web site located at support.sas.com/pubs

You will find product and service details, including

- **companion Web sites**
- **sample chapters**
- **tables of contents**
- **author biographies**
- **book reviews**

Learn about

- **regional users group conferences**
- **trade show sites and dates**
- **authoring opportunities**
- **e-books**

Explore all the services that SAS Publishing has to offer!

Your Listserv Subscription Automatically Brings the News to You

Do you want to be among the first to learn about the latest books and services available from SAS Publishing? Subscribe to our listserv **newdocnews-l** and, once each month, you will automatically receive a description of the newest books and which environments or operating systems and SAS® release(s) each book addresses.

To subscribe,

1. Send an e-mail message to **listserv@vm.sas.com**.

2. Leave the "Subject" line blank.

3. Use the following text for your message:

   subscribe NEWDOCNEWS-L *your-first-name your-last-name*

   For example: subscribe NEWDOCNEWS-L John Doe

You're Invited to Publish with SAS Institute's Books by Users Press

If you enjoy writing about SAS software and how to use it, the Books by Users program at SAS Institute offers a variety of publishing options. We are actively recruiting authors to publish books and sample code.

If you find the idea of writing a book by yourself a little intimidating, consider writing with a co-author. Keep in mind that you will receive complete editorial and publishing support, access to our users, technical advice and assistance, and competitive royalties. Please ask us for an author packet at **sasbbu@sas.com** or call 919-531-7447. See the Books by Users Web page at **support.sas.com/bbu** for complete information.

Book Discount Offered at SAS Public Training Courses!

When you attend one of our SAS Public Training Courses at any of our regional Training Centers in the United States, you will receive a 20% discount on book orders that you place during the course. Take advantage of this offer at the next course you attend!

SAS Institute Inc.
SAS Campus Drive
Cary, NC 27513-2414
Fax 919-677-4444

E-mail: sasbook@sas.com
Web page: support.sas.com/pubs
To order books, call SAS Publishing Sales at 800-727-3228*
For product information, consulting, customer service, or training, call 800-727-0025
For other SAS business, call 919-677-8000*

* **Note:** Customers outside the United States should contact their local SAS office.

The Power to Know.

§sas. | SAS Publishing